# 365 DAYS OF
# HOODOO

## About the Author

Stephanie Rose Bird is a hereditary intuitive, contemporary root-worker, solitary green witch, and visionary. She has been involved with mysticism, symbology, spiritualism, and the occult for thirty years. Bird is inspired by her ancestors, in particular her grandmothers, one of whom was a psychic and the other a Spiritualist minister and herbal healer. Her uncle, a Santeria priest, Babalawo of Shango, taught her the Ifa traditions of the Yoruba people. Bird studies healing, magical, and divination traditions of indigenous people around the world, with a focus on Africa. Her passions include keeping the ancient traditions alive and updating them so that they evolve with us, suiting our current environment and lifestyles. Bird enjoys involvement with the American Folklore Society, the Herb Research Foundation, and the Handcrafted Soap & Cosmetic Guild.

Bird holds a BFA cum laude from Temple University, Tyler School of Art, and an MFA from University of California at San Diego, and has received multiple academic awards. She was an assistant professor at the School of the Art Institute of the Art Institute of Chicago from 1987-2002. Bird offers healing workshops, rituals, retreats, and classes across the country. She is an active arts educator, teaching undergraduate art appreciation and art history in Chicago, giving lectures, conducting goddess rituals, and writing for numerous publications. Visit her at:

Website: http://www.stephanierosebird.com

Blog: http://stephanierosebirdstudio.blogspot.com

Facebook: https://www.facebook.com/stephanierosebirdauthor

Twitter: @StephanieRoseBi

STEPHANIE ROSE BIRD

# 365 DAYS OF
# HOODOO

## DAILY ROOTWORK, MOJO
## & CONJURATION

Llewellyn Publications
Woodbury, Minnesota

FIRST EDITION
Third Printing, 2019

Cover design by Kevin R. Brown
Interior art by Llewellyn Art Department

Llewellyn Publications is a registered trademark of Llewellyn Worldwide Ltd.

**Library of Congress Cataloging-in-Publication Data**
Names: Bird, Stephanie Rose, author.
Title: 365 days of Hoodoo: : daily rootwork, mojo, and conjuration / by Stephanie Rose Bird.
Description: FIRST EDITION. | Woodbury : Llewellyn Worldwide, Ltd., 2018. | Includes bibliographical references and index.
Identifiers: LCCN 2018034726 (print) | LCCN 2018038322 (ebook) | ISBN 9780738755175 (ebook) | ISBN 9780738747842 (alk. paper)
Subjects: LCSH: Vodou—Miscellanea.
Classification: LCC BL2490 (ebook) | LCC BL2490 .B56 2018 (print) | DDC 133.4—dc23
LC record available at https://lccn.loc.gov/2018034726

Llewellyn Publications
A Division of Llewellyn Worldwide Ltd.
2143 Wooddale Drive
Woodbury, MN 55125.2989
www.llewellyn.com

Printed in the United States of America

## Other Books by Stephanie Rose Bird

*Sticks, Stones, Roots & Bones*
(Llewellyn, 2004)

*Four Seasons of Mojo*
(Llewellyn, 2006)

*The Big Book of Soul*
(Hampton Roads, 2006)

*A Healing Grove*
(Lawrence Hill Books, 2009)

*Light, Bright, and Damned Near White*
(Praeger, 2009)

*Earth Mama's Spiritual Guide to Weight Loss*
(Green Magic Publishing, 2017)

*Louisa is a Spanish/Italian name and the feminine form of Louis: "renowned warrior." It is also the given name of my grandmother and great-grandmother, famed warriors of our family, to whom I dedicate this book.*

# Contents

## Chapter 8

## Chapter 9

# Section III—Disturb Me Knot: Shielding, Noticing & Undoing Negativity

## Chapter 10

## Chapter 11

## Chapter 12

## Acknowledgments

Thank you to my family, particularly my children and husband, for being a constant fount of support and inspiration. I appreciate the enthusiasm and open hearts of my dear girlfriends Szmeralda Shanel, Jan, and Chunie. Thanks to Jannette Giles Hypes for fresh energy, insight, and support as my editor and friend. I am deeply indebted to Elysia Gallo for her sharp eye and to Andrea Neff. Thanks to the publishing team at Llewellyn Worldwide for supporting my work and believing in me.

## Disclaimer

The material in this book is not intended as a substitute for trained medical or psychological advice. Readers are advised to consult their personal healthcare professionals regarding treatment. Neither the publisher nor the author take any responsibility for any possible consequences from any treatment, action, or application of medicine, supplement, herb, or preparation to any person reading or following the information in this book.

# INTRODUCTION

My first book, *Sticks, Stones, Roots & Bones*, presented Hoodoo in a practical manner to add magick to the defining passages of life: weddings and funerals, pregnancy and birthing, sickness and health. Later, *Four Seasons of Mojo* expanded the concept to show how to meld Hoodoo with the seasons of the year in accordance with the cycles of life.

*365 Days of Hoodoo* is a return to basics and a solid introduction to Hoodoo for the beginner. At the same time, the text will be educational for the practiced Hoodoo as well. Regardless of your personal knowledge of Hoodoo, presented here are 365 days of tricks, spells, rites, rituals, mojos, and curios to power up your everyday living and advance your exploration of Hoodoo. This book is infused with traditional and historical Hoodoo workings presented in an updated way. It is designed to be used throughout any given calendar year. This is a guide to help you employ Hoodoo in many different areas of your life and in various situations that may arise during the year, such as these:

- **Love Life:** You might need to find love or, once you have it, adjust your relationship. Through this daily guide, you will learn to use magickal Hoodoo tools such as mojo bags, powders and charms to attract love, keep love alive, and break up, if necessary.

- **Friends and Colleagues:** If problems arise with friends and coworkers, this book will equip you with just the right spell to restore order and peace in difficult interpersonal relationships.

- **Work Life:** Getting and keeping a job, blessing your workplace, and dealing with your boss or clients are real issues you may come across in your work life, all of which can benefit from the use of Hoodoo.

- **Money:** Attracting wealth and prosperity into your life and keeping hold of it is very helpful, and you'll find suggestions for how to do this.

- **Luck:** Drawing luck using baths, washes, curios, and zoological materials is an important feature of the Hoodoo's life.

- **Protection:** In our complex world, we all need protection from a variety of worldly and supernatural sources. You will find numerous workings centered on protection magick in this book.

- **Hex/Unhex:** Your work will include noticing, shielding yourself from, and undoing hexes you encounter.

- **Justice:** Everyone craves justice, and from time to time you'll need magickal ways of dealing with the law. Justice work is a unique feature of Hoodoo and is covered in this book.

- **Moving:** Sometime in your life, you will most likely move into a new living or work space. This book shows you how to clear out old entities, such as hants, and then magickally dress and bless your new space.

In this book you'll find the following:

- Magical recipes featuring herbs and curios
- Guidance on creating a Hoodoo garden
- Days that are focused on Hoodoo curios
- Altars for specific days, types of work, saints, and deities
- Appropriate mojo bags for a wide variety of purposes
- Prayers, chants, psalms, mantras, and meditations
- Tricks, spells, rites, and rituals
- Hoodoo for candle and metal magick
- Incense, floor washes, baths, hand and foot washes, grave-yard dirt, needle work, bottles, egg magick, and more

*365 Days of Hoodoo* is designed for newbies and experienced practitioners alike to learn how to shape each day of the year around Hoodoo. Daily Hoodoo work in the form of reflections, rituals, tricks/spells, chants, altars, and mojo bags will help you live your life powerfully as a Hoodoo.

Hoodoo is known as a practice for the everyday person dealing with real-life issues. This down-to-earth, do-it-yourself-style book is one you'll want to have close at hand as you make your way through the ups and downs of each year. Through your daily work, you'll be prepared to move forward courageously, armed with power and infused with the wisdom of the complex nature of spirit on your side.

Hoodoo is a bold tradition that deals with spirit directly, particularly with how your spirit and supernatural spirits come together, positively or negatively, to affect your well-being. The mind-body-spirit connection is a topic that frequently arises in the conversation of holistic health. The Hoodoo's dealings in this arena are propelled by an unflinching and relentless concern for all matters of the spirit, including viewing spirits as an integral and lively component of daily life.

With its focus on spirits, Hoodoo is a mysterious and, in the minds of some, scary practice, since as a society, we tend to shy away from what we don't fully understand. If you are in the dark about the potential healing and everyday problem-solving skills that can be gained through engagement with Hoodoo, you have picked up the right book.

*365 Days of Hoodoo* is designed to shed light on the numerous positive and impactful ways the unique collection of primarily African-American folklore called Hoodoo can be utilized in your daily life. With its gentle guidance and hundreds of useful suggestions, you will be positioned to courageously take control of issues and concerns that once seemed out of your control.

## A Historical Overview

Hoodoo can be traced back to sub-Saharan Africa, particularly Western and Central Africa, as those were areas from which people were taken to the United States and enslaved. My people, for example, hail from central Congo and Western and Southern Africa. Moreover, since there were migrations of people from ancient Kush and Nubia (areas of what is today generically called Egypt) into sub-Saharan Africa, there are also Egyptian, Nubian, and Cushitic influences. Heck, if you delve into it deeply, you will find that astrology, Hindu practices, Appalachian folklore, and many other practices have commonalities with Hoodoo. This practice is open to all, particularly considering that we all originated in Africa, regardless of how skin color has evolved over time.

Hoodoo is an age-old assemblage of practices that have crossed continents and been passed down from one generation to the next. Because of the vitality and strength of its rich traditions, Hoodoo continues to draw a new influx of curious practitioners to the path.

## Ashe and the African Connection

In traditional African societies, many indigenous beliefs center around the lively stories and antics of spirits. Spirits are everywhere and in everything under the sun. Our mother, Earth, is infused with spirits in her plants, stones, trees, animals, and minerals, as well as in natural phenomena such as lightning, rain, and running water. This universal energy force is called *ashe* (ah-SHAY; also *ase*, ah-SAY) in parts of Africa, and it can speak to us through dreams and signs, cure disease, bring malaise, and protect. Through serious and sustained practice comes knowledge and experience that will allow the practitioner to recognize, embrace, and use this energy for enlightening and beneficial purposes.

While Hoodoo incorporates elements of various religions, including Catholicism, it is not a religion. Anyone can practice it regardless of religious affiliation, including practitioners of eclectic forms of paganism. In fact, part of the reason for its welcoming nature is the fact that it can accommodate and speak to people from a wide variety of belief systems and enrich preexisting practices in the process. The primary concern of Hoodoo is not only spirits but also self-determination, which made it an attractive and enduring fixture of black culture in the antebellum South.

## Early African-American Wisdom

Slavery was a truly dark part of our history, as it sought to strip the enslaved Africans of their beloved sense of community, family, and connection to a rich cultural identity. Through Hoodoo, however, we are connected to the strength, adaptability, and do-it-yourself wisdom of early African Americans. Hoodoo is a reservoir of knowledge that, though specialized, is open to all who are interested in learning what it has to offer.

With its wide-ranging applications, Hoodoo not only flourished during enslavement but continued to grow and expand after emancipation, surviving Jim Crow, the civil rights movement, and beyond. It had something of a heyday during the early to mid-twentieth century, an exciting though confusing time for a group of people reconnecting with all that it means to be free.

The wealth of the traditions, stories, lore, and magick within Hoodoo enriches life in every way imaginable. It affords us the opportunity to address matters of physical and mental health in a cost-effective, affirming manner. It also feeds our marked spirit of self-determination.

## What Is Hoodoo?

Hoodoo is a practice that addresses issues and concerns we all can relate to, such as resolving mental, spiritual, and physical health conditions; drawing love and keeping it close; maintaining good spirits and relationships in the home, at work, and in school; attracting luck and protective energies; and setting things right when necessary. Finally, it addresses a significant subject that is as important and elusive today as it was in the distant past: social justice. There are ways of working toward social justice—such a relevant topic in troubling times—in multiple practices of Hoodoo.

## Historical Overtones, Contemporary Practices

As I mentioned, Hoodoo has been practiced for hundreds of years. The practices vary by region, and in some cases by cities and towns within a state. Harry Middleton Hyatt, an Anglican minister and amateur folklorist raised in Quincy, Illinois, left a wonderful gift for students of Hoodoo when he interviewed more than 1,600 practitioners of Hoodoo and compiled their practices into his densely packed five-volume series *Hoodoo, Conjuration, Witchcraft, Rootwork.* All but one of these "informants" were African American. They hailed from various locales across the United States, concentrated in the Southern states, the Midwest, and along the East Coast. This series of books contains over 4,600 recipes and cures; protection, attraction, and lucky potions, rites, and spells (which are called "tricks" by Hoodoos).

This book draws from the wisdom of numerous Hoodoo informants interviewed in *Hoodoo, Conjuration, Witchcraft, Rootwork,* the results of my eclectic studies of African-American folklore and slave narratives, and the impressive Valmor collection of Hoodoo formulas, history, catalogs, and knowledge at the Chicago Cultural Center in Illinois, curated by cultural historian Tim Samuelson.

It is my pleasure to share the tools and equipment you will need to establish your Hoodoo practice. The work presented here has been researched, gathered, sifted through, updated, and inspired by authentic and historically documented Hoodoos as well as my personal practice. It is enlightened by the past but looks toward the future.

## Hoodoo, 365 Days of the Year

Hoodoo is dense, rich, and complex. If you would like to utilize it to its full potential, to indeed tap its ashe, you must practice, practice, and practice some more. *365 Days of Hoodoo* is designed to assist you on your spiritual journey.

## How This Book Works

This book begins with an overview of Hoodoo. This introduction is designed to help you get grounded in the many facets of the practice, including its history, origin, philosophy, implications, and ways it can be used in your daily life.

Dispersed throughout each month are special sections called "Curio of Note" and "Hoodoo Gardening." These important days are designed to create mental space to help you focus in on information about Hoodoo curios and provide step-by-step directions to enable you to grow a garden containing important herbs to use in your practice. If you are not able to garden or if your garden is not ready to harvest when an herb is called for, go ahead and buy from a local health store, supermarket, or nursery, or go online for some of the harder-to-find dried goods.

This book is divided into three sections:

• **Section 1: Hoodoo's Fixin's: Key Components of Your Hoodoo Spells and Tricks** is divided into five chapters that go in-depth regarding the important components for practicing Hoodoo. These include the signature power medicine, called a mojo bag; waters, baths, and washes; fires, candles, and metals; foot track magick; and graveyard dirt, goofer dust, and crossroads and forks in the road dirt.

- **Section 2: Tricks of the Hoodoo's Trade: Spells, Rites & More** focuses on the Hoodoo's magickal workings concerning the issues directly impacting your life. This is a handy do-it-yourself section filled primarily with the ways Hoodoo is employed, and is useful every day of the year. Here you will find attraction, love draw, and relationship Hoodoo; luck, abundance, and prosperity tricks; home and moving tricks; and Hoodoo for the career, business, and success.

- **Section 3: Disturb Me Knot: Shielding, Noticing & Undoing Negativity** is a very important element of Hoodoo. This section is built around how to take control of elements in your life that seem out of your control. It includes the all-important protection magick, hexing/unhexing, banishment, and justice work.

Each section begins with a brief introduction, followed by a month of spells, rites, altars, ceremonies, recipes, and tricks. At the end of each section is a space left for you to write personal reflections. As each section concludes, you are invited to check in with yourself by answering a few questions on your development before you move on to the next section.

## Workin' It

Knowing how this book works is useful, but realizing that it is you who will work its contents is essential. Ideally you will start work on the first day of the year (any year of your choosing)—that is day 1. Then you will travel through each of the days of the year until you arrive at day 365.

Hoodoo is fluid, and I honor that fluidity. Therefore, while I suggest that your day 1 be January 1, your first day can be any day of your choosing. You should start when you are ready to commit fully to utilizing the book daily and taking time for self-reflection. It is important to understand that the skills become progressively more involved, and for that reason the book is designed to be followed from beginning to end. However, not every reader will have the need for every practice presented on a specific day. To the same end, each practice can stand alone and be used as the need arises.

Use *365 Days of Hoodoo* as your handbook of daily Hoodoo inspiration, a workbook of self-reflection, and a reference book to return to as needed. Mark pages you want to return to when the conditions are right, such as a certain moon phase or once an ingredient can be acquired. It is recommended that you keep a journal of your Hoodoo journey. Use the journal to make notes about your experiences, keep track of page numbers you plan to return to, make shopping lists of materials, or record whatever else you feel led to include.

Ultimately you will have learned about the essential tools and the language of Hoodoo, as well as an array of rites, altars, spells, tricks, ceremonies, recipes, gardening, and lore. If exact measurements are not given, this is an opportunity to pull on your intuition, listen to spirit, and call to the ancestors for their wisdom. Be mindful! By day 365 you will understand and be prepared to practice Hoodoo to improve and support your life and enrich your lifestyle. You will be on the road to becoming a Hoodoo.

The work given here is based strictly in Hoodoo. Other traditions may call for opening and closing rituals not practiced by traditionalists. If you want to include opening or closing rituals, that is up to you and your level of eclecticism.

## Common Sense and Best Judgment: Your Responsibility

It is important to keep your practice within health, safety, and legal boundaries. For obvious safety reasons, don't leave burning candles unattended.

Remember that when using herbs and botanicals, allergies can be possible. While placing plant matter in a mojo bag isn't likely to cause harm of any sort, if you are considering taking any herbal product internally, you should clear it with a doctor first.

Collecting graveyard dirt under the moon could be against the rules of the cemetery, and it also might not be safe. There are a wide variety of graveyards, however, which will affect your ability to gather the dirt. If you have a family graveyard property, you are in luck. Most likely you can collect dust as needed. In other situations, if you are outgoing, you can develop a relationship with local gravediggers in order to gather soil at specified times. However you do your grave magick, do so with respect to all.

If you are collecting footprint dust of another person, consider that it could be misperceived as stalking. If you are circling a home you want to buy, think first about whether it is trespassing. Security systems, motion-activated lights, and neighborhood watch groups could all be present. These are just a few of the things to consider that may not have been an issue at the time the tricks were originally created. Always be aware of local laws and don't put your safety at risk.

# SECTION I
# HOODOO'S FIXIN'S:
## KEY COMPONENTS OF YOUR
## HOODOO SPELLS & TRICKS

Like other practices, Hoodoo has components and elements that are frequently used. These tools of our practice make it distinct. In this section you will learn what these tools are and how to employ them.

# CHAPTER 1
# MOJO BAGS: DAYS 1-31

Contained within the corpus of Hoodoo is a broad-based, in-depth knowledge of the workings of nature and the environment. Beneath this umbrella there are spirits, humans, animals, plants, stones, metals, deities, the ancestors, and the elements. Beyond these complex individual components there is a conglomerated energetic force that has come to be known as *mojo*. Mojo is of the soul; it has soul, and impacts, reflects, and feeds upon it.

*Containment* is a beautiful and primal concept important to Yoruba medicine. The Yoruba are an influential West African tribe, some of which were enslaved and brought to the Americas. Containment is particularly useful when different elements need to be brought together. One of the oldest and most valued sacred objects used by practitioners of magick across the globe is the humble satchel, or bag. In fact, the bag is an ideal object for containment. Within it, there is an enclosed space or world that seals off the possibility of outside interference. This inward-facing, dark, and limited area is the perfect space in which to concentrate power.

Within a cinched bag, synergy can be seeded, fed, left to ripen, and then harvested. Knowledgeably blended individual conjuring objects culled from physical, spiritual, and mental engagement with nature and the spiritual realm are powerful from the start. Inserting them into a contained environment where they can come alive and develop a symbiotic relationship with one another magnifies their power potential. A carefully crafted mojo bag is a very potent object.

Activating this newly developed extension of the self helps render the contents' magickal potential useful. Through touch, sight, sound, scent, dreaming, and attentive thought, the bag's mojo is nurtured into being. The practitioner of Hoodoo needs to utilize numerous items, alone and in combination, to work magick and undertake conjuration.

The mojo bag is the perfect vessel for this work. It embodies the Hoodoo and is quite capable of yielding their intent. This month is devoted to the mojo bag. Here you will explore, study, experiment with, and experience the myriad possibilities of this staple in the practice of Hoodoo.

## 1. What Is a Mojo Bag?

Your first day is a day of contemplation of one of your most important Hoodoo tools: the mojo bag. What is it exactly? It is many things. The mojo bag is one of the most intimate allies of the Hoodoo. Mojo bags are collections of power. They can be used for protection and drawing. *Drawing* is a type of magnetic attraction power frequently used in Hoodoo. Mojo bags can draw luck, love, success, money, prosperity, and much more.

The bags are built around the concept of *animism*, the belief that plants and seemingly inanimate objects are alive and have a soul. These bags bear a striking resemblance to figurative sculptures from Central Africa. Both are stocked with potent components, including herbs, curios, zoological parts, coins, types of metals, and metallic and magnetic powders.

In Africa, these sculptures are assembled by a healing specialist called a *ngana* (priest or priestess). They are not only filled with plants and objects considered powerful but are also prepared with knowledge, intent, and a powerful understanding of earthly concerns and their relationship to the spirit realm.

You will begin the journey of collecting your Hoodoo materials on day 2. For today, contemplate how this practice will connect you to traditions of past and present Hoodoos and ancient magick. Meditate on what this exercise will mean to you and how it will positively affect your future.

Today, locate a source of oil of clove (clove oil) and Van Van oil to be used later for luck.

## 2. The Flannel

There are several different names for a mojo bag, one of which is a *flannel*. This word has a double meaning, as the bag is also made of cotton flannel fabric. Flannels are generally created from solid colors rather than the types of plaids commonly used to make flannel shirts. The old-time Hoodoos most frequently call for putting your magical ashe-filled items into a red, yellow, or green flannel.

Flannel is a relatively inexpensive, easy-to-obtain material. It is also easy to work with. The fact that it is very soft to the touch is also important. It feels good to the hands and can be worn close to the skin, tied off the waist or knees, or even put inside a bra.

Magical bags in the mojo family need to be maintained and sparked in order for them to act. Flannels work well in this regard, as you can easily stick needles and pins into them for your specific purposes.

Today is a good day to obtain your flannel. Get a yard of red flannel from a carefully selected source. I like recycling and upcycling from old clothing. It is also enjoyable to hunt for it in secondhand stores and flea markets. You can get it from a craft shop or sewing store. Fold your flannel in large segments. Put it under your pillow tonight and keep it there for nine days. This enables you to imprint your energy into the fabric.

### 3. The Power of Red

Red is a vibrant, compelling, and powerful color. The Yoruba people of Nigeria and nearby regions of Yorubaland have a complex belief system called *Ile Ifa*, or simply *Ifa*. This belief system incorporates red as a symbolic conceptual component called *pupa*. In Yoruba medicine, red embodies motivation, action, strength, and vitality.

Africanisms are holdovers of African beliefs and practices that are now found in the African diaspora. Many thousands of black people who were brought to the United States and enslaved have Yoruba ancestry. The preference of red as the predominant color of the Hoodoo's mojo bag is not arbitrary. It is most likely an Africanism.

As you seek out the perfect flannel material for the construction of your mojo bag, be sure to collect a variety of bright, potent reds, so your bag will be the most effective vessel to hold its magical contents.

Red is a royal color in Africa, and it is emblematic of the life force, as it is the color of our blood. Shroud your precious parcels of ashe-dense curios, herbs, roots, metals, and stones in a red mojo bag that you make yourself.

Today, begin collecting pieces of ribbon and cord (especially red ones) for tying up mojo bags.

## 4. Explore Related Traditions

When learning about new techniques and spiritual practices, it is always useful to look at neighboring traditions. To do so requires only an open mind. When thinking of the way a mojo bag works, the Native American medicine bags used by shamans and holy people immediately come to mind.

Native Americans of certain groups like the Lumbee, Cree, and Eastern Cherokee had a lot of cultural exchange with African Americans. Our soul food incorporates corn dishes such as corn bread, hominy, and succotash that are borrowed from Native American cuisine.

Being indigenous people, both groups traditionally lived very close to Mother Earth. It is likely that enslaved Africans found common ground in the spirituality, herbal healing ways, and power objects such as the medicine bags (bundles) and bandoliers (long-strapped medicine bags) of the Native Americans they encountered. Medicine bags hold a collection of items that possess spirit, including hair and fur, animal parts, wild grasses, herbs, seeds, stones, tobacco, dirt, and coins—items just like those in a mojo bag.

The Bamana of Western Sudan have warrior bags that fight ill intent. These bags, while not mojo bags, have a similar form and intent. They contain *bilongo* (medicine) and have a *mooyo* (soul). They must be closely guarded, nurtured, and fed by their owner to keep their contents alive and accessible. They are primed to act on their owner's behalf by following a certain protocol.

## 5. Hunting and Gathering Materials

This is a lovely exercise that could have long-term meaning for your Hoodoo practice, especially if you love natural objects. Go to an undisturbed location, such as a forest preserve, nature conservancy, or wooded area. Walk mindfully for at least thirty minutes, collecting objects that call out to you. Mindful walking requires only that you stay in the moment rather than thinking about the past or worrying about the future. Objects like those found in African sculptures and bags, as well as in Native American medicine bundles, will work nicely. Place the items together in a favorite bag or satchel of your choosing for now. These items can be used later in your personal mojo bag.

## 6. Reflect and Learn: Understanding Ashe

Today is a day for reflection as you equip yourself with the knowledge necessary to practice Hoodoo. Various groups of indigenous people honor the intrinsic power of nature and natural objects rich in ashe. Ashe is the invisible power of nature. It is a type of natural energy filled with potential. Ashe is prevalent in a wide variety of plants, natural objects, lightning excreta (things touched by lightning), and fluids (bodily and humanmade).

The Igala people of Nigeria believe that all plant life is filled with medicinal healing powers that can be used to treat matters of the earthly and spiritual realms. This concept stems from the notion that the objects are animated with life and imbued with ashe. The literal translation of ashe is "So be it" or "May it happen," yet since ashe is the divine energies of the universe manifest, it is a term whose true meaning can't be translated into mere words.[1]

The Yaka, Kongo, Teke, Suku, and Songhai people insert a variety of ashe-dense items into a cavity in the belly of their figurative sculptures.[2] Mojo bags are a type of power object utilized in Hoodoo, whereas in parts of Africa, shields, masks, figurative sculptures, amulets, and charms are power objects that possess ashe. Though Hoodoos might not speak directly about African ashe or animism, the beliefs are deeply embedded in the practice and are apparent in our mojo bags.

Today, locate a source of and purchase cinnamon chips, Adam and Eve root, and male (pointy) High John the Conqueror root.

## 7. Wearing Flannels

Flannels are worn or carried on various parts of the body. You can think of a flannel you wear as a part of your warrior gear. Mojo bags make the inexplicable facets of life easier to understand and manipulate, if need be, through the accumulative power of the objects they contain, such as those you've recently collected. Every day we face challenges and do battle of one type or another. Mojo bags draw, attract, protect, guide, and assist.

Flannels, which vary by purpose, are worn or carried on various locations of the body. For example, you'll want your mojo

---

1. Thompson, *Flash of the Spirit*, 7–9.

2. Anderson and Kreamer, *Wild Spirits, Strong Medicine*.

bag where you can feel and touch it. This will likely be in your front pocket or purse. The *nation sack* is a specialized Hoodoo tool for women. This can be carried in the bra or tied off the waist. Some mojo bags benefit from being carried in the upper pocket of a jacket or shirt, since they need a good talking to. This placement also carries over to the *jack*, which you will encounter in a bit.

Each bag has a purpose that matches your intent. I will let you know exactly where to wear your mojo bag or similar power object for your Hoodoo work when placement is vital to its efficacy.

Today, locate a source of and purchase five-finger grass (cinquefoil) and black snakeroot herbs. *-need to find*

## 8. Curio of Note: The He and She Known as a Lodestone Pair

Some curios, including herbs, have a specific gender. A *lodestone*, which is a naturally magnetized piece of the mineral magnetite, is a gender-specific magical object. It varies in shape and color and may be painted. Different colors are coordinated with the Hoodoo's goal.

The male lodestone, simply called a *he*, has masculine energy and a phallic shape. The female lodestone, or *she*, has feminine roundness that is suggestive of breasts or the pregnant belly. By bringing together the he and she, Hoodoos capitalize on their power. The pair of lodestones, united in the act of intercourse, are an important drawing fixture in Hoodoo when placed in mojo bags.

Today, locate a source of and purchase a lodestone pair. It's best to go to a brick-and-mortar store to select your he and she.

Procuring your magical items in person puts you in control. You can feel what you are drawn to and see how the pair interact. Once you have observed the offerings and felt which ones you are drawn to, make your selection and practice putting them together. If this is not possible, contact an online store and speak to the shopkeeper. Ask them to use their expertise to match a pair to your specifications.

After obtaining your he and she, feed them according to the purpose of your mojo bag. Popular traditional foods for lodestones include whiskey, chamber lye, and Hoyt's Cologne. After briefly soaking the pair in the feedin' potion, dry them off completely so they don't rust.

## 9. Nation Sack

A nation sack in Hoodoo is a type of mojo bag specific to people who identify as women. Its use was established in Memphis, Tennessee. A man cannot touch a woman's nation sack; it is solely hers. This intimate bag may hold cherished as well as necessary items for its owner in lieu of a purse, including feminine products, lipstick, perfume, and money, along with the customary mojo bag materials for conjuration and drawing magick. It may also hold her partner's underwear remnants, hair, and other intimate items.[3]

### Nation Sack Tips

1. Your nation sack can go in your purse, but it is safer hung from a belt or cord around your waist, under your clothing. Some women stick them in their bra.

---

3. Hyatt, *Hoodoo, Conjuration, Witchcraft, Rootwork*, 1,450.

2. This type of mojo must be put on for the day, after showering or bathing, and is not to be taken off until bedtime, so wherever you place it, make sure it is comfortable.

3. Making a nation sack from an intimate garment increases your connection to it. This material may come from your partner or your intimate apparel or even a sock. You can then roll it up tightly and tie it off into a bag, or sew it up.

4. Letting your nation sack fall into the wrong hands, or indeed anyone else's hands, is extremely dangerous.

Today, locate sources of lodestone powder, anvil dust, and steel dust in your environment. Purchase these items if there is no other way for you to obtain them.

### 10. Zoological Curios

*Minkisi* (*nkisi*, singular) are Kongolese power figures.[4] They, like mojo bags, are essentially charms under the influence of spirits. African power figures have a cavity that is stuffed with dirt from elephant footsteps, snake scales, animal sexual organs, nail and hair clippings, and bits and pieces of deceased sorcerers and warriors.[5] These items are activated by driving nails into them. The figures are covered with power-animal skins and embellished with natural grasses, metal, nails, beads, bells, and cloth.[6]

Like African power figures, mojo bags also contain zoological remnants such as a rabbit's foot, a raccoon's penis, alligator teeth, chicken bones such as a wishbone, lightning excreta, and

---

4. Thompson, *Flash of the Spirit.*

5. Anderson and Kreamer, *Wild Spirits, Strong Medicine.*

6. Ibid.

foot track dirt, which is essential to foot track magick, a practice we will explore in chapter 4.

The use of animal parts is historically acceptable; however, vegetarians and environmentalists may prefer using animal sculptures and images in place of actual animal parts. Our environment is fragile, and animals within it should be treated humanely and with the utmost respect. As substitutes for actual animal parts, you can purchase animal toys, replicas, or idols or make them yourself from self-drying clay. If you choose to create your own from clay, you are again harkening back to the African power figure tradition.

## 11. Libations and Feeding

Mojo bags are packed with ashe, yet they must be fed to stay alive. Mojo bags require special care, attention, nurturing, and food for their souls to stay vibrant and useful. Our bags are fed substances used for libations (such as whiskey), colognes, and sweet waters. They are fed herbal powders, dust, and magnetic or metallic powders.

Libations are tribute rituals used in many different African diasporic spiritual practices. A libation is a poured spirit in combination with an incantation, song, or prayer that invokes a deity, lwa, or orisha. They are also used to honor the ancestors. Libations connect to the idea that all is alive on the earth, as well as above it and below the ground. Ancestors, deities, and spirits can be engaged, pleased, and praised by feeding them specific types of foods and libations. Two common types of feedin' potions used in Hoodoo are whiskey and chamber lye.

In Hoodoo, spirits (alcoholic beverages) are used as offerings on spiritual altars. The spirits are poured directly onto the flannel or its contents to dress and feed mojo bags. This action is similar in form and intent to libations but is called feeding.

Today, locate a source of and purchase a small horseshoe charm to place inside a bottle of Jockey Club cologne in the future.

## 12. Contemplate Containment

As a Hoodoo, you'll need to make many mojo bags. A fundamental principle of Yoruba medicine is the separation of what is contained or hidden from what is exposed or revealed.[7] The hidden is the unseen metaphysical world. When you contain magical items in a red mojo bag, you are engaging in an Africanism of Yoruba origin.

The red or other symbolic color of your bag shows spirits and humans that they are encountering a power object. The items within your mojo bag maintain their unique energies because they are protected, shrouded, and contained.

### Directions for Making Your Personal Mojo Bag

Take the items from the hunting and gathering materials exercise on day 5 and place them in the center of the red flannel. Decide which closure method you want to use. Gather up the edges of the flannel and close up the bag using one of these methods:

1. The simplest way to make a mojo bag is to obtain a piece of red flannel about six inches square and tie it off with a piece of twine or thin ribbon.

2. Another way to make a mojo is to fill a red flannel bag with its contents and then sew it together.

---

7. Thompson, *Flash of the Spirit.*

3. Here is an illustrated method for constructing a mojo bag that is easy to feed and refill.

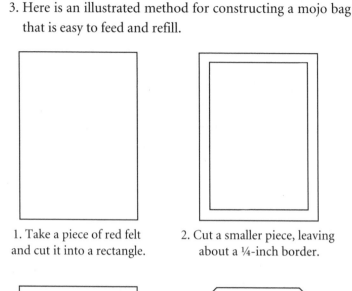

1. Take a piece of red felt and cut it into a rectangle.

2. Cut a smaller piece, leaving about a ¼-inch border.

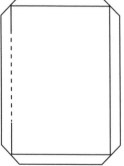

3. Sew the two pieces together, leaving a two-inch opening for stuffing.

4. Cut the corners at an angle, then turn the bag inside out.

**Mojo Bag Construction**

## 13. Activate Your Hand

By now, you can see the relationship between the names of mojo bags and their making. There is a close relationship between a Hoodoo *hand* (another name for a mojo bag) and our anatomic hands, which we will discuss in more detail on day 18. In many ways, Hoodoo hands can do a bit more than human ones if your intent is to spark action on the metaphysical plane. A hand is a magickal helper. It aids you in obtaining your wants, needs, and desires.

Don't consider the purpose of your hand a done deal just because you have made one. It needs to be activated. To activate it, stroke, squeeze, and feel it so you are constantly reminded of it and its power is with you.[8] Sometimes you'll want to talk to your hand as well. Tell it what you desire from it and clearly state the purpose of its creation. This helps mobilize its collective items to do your bidding.

Hands must be dressed and powered up by their user. Knowing specifically what you want enables it to act on your behalf. The contents of the hand also help unite it with its designated purpose, but those contents need dressing.

Your bag needs to be charged and recharged or it will die, much like your phone or computer. Recharging is accomplished through feeding.

## 14. Feedin' Potions: Whiskey and Chamber Lye

Spirits is a synonym for alcoholic beverages, which makes for a very interesting relationship between the two. Hoodoo is a practice that is keyed into the use of spirits of both sorts. Spirits are

---

8. Hyatt, *Hoodoo, Conjuration, Witchcraft, Rootwork*, 519.

employed as feedin' potions for the mojo bag, and whiskey is a favorite.

While originating in Scotland, whiskey flourished in the United States at home distilleries during the heyday of Hoodoo. Hoodoo is enjoying a second heyday, and so is whiskey.

Be sure to get hold of some high-quality whiskey, because you'll be needing it to feed your Hoodoo items in and outside of your mojo bags.

You can tell by the names of the potions and cures used that Hoodoo has been around for a very long time. Back in the day of outhouses, when there was no indoor plumbing, folks relieved themselves in vessels in their bedroom chambers.

Chamber lye is urine. Humans and animals mark their territory with various types of bodily fluids. Chamber lye is a popular fluid for many different types of Hoodoo. Moreover, this substance is used to soak, charge, and feed items in the mojo bag.

Sometimes you'll be asked to soak a root or curio in chamber lye, and you may do so in a glass jar with a top. Otherwise, use the substance carefully by dropping it out of a dropper until your root or curio is saturated.

## 15. Curios of Note: Anvil Dust and Steel Dust

There has always been great admiration in Africa for metalsmithing and the magick within the alchemical process of metallurgy. This is inherent in the reverence of the warrior orisha Ogun in the diaspora.[9] There is a unique carryover from the Yoruba's spiritual and philosophical beliefs in the Hoodoo's predilection for using powders of Ogun, including anvil and steel dust.

---

9. Thompson, *Flash of the Spirit*, 57.

Metalsmiths were highly respected in the past, and for a time it was a sought-after profession by early African Americans. The process of metalsmithing and ironworking is looked upon as a mysterious metaphysical activity. Therefore, metal and iron bits feature prominently in several magickal paths, including Hoodoo.

Anvil dust and steel dust add Ogun's potent ashe to the contents of your mojo bag. Make sure to have metallic powders (also referred to as *dusts*) on hand as you work your way through this Hoodoo year of magick. Aligning your practice with processes utilized by the makers of ironwork and steel puts your mojo in a position of indelible power.

## 16. Hoodoo Hunter and Gatherer

Begin your mojo workin' collection today. Check your pantry for baking soda, white cane sugar, and whole garlic cloves. If you do not have these items, purchase them. Buy a good-quality whiskey. Search for suppliers of Florida Water, rose water, Hoyt's Cologne, and Jockey Club cologne for future use. Gather red and other flannels that feel good to your hands. You will also need pins and sewing needles. Devil's shoestring and real silver dimes (minted before 1964) should also be on your list.

As I've mentioned, look for your supplies locally first. If that doesn't work out, try buying from individual sellers on eBay or Etsy. This makes your search a little more laborious, but it also helps you be more in control of what you are buying and from whom. I am particularly fond of Etsy because it is the home of creators and makers as sellers. If that or the other options don't work out, then I would look for online suppliers, remembering that shopping around is always best. Try to see yourself as a

Hoodoo hunter and gatherer when seeking out magical supplies. Authenticity and good vibes with your supplier are important.

Make sure to keep track of your suppliers by making notes in a journal or other safe place. Once you have found reliable sources, you will want to make sure you do not have to repeat the search each time you need to make a purchase. If you are not happy with an item, make note of that too. Then you will not make the mistake of purchasing that item from that source again.

### 17. Luck Draw Mojo

As you have read and hopefully have directly experienced by this point, mojo bags can be called upon to do many different things. They are extensions of your own hands and of your physical body. Because of this invisible and potent connection, the mojo bag is to be closely guarded, fed, and nurtured.

Here is a luck draw mojo for increasing luck (especially in money matters) that brings together some very potent items known to bring good fortune, including garlic, lodestones, and anvil dust. Anvil dust can be purchased, but originally it was the fine black iron dust that settled around a blacksmith's anvil as a natural byproduct of hard work. Magnetic sand is sometimes used as a substitute.

- Lodestone is known for drawing and attracting things to you.
- Garlic protects you from evil and from anyone trying to destroy the potency of your mojo.
- Red is a symbol of life, warning intruders to stay away from your stuff.

- Sugar is a peaceful, spiritually sweetening agent.
- Anvil dust draws luck and winnings.

Put a lodestone pair and an entire clove of garlic in a red flannel. Sprinkle with anvil dust and white cane sugar. Sew the flannel together. Douse with whiskey to feed it and bring it to life. Speak to it. Tell your new creation the intentions you have for it, and ask for what you want. Rub it kindly to speak it into acting on your behalf.

## 18. Handy Flannel

Mojo bags have many different names, as you've learned. I frequently think of my mojo bags as flannels and hands. We discussed flannels previously, so now let's stop to consider how and why a mojo bag relates to our hands, and serves as one.

You may be familiar with the *ajna*, or third eye. This eye sees what our other two eyes miss. It is an eye that sees the unfamiliar and things from the spiritual realm. It is a sensing and guiding device.

Similarly, the hand in Hoodoo relates to our hand in a multilayered manner. Through our hands we search, feel, find, sense, gather, hold, mold, make, communicate, sign, ask questions, curse, point, nurture, show love, fight, dance, and more.

Our physical hands set us apart from most other mammals because of our opposable thumbs. Our hands assist us in practically every aspect of our lives; therefore, using hands in a magical sense, as a Hoodoo tool, is fitting.

Our Hoodoo hand holds our intent, wishes, prayers, hopes, will, power, fate, and protection. The Hoodoo's hand reaches out, as an extension of ourselves, into the seen and unseen worlds. It represents us and serves as a magical signature. To make by hand, we make magical power objects, potions, powders, and other tools essential to the Hoodoo.

Take time today to research sources of chamois skin, chamois cloth, and synthetic substitutes. Find a quality supplier and purchase enough to make a mojo bag. Chamois is used for polishing various items, including cars, and as a drawing material for artists, so you can find it at either type of supplier.

## 19. A Gambling Luck Hand and a Job Fixin' Toby

Luck seems out of our control, yet it is close at hand. Making your own luck by drawing it to you is empowering. It is not as difficult to do as it might seem. Working on honing, shaping, and crafting your luck at will is a favorite Hoodoo trick.

Most likely you use your hands when gambling or playing games of chance. Here are some fixin's for a gambling luck hand from an old-timer from Algiers, Louisiana:[10]

- Black snakeroot
- Devil's shoestring
- High John the Conqueror root
- Cinnamon chips

Put these ingredients inside a super-soft chamois skin, along with a real silver dime (minted before 1964).

Dress with Van Van oil. Carry it in your front pocket. Squeeze your hand as you play, and luck will surely come your way.

Sometimes gambling luck might not be what is called for. Perhaps you have a money-making opportunity in the form of

---

10. Hyatt, *Hoodoo, Conjuration, Witchcraft, Rootwork*, 547.

a new job. In that case, this *toby* (yet another name for a mojo bag) is a formula from a Hoodoo from Charleston, South Carolina.[11] It uses your lodestone pair (your he and she) to draw luck for a job interview.

- Your lodestone pair (your he and she)
- Lodestone powder
- Flannel
- Hoyt's Cologne
- Red ribbon or cord

Dress your he and she with some lodestone powder to charge them up, and put them inside a flannel. Dress with Hoyt's Cologne, then tie off with red ribbon or cord. Put this guy in your pocket and squeeze him as much as possible on the way to, during, and after your job interview.

## 20. Five-Finger Grass Rite

Five-finger grass is an herb that is also called cinquefoil. It has five-lobed leaves and five-petaled yellow flowers. Its shape mimics our physical hand, so it is perfect to use in the creation of a magical one. Five-finger grass is an easy-to-grow garden herb for your Hoodoo garden.

You won't need many items to create this traditional protective hand inspired by Harry Hyatt's informant from Wilmington, South Carolina,[12] and once you've done so it will be difficult for others to harm you.

---

11. Hyatt, *Hoodoo, Conjuration, Witchcraft, Rootwork*, 600.

12. Hyatt, *Hoodoo, Conjuration, Witchcraft, Rootwork*.

Hoodoos often use psalms as their incantations while doing tricks, rites, and spells. Psalms are sacred songs or poems from the book of Psalms in the Old Testament of the Bible that are used in worship.

Write Psalm 23 on kraft paper using a #2 pencil. The psalm is as follows:

### A Psalm of David

The LORD *is* my shepherd; I shall not want.

He maketh me to lie down in green pastures: he leadeth me beside the still waters.

He restoreth my soul: he leadeth me in the paths of righteousness for his name's sake.

Yea, though I walk through the valley of the shadow of death, I will fear no evil: for thou *art* with me; thy rod and thy staff they comfort me.

Thou preparest a table before me in the presence of mine enemies: thou anointest my head with oil; my cup runneth over.

Surely goodness and mercy shall follow me all the days of my life: and I will dwell in the house of the LORD forever.

Put some five-finger grass inside your bag. Purposely recite the psalm, with your intent in mind, as you tie up your bag. Now you've got yourself a very protective hand.

## 21. Nails

While Ifa and Santeria are different from Hoodoo, the Yoruba essence that connects the practices is alive within it. This is natural, since many African Americans come from cultures directly influenced by the Yoruba, and we have shaped Hoodoo.

You will notice that your mojo bags call for nails, typically coffin nails, and sometimes there is work with horseshoe nails. Iron-containing implements, tools, vessels, and weaponry contain and share Ogun's fierce energy as the god of war. Nails are activating. They penetrate surfaces, fix things into place, bind pieces together, and permanently hold what we want contained. Piercing Ogun energy is present in nails, needles, arrows, swords, machetes, horseshoes, hoes on which we make hoecakes, and the iron skillets used to cook other types of soul food, as well as in brews, potions, and tricks.

Nails are useful in mojo bags. They have inherent strength because of the Ogun ashe they contain. Nailing, or the inclusion of nails, is about action, protection, and making things happen. This action is reinforced by the specificity of the type of nail used. Coffin nails bind and protect; they are also warrior's tools. Horseshoe nails bring luck and prosperity. Remember, though, that only those who are fully spiritually engaged and folks with a great facility with their hands will benefit from the power of nails offered by the lord of war.

## 22. Pins and Needles

Pins and needles are used for constructing mojo bags, but they go beyond the utilitarian function intended. Both do-it-yourself tools contain the same Ogun energy and ashe as nails. As with nails, pins and needles are useful for penetration, piercing, binding, and activating previously inert energy.

Hoodoos love making, binding, and fixing things. To give our magickal items the boost they need to be as potent as possible, we make things ourselves more than buying them ready-made. By doing it yourself, your energy becomes even more prevalent in the creation. Pins and needles are tools you'll need for candle magick and mojo bags.

Take some time to gather a good collection of pins and needles. These will be used for constructing and sewing together mojo and other types of Hoodoo bags, and for magical work to come. If you are fortunate, you may have a sewing box you inherited from a family member. Using items owned by ancestors in your creation work will strengthen your connection to the work. While you're at it, find, purchase, or make a pin cushion, and obtain a thimble to protect your hands as you work as well. Then, as projects arise, you'll be good to go.

## 23. Ogun Praise Chant

Do you have Ogun on your mind from the reading and gathering you've done over the past few days? Good! Today we will do a praise chant to please and engage Ogun. You can use this chant when doing Hoodoo involving nails, needles, and pins. This praise chant is from the ancient town of Ketu: [13]

> Ogún, allied to the man with a quick hand
> Ogún, owner of high fringes of palm fronds
> Ogún ties on his cutlass with a belt of cotton
> Ogún of the sharp black cutlass
>
> Hoe is the child of Ogún
> Axe is the child of Ogún
> Gun is the child of Ogún
>
> Ogún, salute of iron and stone
> The blacksmith of all heaven.

---

13. Thompson, *Flash of the Spirit*, 53.

## 24. Curio of Note: Money for Your Mojo

Coins and other types of currency, including cowrie shells, are used in West Africa and the diaspora for spiritual purposes. Money is needed by the spirits, particularly the ancestors, to carry out their activities. Moreover, money is a way of paying tribute to the assistants for helping with your magick work. In other African diasporic practices, coins in general are used as an offering to spirits, lwa, and orisha.

The dime appears repeatedly in Hoodoo as the preferred money offering to make tricks and rites go just the right way. Not just any type of dime will do. The dime should contain silver, which means you'll want to get hold of dimes minted before 1964. Begin to gather and set aside these silver dimes when you come across them.

Silver is a revered metal in diverse magical paths. Silver is used to invoke deities, lwa, orisha, and the ancestors. It is also used in love, luck, and money drawing and in protection magick. It is a psychically oriented metal and embodiment of moon goddesses.

## 25. Money Moon Bath

To charge your dimes for Hoodoo, place them outside in a crystal or glass dish two days before a full moon. Leave the bowl of dimes outdoors for three nights, with the third night being the full moon.

Wrap your dimes in red flannel and bring them indoors. Now they are ready to be used in the construction of specific types of mojo bags.

## 26. Divination Jack

Divination, signs, and prophecy are important practices in Hoodoo. The courageous practitioner is willing to participate in divination, learning to read signs and then dealing with the prophecy. Some folks like simple yes-or-no questions answered from the spirit realm. By activating and stewarding a deep relationship with a specific collection of conjuration items wrapped into a ball shape, you can build a prophecy aid. A jack is like a mojo bag, but it is used primarily as a divination device.

Here are some tips for using a jack that were shared by a Hoodoo from Hampton, Virginia, in the 1930s:[14]

1. Jack hangs around the neck, or if he is a wish-granting Jack, he can be carried in the purse, after wishes are whispered to it.

2. Typically, he is small on one side; larger and longer on the other end.

3. Be sure to hold Jack by the string and off your neck when you are asking questions.

4. Notice in which direction he swings to determine the answer.

5. Jack can be used as a honing device to find money. To use the bag in that manner, insert nine pins into him.

Keep Jack well fed and safe. You want to maintain a long-term relationship with him. He will work like a pendulum. You can assign *no* answers to him swinging more to the left and *yes* to him leaning more to the right. Consult Jack when in a quandary about where to go and what to do.

---

14. Hyatt, *Hoodoo, Conjuration, Witchcraft, Rootwork*, 190–191.

## 27. Hoodoo Gardening: Adam and Eve Root

Adam and Eve root, also called Eve, Adam, and Son root, is very useful in your love draw mojo bag. It is the perfect plant to grow in your Hoodoo garden. Adam and Eve plant (*Aplectrum hyemale*) is in the orchid family. It is also appropriately called putty root, as a mucilage from it is used to create a strong binding glue for clay vessels. The root grows in colonies underground, coupling and multiplying at will. It releases a binding substance, indicating it can be used to bind others together, including couples.

Back in the day, Hoodoos went out to the woods and tapped the earth for the roots needed for their workings. However, with the strong demand for this love draw plant and overutilization of its habitat, its status in the wild is fragile.

The flowers are truly intriguing in appearance and biology. They are tricolored and have a curious appeal. They are hermaphrodite, having both female and male organs, which are pollinated by insects.

Adam and Eve root has traditionally been macerated and used for healing boils. It has a pain-relieving quality, as an analgesic, which shows that it helps to act on our head, addressing our mental state.

### Growing Adam and Eve Root

Adam and Eve plant can be purchased as a bare root from many suppliers. It is native to Tennessee and grows well in the southern United States generally. It prefers shady, moist areas in zones 5–8. I have found that it is sold on Etsy and at online nursery suppliers. These plants are considered easy to grow and are not picky about their garden space, though they have a predilection for establishing a symbiotic relationship with certain types of fungi.

## 28. Curio of Note: High John the Conqueror Root

While the mojo bag is the most recognizable object used by Hoodoos, High John the Conqueror root is most frequently placed inside it. This root's prominence in the practice speaks volumes about the folkloric nature of Hoodoo. This plant's enduring use is an excellent example of sympathetic magick and correspondences in Hoodoo.

### The Story of High John the Conqueror

By now you are familiar with the large measure of determination and the spirit of survival alive in Hoodoo. This spirit of survival is so strong that it helped African Americans through capture, enslavement, Jim Crow, the civil rights movement, and, most recently, the Black Lives Matter movement. High John is believed to have been an African prince who was captured and enslaved, yet his clever spirit could not be broken. High John is also thought to have been a trickster, which enabled him to evade his masters and survive. His spirit lives on in the tales of Br'er (Brother) Rabbit and Uncle Remus.

### The Height of Sympathetic Magick

When an herb's appearance, qualities, elements, or usage coordinate with the type of magick performed, it is called *sympathetic magick*. High John the Conqueror root is a plant part that is extremely tough and difficult to break down and process. It has a heart-shaped leaf, is used for protection, and is worn at times in a pocket near the heart. The flower is hermaphrodite, reddish, and trumpet-like—clearly it has something important to say and do. Additionally, it is evergreen (always useful) and a vigorously growing climber.

## 29. Bodyguard

We all need a good bodyguard from time to time. Any practicing Hoodoo would agree that protection is a necessary, if not essential, part of the Hoodoo practice. Here is a traditional protective bodyguard in the form of a mojo bag that draws on the melding of potent High John the Conqueror root, chamber lye, silver, and Hoyt's Cologne. Try to create this when the moon is full. Gather the following items:

- Chamber lye (your urine)
- Glass jar with lid
- A silver dime (minted 1964 or before)
- High John the Conqueror root
- Red flannel
- Ribbon, twine, or cord
- Hoyt's Cologne

Collect chamber lye in the glass jar. Put the dime and High John the Conqueror root in the glass jar with the chamber lye. Fix the lid tightly on the jar and soak overnight. In the morning, remove the dime and root and pat them dry with a paper towel or rag. Place the dried material inside a red flannel. Fix it tightly with the ribbon, twine, or cord. Feed several drops of Hoyt's Cologne to the mojo bag. Tie the bag around your waist and feel safer thanks to the confluence of the powerful components from which it is made.

### 30. Jomo

While the origin and definitive meaning of the word *jomo* are shrouded in mystery, two things are clear. A jomo is a type of power object related to a mojo bag. The word itself is an anagram of the word *mojo*, meaning the letters have been rearranged to make a new word.

I mentioned previously that there is division in the magickal world of the Yoruba between the hidden and the revealed. The manipulation of words to suit our purposes is an enduring Africanism that lives on in the United States. Of course, during enslavement, Hoodoo and similar practices were outlawed. Therefore, for Hoodoo to survive, secrecy was essential.

Coding has been something useful to cultural African survival in the Americas. African Americans' masterful use of word play and double entendre is evident in Negro spirituals' usage to send messages about the goings-on of the Underground Railroad. An anagram such as jomo may have been another way to hide Hoodoo work so it could survive and flourish into the future.

Mojo bags are called different things by different practitioners, as I've mentioned. This choice may be solely at the discretion of the Hoodoo, or it may vary according to the bag's specific purpose or its relationship to a person, or from one region to the next. The following is a vintage jomo formula derived from an account of an informant out of Waycross, Georgia.[15] It blends crossroads magick with luck draw to draw luck to the home.

---

15. Hyatt, *Hoodoo, Conjuration, Witchcraft, Rootwork*, 595.

### Lucky Jomo

Head out to the crossroads of your choice between 12:00 and 1:00 a.m. Gather up some crossroads sand. Put it in a flannel and fix the bag tight. Hang this over your mantel.

## 31. Lucky Gamblin' Toby

This mojo type of bag is a New Orleans–style hand for you to use in games of chance. This is an original toby, whose contents were shared by an informant from New Orleans, Louisiana.[16] It incorporates powerful items we have discussed, along with a very old type of wonderfully scented cologne, used specifically in gambling magick, called Jockey Club. Jockey Club cologne used to have a small horseshoe inside, but you can purchase one and add it to your cologne bottle.

- Baking soda
- High John the Conqueror root
- Your he and she (male and female lodestones)
- Red flannel
- Oil of clover
- Jockey Club cologne

Sprinkle some baking soda on your High John the Conqueror root and a bit on your he and she. Sew them up into a red flannel. Feed them oil of clover. Each time you use this lucky gamblin' toby, do a spiritual hand wash before touching it by mindfully pouring some Jockey Club cologne on it.

---

16. Hyatt, *Hoodoo, Conjuration, Witchcraft, Rootwork*, 655.

# CHAPTER 2
# HOODOO WATERS: DAYS 32-62

The liquid water at the surface of our sacred mother makes our planet special within our solar system. Earth-based spirituality celebrates the gifts of the earth in its manifestation as the Great Mother. Water enables Earth Mama to support life—intelligent life at that. The existence of water and the amount of it at our disposal creates, supports, and sustains life as we know it.

Many different magickal paths acknowledge and use the elements: earth, air, ether, water, and fire. The elements help us breathe life into our work. Hoodoos enjoy incorporating the elements into tricks, spells, and rites specific to the practice. Various types of liquids are heavily utilized, with watery fluids being chief among the substances recognized as encapsulating metaphysical essence.

This chapter is devoted to the exploration of the ways waters and other liquids have been used and can be used in your Hoodoo practice. The natural fluidity of watery substances enables you to craft potions, brews, medicines, baths, washes, libations, and magickal elixirs that effect change. Water is an excellent vehicle for Hoodoo. The ability to skillfully manipulate liquid substances for conjuration is an important aspect of your work.

Waters and liquids useful to the Hoodoo come from a wide variety of sources. It will take energy, engagement, and at times intuition to know exactly when and where to acquire your water and other fluids. These mystical substances, whether collected from nature, handmade, or purchased, have specific qualities, correspondences, and affinities with other items. They also have varied rites and tricks with which they are associated. Now is the time to delve into this unique corpus of knowledge, which will fuel and propel your Hoodoo practice.

Here are some of the things you will do this month:

• Grow to appreciate natural existing waters, such as running water like streams, rivers, brooks, and waterfalls, for their inherent possibilities and their relationship to deity.

• Explore the many implications and uses of the sea and ocean.

• Work with weather-related waters derived from rains and lightning storms.

• Experience the ashe-rich blending of Hoodoo's conjuration herbs with water to create powerful decoctions, tisanes, and teas.

• Learn how to use holy water and floral waters to purify, cleanse, and bless the household through floor washes and other applications.

• Explore ways of employing waters of the household, such as dishwater for protection and unhexing.

- Create hand and foot washes for drawing, cleansing, and protection.

- Make ritual baths for a variety of purposes.

- Learn about old-fashioned and newer colognes used in Hoodoo.

- Become familiar with traditional procedures and age-old techniques for employing waters every day you work your magick.

## 32. Contemplate Water

Examining the ways that water is viewed by sub-Saharan Africans is useful to understanding its role in Hoodoo. Looking to West Africa for ways that water is viewed metaphysically is telling. For example, in the Yoruba cosmology, water represents the unique strangeness of the spiritual realm. From their point of view, we can see through it yet only understand it on a surface level. It is a glass mirror that we may look through but not fully comprehend. The sea mother and father orisha figures Yemaya and Ologun, respectively, represent the energies of the upper and the lower ocean in Ife. The orisha Oshun has a deep relationship with the running waters of rivers. Oshun is beautiful, otherworldly, light-skinned, and depicted as being foreign, likely because of her connection to water.

In Hoodoo, there is also a wide range of ways the varied qualities of water and other liquids are used. Hoodoos collect water that has fallen from the sky during ordinary rain showers and during or after storms. Rainwater, thought of in diverse mythologies as tears from the heavens, is a valuable magickal tool. Lightning water (rain collected during a lightning storm) is also obtained. It is utilized in baths for empowerment and to invoke change. You will notice that many Hoodoo tricks call upon the forces within running water such as brooks, streams, and rivers.

From the mundane tap water to the mystical lightning water, let's explore ways of empowering our practice and enriching life by employing water.

## 33. Start Your Water Stash

Today, begin to consider water through the eyes of a Hoodoo. Water has a wide range of applications and qualities. As a healing bath or rain shower, it can be refreshing, renewing, and soothing. On the other hand, water in the form of a tsunami or flash flood can threaten and take lives. As a Hoodoo, your task is to capture and use these properties in your work.

This is the time to collect vessels that will hold your waters. Gather some sterilized glass jars to reuse as containers for your collection. Purchase or create blank labels on which you can note the type of water, date collected, and location from which it was obtained. Use a waterproof marker and waterproof labels for your notations.

Identify a source you will tap to secure your running water. In your tricks, spells, and rites, you will need a good source of running water. Is there a nearby spring or creek you can visit? Start paying closer attention to the weather, no matter the season. Are you experiencing or expecting showers or a storm this week? If you are, be prepared to collect water.

This can be done over a longer period than just one day, of course. Collect rainwater, morning dew, tears, sweat, slobber, and lightning water. Dishwater and bathwater will also play a role. After obtaining a water sample, label it appropriately, seal the container tightly, and store in a cool, dry place.

## 34. Reflection and Journaling

The surface of a mirror is likened to water in various types of mythology. It returns the reflection of the gazer, but there are secrets in its depths if you can see past the reflection.

Today, begin your water work with its metaphysical representative—the mirror. Consider where to find a good mirror. Antique mirrors are especially useful. Check your attic or basement, ask an aunt or grandparent, or head out to a thrift shop or antique store. The older your mirror the better. (Even the back of a mirror is useful. It is scraped and the silver residue from it is used to perform various tricks.)

Hold your mirror and practice grounding and centering. Take four to five cleansing breaths. Gaze into the mirror for about ten minutes. Let your eyes soften and become unfocused. The goal is to see beyond your image. What do you see? Write it down.

To fully immerse yourself in the power of water, you need to set aside time for journaling. Here is a guided brainstorming session to get you started.

### Water Brainstorming Session

- How do you hope to align yourself with the qualities of water?

- Are there any water deities, lwa, or orisha you relate to, and why? If not, are there any water-related spirits you plan to explore, and why?

- How is water currently important in your spiritual life?

- What are some ways that you know water is used in relation to spirituality?

• What types of watery substances have the most value and resonance in your life currently?

## 35. Procedures for Using Water

There is a set of procedures for using Hoodoo that you need to know to use your waters effectively. As you move through this chapter and through section 3, you'll frequently see the following procedures for using your waters.

### Downward

When taking a spiritual bath, you will want to spiritually cleanse yourself by pushing the healing water downward. Practice downward strokes as you cleanse your body so it becomes second nature. You want water to pour down your body to rinse. Downward motion in the spiritual bath clears negativity. You will be truly cleansed as the water drains from body to tub and eventually down the drain.

### Prayers/Psalms

Incantations are used to support healing water treatments. Typically, prayers are said, and most frequently in traditional Hoodoo, those prayers are psalms from the Bible. You will also be given alternate incantations to use.

### Numerology/Counting

Timing is everything. When taking a cleansing wash, you will be directed to count. There are specific amounts of times to cleanse in the spiritual bath or other types of washes. The number of times is usually an odd number. There are special times of the day when this type of cleansing magick is to be performed as well. Much protective work takes place just before or at sunrise, as you would intend to beat the evil Hoodoo by doing your healing work before they do their work against you.

## 36. Holy Water

Holy water is water that has been sanctified, cleared of any evil influence, and blessed by a priest or other holy person. It is used in Catholicism to clear and purge a person or place of demons and other evil beings. Holy water is not only sanctified but also capable of clearing a home environment of negative influences and bad juju, making it a peaceful water that packs a huge spiritual punch.

### New Orleans Uncrossing Peace Water Rites

- Sprinkle holy water in the four corners of your home.
- Put some holy water on a rag or sponge and wash your front door with it for three mornings in a row.

These simple rituals bring positive energy that yields peace and brings success to the inhabitants of your home.

### Holy Water Bath

- Begin early, before the sun rises.
- Add holy water to a shallow bath.
- Cleanse yourself, using downward motions, so the bad influences you have encountered drain off you and into the water.
- Set an intention or make a wish as you wash in the holy water.
- Collect the used bathwater in a large basin or jug.

- Throw the water in which you have bathed toward the sunrise.

Take daily notes of which of your troubles have gone away. Do this with integrity and belief in your ingredients and in the rite. Believe that your trouble has been removed. Rest assured that you are cleansed and your problems have been returned to the universe, purified by the first light of day.

## 37. Alternate Holy Water Cleansing Ritual

If you find yourself unable to use holy water because it is a part of a religion you do not believe in, substitute other waters considered holy in different sorts of earth-based spirituality or pagan practices, such as rose water or a kosher (or sea) salt water, in which a silver dime has been steeped overnight. You will need to purify the water, salt, rose, or other herb before adding it to the bathtub, so that the whole blend is pure and ready to do its good work.

As you run the water, recite this pagan prayer:

*Blessed water deva,*
*May your fluidity and graceful cleansing gifts*
*permeate my healing waters.*
*Earth Mother and Father Sun,*
*I call upon thee:*
*Purify these sea salt crystals (or water of the rose, or herbal water)*
*in your bountiful and beautiful image, I pray!*
*Blessed be!*
*Blessed be!*
*Blessed be!*

Blessed water, without any accoutrements, is a sacred substance, and is particularly effective when paired with numerology. If you or your living/work space need cleansing, try the following rite.

### Traditional Hoodoo Rite

The old folk would take three buckets of water and throw it at 6:00 a.m. toward the sun, after saying prayers. You can do this for nine mornings to purge evil from your life.

## 38. Curio of Note: Bluing with Anil Balls

Amplification may be needed to strengthen your work. Herbs, stones, bits of metals, or other Hoodoo tools will often be added to your waters to increase their strength. As you know, colors are symbolic in Hoodoo. In the past month you became familiar with the power of red and learned about how it is employed in flannels and mojo bags. Now we will consider the color blue, bluing, and the use of anil balls in Hoodoo.

When you set out a pan or bowl of blue water or scrub your stoop with it, you are engaging in a practice based on the age-old belief that blue is calming and peaceful. Blued water can thwart bad intent and actions against you. This association between calm, unhexing, and blue is most likely related to blue being the color of ocean and sea water. The oceans and seas coordinate with hundreds of primordial figures, including gods and goddesses, lwa, and orisha, as well as the Virgin Mary. These correspondences vary according to the belief system.

Hoodoo, being a mélange of beliefs but with a strong African foundation, incorporates bluing as a plea to the spirits and ancestors. Using the solution of bluing and water, which is sacred on its own, sends a symbolic message to the universe that you are a seeker of peace.

## 39. Peaceful Home

As a Hoodoo, you can use blued water, created from anil balls, to cultivate a peaceful, quiet, nurturing, and calm environment in your home.

In the original Hoodoo recipes, bluestone was used. Bluestone is copper sulfate. The reason it is no longer used is because it is toxic. Seeing that we now have a safer option, today's Hoodoos go for anil balls. They are available on Etsy and eBay, among other websites. Once you get a good source of blue (anil) balls, use them like this:

• Add some blue balls to a bucket of water and stir. Make sure you have a nice rich blue.

Use this solution to do the following:

1. Scrub your walkway and stoop. Replenish the blue water until you've done the job well.

2. Put a good-size bowl of blue water under your bed to stop bad dreams and evil juju from getting into you as you sleep. Replenish every day for six days.

3. Burn anil balls in the house or wear them in a small pouch hanging from the neck. This will protect you and banish evil work done against you. This is great for unhexing!

4. If you've walked over an evil Hoodooed object, take a bath in very dilute blue water mixed with a bit of sulphur. When you've finished bathing, throw some of the bathwater outside to dispose of the bad energy.

## 40. Dishwater Rite

Hoodoo is a resourceful practice with a strong focus on domestic affairs, the atmosphere of the home, and the happiness of those living within it. While other traditions will simply have dishwater drain down the sink, in Hoodoo the water has a keen relationship to those who have eaten on the dinnerware and with the flatware. The water magickally transforms once the dishes are in it. The water goes from being utilitarian to mystical because it contains some of the residual fluids (saliva, for example) of those who have eaten. Dishwater, like spiritual washes and spiritual bathwaters, has power that can be wielded because it contains the mojo of the occupants of the house from which it was created.

If a person has your foot track, they can do powerful spells against you. To defeat this type of negativity in your life, you will need dishwater to set it right. This rite is inspired by Doctor Maguin of Charleston, South Carolina.[17]

1. Wash your dishes in a plastic tub or basin.

2. Throw the dishwater over your right shoulder outside once the washing of the dishes is complete.

3. Walk backward, all the way off the property.

4. Repeat this three mornings in a row (dish washing, throwing the water, walking backward).

## 41. Luck Reversal Bath

There is a lot of emphasis on luck in Hoodoo. Fortunately, luck (and particularly bad luck) isn't seen as being stagnant or

---

17. Hyatt, *Hoodoo, Conjuration, Witchcraft, Rootwork*, 434.

something that just is. In Hoodoo, good luck can be drawn to the person seeking it, whereas bad luck can be reversed, particularly if that bad luck comes from a bad Hoodoo trick. Before you start, gather enough clean, dry jugs to hold eight quarts of liquid, plus the following ingredients:

- 8 quarts water
- Dime size of saltpeter
- 1 teaspoon kosher salt

Heat the water until steaming but not boiling. Add the saltpeter and kosher salt. Stir until dissolved.

When you are ready to begin the rite, draw a very hot bath. Swish and swirl the mixture into the bathwater while focusing your intention to reverse your luck.

Enter the bath. Recite the following incantation as you bathe. Remember to always rub yourself downward as you cleanse: clean your face, down your body, to your toes.

*Luck, O sweet luck,*
*I call your name.*
*Luck with force and power to make change,*
*Walk with me and talk through me.*
*With your help, all that can and should be will be!*

Exit the bath and fill your jugs with the bathwater. Take a bath incorporating this same water daily for eight more days, repeating the incantation each time.

On the ninth day, fill the jugs with the water from your final bath. Take all the water outside and throw it toward the sun.[18]

---

18. Hyatt, *Hoodoo, Conjuration, Witchcraft, Rootwork*, 474.

## 42. Hoodoo Gardening: Just Rosy

Many people have asked me what plants should be included in the Hoodoo's garden. Rose bushes should be a staple, because they have multiple functions. You can use the petals and also rose water in your magickal rites and spells. I suggest getting yourself a variety of gardening catalogs and reading up on roses that grow well in your area.

- Roses are perfect for love draw, and as a systemic nervine, they create a calming environment and will calm your nerves.

- Using roses in the concentrated form of rose water is a handy way to envelop yourself and your implements and home in their healing ashe.

As you investigate various types of roses, keep an eye out for these medicinal and fragrant varieties: Apothecary's Rose, Belle de Crecy, Bulgarian or Damask, Celestial, Kazanlik, Madame Isaac Pereire, Guinee, Souvenir de la Malmaison, and Great Maiden's Blush.

## 43. Beloved Perfumes and Colognes

From the mid-eighteenth century through the mid-twentieth century, there was a beautiful array of alluring scents available, different from those made today. These scents captivated Hoodoos. From wherever they hailed, Hoodoos would set out to five and dimes, apothecaries, and drug stores to get their favorite formulas for magick making. There were even door-to-door salespeople who made these delightful items available. Times have changed, but these scents are still available today.

**Hoyt's Cologne** is shared as a multipurpose scent by numerous Hoodoo informants through Harry Hyatt's research, sometimes written as Hearts Cologne because he was recording the spoken words of his informants reflecting regional dialect. Hoyt's Cologne, developed in 1868, was treasured in Early America and by Hoodoos. In Hoodoo, it is used for luck draw, success, and love. It has a very evocative scent.

Splash it on your hands and rub or clap them together before going out to draw good luck.

**Jockey Club** was developed by Caswell-Massey, an American personal care and apothecary established in 1752. This cologne was introduced in 1840 and is used for good luck with horse gambling, among other games of chance. At one time it had a small horseshoe inside. It is pleasantly unisex-scented with essential oils of bergamot, geranium, amber, ylang-ylang, sandalwood, and musk.

Before setting out for your equestrian gambling activities, dab this cologne on your mojo bag or pulse points. If you'd like, put a very small gold horseshoe charm inside the bottle to enhance its luck draw properties.

### 44. Multipurpose Washes

Washes are another unique way that Hoodoos engage with the element of water magickally. Here are a few that you will come to find useful:

**Florida Water,** developed in 1808, is a dearly beloved spiritual cleanser that feeds the ancestor spirits while clearing away negative spirits. Florida Water is also popular in Santeria.

With refreshing orange, calming lavender, and grounding clove, it is a bracing tonic.

Add Florida Water to a bowl to place on your ancestral altar. Cleanse the floor, altar, and bath before spiritual work by adding it to some water first and using it as a spiritual cleanser.

**Chinese Wash** contains the energy of the bush (wild, unspoiled lands) because of the unique combination of grass essential oils in its formula. Chinese Wash is used for various purposes. It has a fresh high-frequency scent.

To use Chinese Wash, add it sparingly to your cleaning bucket or mop. It washes away bad juju used against you and your family. Cleanse your work space, home, and car as you restore positive vibrations with this spiritual wash.

**Kananga Water** is created from ylang-ylang, an uplifting, activating feeding herb.

Use Kananga Water for home protection, ancestor worship, and spiritual cleansing by using it in a floor wash, on a mop or natural sponge, or placed out in bowls.

### 45. Bodily Fluids

We tend to think of ourselves as skin, bone, organs, hair, and nails, but our breath, spirit(s), and many types of excretions also make us all that we are. Excretions help us extend ourselves into different spaces and situations. Body excreta also have specific scents. Our aromatic qualities can have a strong influence on many things. Mood and even mate choices are affected by scent. Our sweat, urine, breath, saliva, breast milk, skin oils, and sexual secretions all contain scent-communication chemical compounds. In fact, humans contain denser concentrations of scent glands on the skin than almost any other mammal.

This influence of fluids goes way back in history and extends across the globe. African warriors have collected excreta for various purposes, such as deer's tears after it is killed to capture their fear, and sorcerer's sweat for its distinct qualities. They realize that each type of body fluid, rendered at a specific moment in time, has a strong manner of acting on us if yielded magickally, whether we are keyed into that power or not.

As you move forward, you will come across work that utilizes secretions and excreta as a subtle, and sometimes not so subtle, tool in the comprehensive arsenal of your Hoodoo practice. Stay attentive to and aware of opportunities to collect specific types of fluids from humans and animals in the specimen jars you've collected.

## 46. Hoodoo Gardening: Milkweed

Tomorrow, I will share an old-timey toddy that includes milkweed herb. Today, let's explore milkweed and why it might have been selected for use in this drink to restore balance where there is evil in a relationship.

Milkweed (*Asclepias syriaca L.*) grows easily in fields and wastelands and on roadsides in the eastern United States, growing as far west as Kansas and to Saskatchewan, Canada. Its actions are diaphoretic (promotes profuse sweating). Milkweed is a diuretic (encourages the body to release water and salt through the urine), emetic (vomiting), and purgative (a laxative) tonic. This is the plant treasured by monarch butterflies each year on their migration journey. The milky fluid inside its pods resembles semen.

Make no mistake, milkweed will help get rid of waste held by the body. It is very cleansing all around.

- Milkweed as a flower essence helps sort out strong dependency on others, making way for independence and balance in a relationship.

- The rootstock and young pods of milkweed are the parts used medicinally. Use of these parts is not recommended for those who are pregnant or nursing, children, elders, or those with high blood pressure or on heart medication.

- If you are worried about using milkweed's medicinal parts and don't belong to the categories just listed, use the milkweed flower essence.

### 47. Clearing Broken Relationships

Let's face it, people can do great harm through intentionally evil acts that weaken the bond of their relationship with their partner. If that happens to you, particularly if something is done, like an affair, and you still want to repair the relationship, you can use water, minerals, and herbs in the following manner inspired by traditional Hoodoo practitioners to restore balance so you can move toward a repaired relationship.

1. Start this work on a Friday. In a very large stock pot, boil your bed clothes, little by little.

2. Spritz the bed clothes with your homemade rose water and hang them outside to dry naturally.

3. Powder your mattress very lightly with a bit of baking soda.

4. Make a hot toddy before bedtime of milkweed (read yesterday's description and warnings), High and Low John the Conqueror roots, and whiskey. Simmer the milkweed pod and High and Low John the Conqueror roots in a large pot of water, then strain. Add a shot of whiskey and stir. Take three sips of this three times a day on Friday night, Saturday, and Sunday as you discuss how to repair your relationship and reflect upon your independence.

## 48. Madam Collins's Reversing-Evil Bath

If the acts that have taken place have affected the male partner's ability to perform sexually, try this altar/bath.

With a small amount of rose water, cleanse the surface upon which the altar is to be built. When the area is dry, lay down a silky piece of white fringed cloth. Put powdered mustard, saltpeter, and baking soda in a bowl. Bless it in the name of the Father, Son, and Holy Spirit, or do an alternate pagan trinity blessing. The person must bathe on Monday, Wednesday, and Friday in a gallon of water, adding four tablespoons of the bowl's ingredients and washing downward only.[19]

## 49. Lightning Water Rite

Oh, the possibilities of lightning! It can take something that existed for a very long time in a specific way and transform it in an instant. People around the world have been transfixed by lightning for thousands of years, and this fascination is shared by Hoodoos. Here is a very old, unusual way to trap the magickal possibilities of lightning from Algiers, Louisiana, by making lightning water.

---

19. Hyatt, *Hoodoo, Conjuration, Witchcraft, Rootwork.*

I mentioned in chapter 1 that one of the objects sought after for its inherent magickal potential is anything touched by lightning. As always, you are the hunter and gatherer; I'm sure you won't find this in your local store. For the lightning water used in this rite, you need to find a tree struck by lightning in a specific way. This can take some time if you did not witness the strike. You must get two pieces of lightning-singed bark. You'll need some smooth burnt bark from the east-facing side of the tree and some rough burnt bark from the west-facing side.

Bring this back to your kitchen. Fill a large stock pot full of water. Boil the pieces of wood together in the pot. Let cool. Remove and discard the wood.[20]

Bath in this lightning water for any type of physical complaints you may have, or share it with someone who needs it.

## 50. Edward Marshall's May Day Wash

Most likely it is not May Day (the first day of May) today, but since May Day is a special day in Hoodoo, familiarize yourself with this work today. You can work magick specifically for May Day using running water. This is a very simple but effective rite inspired by work reported by the Hyatt informant Edward Marshall.[21] It combines the energetic fresh start promised by the first day of May with the healing quality of running water.

Go to a river. The Mississippi River is preferred, so if it's possible to go there, your work will have a very powerful effect.

---

20. Hyatt, *Hoodoo, Conjuration, Witchcraft, Rootwork.*

21. Ibid., 381.

### May Day Ritual

Identify your worries. Get in touch with the things that are weighing you down, as you approach the river.

Walk into the river. Let the moving water absorb your worries through your feet.

Recite (while you're in the river):

> *Thank you, Earth Mama,*
> *for the running of your waters*
> *and your absorbing soils.*
> *Thank you for taking away*
> *all that I've given you this May Day!*
> *Blessed be!*

Wash your hands, feet, and face with the river water.

Now get out of the water, and on the riverbank shake off your worries, just like you've seen animals do after a bath or swim.

Watch the current as it takes away your troubles.

## 51. Hoodoo Gardening: Sacred or Holy Basil

One of the beautiful things about Hoodoo is its ability to open up new dimensions in pleasure, health, and happiness. Moreover, Hoodoo absorbs and utilizes eclectic traditions from around the world, including Hinduism. I must admit, I use to have a fixed perception of basil. In the West, we think of basil primarily as a culinary herb used in Italian dishes, a salad, or perhaps a sandwich. In India, one type of basil is a sacred herb, and I want you to use it to replace what was traditionally used (sweet basil) over the next few days. I'm recommending a specific type of basil because it has a high spiritual charge and will bring great efficacy to your work.

The Latin word *basilicum* translates roughly as "royal" or "princely." In India, this royal herb is called tulsi (*Ocimum sanctum L.*). It is also referred to as Bhutagni (destroyer of demons) Tulsi, or holy basil, is thought of as a divine incarnation of the Goddess herself. Generally, worshipers of Vishnu perceive the plant as the goddess Lakshmi, devotees of Rama see it as Sita, and Krishna bhaktas view the herb as Vrinda, Radha, or Rukmani.[22]

There are numerous legends in India that revolve around sacred basil. In the classic Hindu myth *Samudramathana* (the "Churning of the Cosmic Ocean"), Vishnu obtained tulsi from the rough ocean waves as a vital aid for all beings.

## 52. Hoodoo Garden Rite

Visit your local garden center or order tulsi seeds (sacred basil) from an online supplier. In temperate zones, it can be grown from seed in a moist, peaty soil, beginning indoors during April. This herb is a vigorous grower, usually reaching eighteen inches in height. It should be placed outdoors in mid-June in pots or window boxes or directly in the garden. Grow tulsi outside your home or business as a natural amulet to encourage blessings and protection. Pinching back the top of the plant ensures healthy growth and prevents an unattractively tall, leggy appearance. Use pinched clippings in culinary ways or in magickal Hoodoo recipes like this one:

Pinch off four to five tulsi leaves and add to simmering water. Steep for seven minutes. Strain this through your head scarf or a handkerchief into a bowl. Pass your hands over the bowl. Pull the steam overhead, cup it, and breathe in the aroma. Chant:

---

22. "Tulsi and Rudraksha," *Hinduism Today.*

*Basil, sweet and kind basil,*
*share your goodness with me.*
*Cleanse my body and free my mind from bad spirits.*
*Let my soul be pure and natural as can be.*
*Bad spirits, you are banished; stay away from me!*
*Basil, sweet and kind basil,*
*share your holy goodness with my body and soul!*

Sit in a bath, water to hips. Add the brew and cleanse yourself with downward strokes. Envision all ill intent moving downward and off your body with each stroke. Save the water in a basin or jugs. Throw it back to Earth Mama, nine mornings in a row, anywhere desired.

## 53. Hoodoo and Evergreens

There is a broad conception of what is living and the idea of life in traditional African-American beliefs. This can be seen in our "living" mojo bags. In African-American folklore and Negro spirituals, the notion of "ever-lasting life" is a noted concept. During the brutal times of enslavement, the collective thought was that surely there was something better waiting when we passed on.

Oil of turpentine (not gum turpentine) has an important place in early African-American culture and folklore since it comes from evergreens, particularly pines. Pines are uplifting and they connect the ancestors and spirits below the ground to the living on earth. Oil of turpentine gets rid of aches and pains and can clear up numerous other physical conditions.

Trees play an important role in our spirituality and beliefs. The conifer is emblematic of the continuation of life through all the seasons since it stays green. The growth of pines and spruce, for example, is very upright. To contemplate the tree and align with its bearing puts you in an upright position. Pine and spruce essential oils are mood-elevating.

The trees have a certain growing cycle, and getting engaged with it is fruitful. During the early spring, pines put off light-green shoots. Gather those shoots for the coming days if they are available. You will also need oil of turpentine; rain or spring water; essential oils of white pine, spruce, and ocean pine; and soapwort root (preferably dried, precut, and sifted).

## 54. Turpentine Holy Ghost Hand Wash

You don't always have to submerge yourself in the tub to have a cleansing. Hand washes are popular in Hoodoo as well. Add just a very few drops of oil of turpentine to a nice full basin of very warm water, as the oil is caustic. Say the traditional Lord's Prayer, create your own version, or try this version from the New Zealand Prayer Book[23] as you wash your hands in oil of turpentine water:

> *Eternal Spirit*
> *Earth-Maker, Pain-bearer, Life-giver,*
> *source of all that is and that shall be,*
> *Father and Mother of us all.*
> *Loving God, in whom is heaven.*
> *The hallowing of your name echoes through*
> *the universe!*
>
> *The way of your justice be followed by the peoples*
> *of the earth!*
> *Your heavenly will be done by all created beings!*

---

23. Anglican Church in Aotearoa, New Zealand and Polynesia, "Today's Lord's Prayer," 181.

*Your commonwealth of peace and freedom*
*sustain our hope and come on earth.*

*With the bread we need for today, feed us.*
*In the hurts we absorb from one another, forgive us.*
*In times of temptation and test, spare us.*
*From the grip of all that is evil, free us.*

*For you reign in the glory of the power that is love,*
*now and forever.*

*Amen.*

Say this prayer with strong intent the entire time you are washing. Let the power of the words wash over you like a wave. Then take the basin and throw your water to the east: with it goes the trouble, hex, or bad juju put on you.

## 55. Pine Floor Wash

In this formula, you are going to blend young green pine shoots with the refreshing energy of rainwater to produce a pleasing floor wash.

Gather these ingredients:

- A large brown paper bag of pine shoots
- ½ cup soapwort root (preferably dried, precut, and sifted)
- Rainwater
- Springwater (optional)
- Rose water
- ½ teaspoon white pine essential oil

- ½ teaspoon spruce essential oil
- ¼ teaspoon ocean pine essential oil

Fill a stock pot with pine shoots. Add soapwort and rainwater (or a mix of rainwater and spring water) to fill the stock pot, leaving an inch or so at the top so it doesn't overflow.

Over medium-high heat, bring the water near a boil. When it starts to bubble, cover with a well-fitted top. Simmer for twenty minutes. Simmering decocts, or extracts, the medicinal and active substances from the shoots and soapwort. Remove from heat. Let cool until it is hot but still touchable without burning yourself. Spritz your besom with rose water and sweep the rooms to be cleaned as the water cools. Strain the contents of the pot into a wash bucket. Add the essential oils and mop your pre-swept floor as you focus on bringing bright new energy to your living space and say the following:

> *Let this space be cleansed,*
> *in, out, and through,*
> *Spiritually and psychically and mindfully.*
> *Blessed be!*
> *Let this space be cleansed.*
> *May joy, bright energy, and love flood in.*
> *Blessed be!*

### 56. Hoodoo Gardening: St. John's Wort

The botanical name for St. John's wort, a plant that has been used for at least 2,400 years, is *Hypericum perforatum*. Another name for the plant is *Fuga daemonum*, or "scare the devil."

The flowers, which are gathered on St. John's observed birthday (June 24), are bright yellow, reminding us of their relationship with the heavens, especially Father Sun. When soaked in olive oil (a holy oil), a blood-red is produced, which is useful for creating anointing oil called Blood of Christ. St. John's Day is very close to the summer solstice.

St. John's wort flowers are thought to produce truth, and as such, they were put in the mouths of the accused, during the burning times, to get confessions. The flowers, which bleed a red sap suggestive of their power, keeps the devil and devilish objects at bay and are used cross-culturally for protection. They are also used specifically in Hoodoo to reverse crossed conditions; for strength, love, and fidelity rites; and for power and success.

Try your hand at growing St. John's wort. Start today. Look to see where you can find the seeds. Once you get them, soak them overnight and then plant them in a pot, following the packet directions. To complete tomorrow's project, procure flowering St. John's wort or return to the following spell when your own plants are mature. Should you desire taking it as a tea for depression, please check on contraindications before using.

## 57. St. John's Wort Anointing Oil

Once your St. John's wort plant has flowered, collect the flowers on their stems after noon but well before dusk. Bring them inside and tie them together firmly but not too tightly with twine. Hang your bunch upside down to dry in a cool, dry place away from sunlight. Once dry, add them to a container (a Mason canning jar is perfect) with eight ounces or so of olive oil. Let the flowers steep for four to six weeks in the oil. Strain the flowers out of the oil and you'll have a terrific anointing oil for candles, yourself, or clients. Set some dried flowers aside for use in other projects.

## 58. St. John's Wort Home Protection Spell

While the oil you made yesterday is steeping, here is a protection spell with St. John's wort to employ for yourself and your home. As the spell suggests, you will want to create a mojo bag to hold the St. John's wort after rubbing the flowers about the house.

*St John's wort flannel, keep evil Hoodoos at bay,*
*I gathered you respectfully on Midsummer's Day.*
*Evildoers, your Hoodoo shall bring no harm,*
*I've gathered St. John's plant as my magickal charm:*
*We rubbed the home from pillar to post with the*
*powerful red-juiced flower.*
*Now even lightning and thunder haven't the power*
*to harm our peaceful home.*
*St. John's wort, warm and kind,*
*around our necks, a hand protects our home, body, and mind.*

## 59. Queen's Delight Cleansing Bath Ritual

Dirt daubers (or mud daubers) are an awesome type of wasp that can kill black widow spiders, among other insects. They live primarily in the South but can be found all over North America. These usually nonaggressive wasps build their nests from mud. Considered a pest by some, they are a boon to Hoodoos, who use the nests for a variety of purposes, including strength and love, power and protection.

The nests can be found in corners and crevices of structures, especially under porches and overhangs. The nests generally empty in early spring or midsummer once the adults emerge and abandon them.

This spiritual traditional bath[24] is used to reverse crossed conditions.

Procure nine dirt dauber nests. If you don't live in the South, ask a friend or relative if they can send these to you, being careful that the nesting season is over and the nests are empty. This is done to honor Earth Mama and to protect this valuable species. Put the empty nests in shallow bathwater until they get soft and break apart. Strain. Stand in the bath and rub your body in a downward direction with your St. John's wort anointing oil. Apply the dauber mud to your body. Rinse all of this off with warm water and soap.

## 60. War Bottles

There are all different types of Hoodoos and a depth to the practice that encompasses peacefulness as well as the warrior spirit. We need both in this complex world. One of the tools of the warrior is the war bottle. War bottles contain liquid, along with herbs, curios, and sometimes animal matter such as blood or feathers. The containment of these substances in a tightly fitted vessel blends and merges their magickal and spiritual qualities. Left long enough, the substances begin to break down, becoming alarmingly funky. These aren't just stagnant; they can be activated, often placed where someone will move something and break it, letting out the strong odor and ill intent, or even need to step over it once broken.

Swamp, blood, waste, dark intent—all of it nestles uneasily in the war bottle. Use these with discernment, because when war can be avoided, that is the best option. When you must move forward and strike, war bottles are thrown at the enemy's porch,

---

24. Hyatt, *Hoodoo, Conjuration, Witchcraft, Rootwork*, 1,058.

a tree on their land, or an outbuilding, as a warning and energetic strike.

If you need some protection from an enemy or after a Hoodoo war has started, try this traditional Hoodoo bottle:

Fill a bottle that has a tight-fitting cork closure with your chamber lye. Write the person's name on white paper with red ink and put it in the bottle. Add a bit of sugar. Cork the bottle. Put it under the east side of their house, upside down. This should take the edge off.

## 61. Confusion Water

Sometimes you'll want to throw your enemies off course, to confuse them and help them forget what they were doing. This type of old-fashioned confusion water will help with that.

You are going to start with the name of the main person who is bothering you and write that down on a sheet of brown paper (kraft paper or a piece of a brown paper bag), using a #2 pencil. Then write the rest of the names (if any) on the same sort of paper. Next, put some water on the stove in a medium-size pot. Turn it on medium high. Tear the names apart, into strips. Put them in the boiling water. Say the following spell:

*(Name of person), your evil is willed to stop.*
*I bind you.*
*I banish you too.*
*Your negative energy will go away,*
*out from my life this very day.*
*Mark my words,*
*do as I say,*
*in the name of goodness, with all my power, in truth!*

Boil the paper down. As the water evaporates into the air, so does their evil intent. Moreover, the bubbles cause a fuzz to develop in their heads. They forget what they were trying to do to you. They are confused. This is a subtle but effective type of war.

## 62. Madam Griffin's Juju Curative Water

The confluence of superpowerful ingredients in this potion by Madam Griffin, from Norfolk, Virginia,[25] makes a very attractive curative. One of the very special parts of this formula is that it incorporates a gourd—a direct carryover from West African tradition, where it is revered.

Go outside to your garden or a roadside, garden plot, or wild patch of land in your neighborhood. You will undoubtedly find some milkweed growing. It is identified by its bulbous, slightly triangular pods. It grows readily across the United States. You'll also need to gather together cedar berries from a cedar tree. Then you need rattlesnake dust (ground-up skin sheds) and black master root (*Astrantia major*). This herb is commonly called master root or masterwort. You can purchase this from a Hoodoo supplier.

Take these items and add them, along with the milkweed, to a cauldron. (A cast-iron Dutch oven with a fitted top will serve just as well.) Add an ample amount of water. Simmer for fifteen minutes, let cool, and then strain. While it is cooling, hollow out a bulbous-shaped gourd.

Add this brew to the bathtub. Wash yourself using downward strokes. Using the gourd, ladle this brew over yourself to get rid of soap.

---

25. Hyatt, *Hoodoo, Conjuration, Witchcraft, Rootwork*.

# CHAPTER 3
# FIRE, CANDLE & INCENSE RITES: DAYS 63-94

The use of fire is an important aspect of Hoodoo. Fire is primal, ancient, and useful and lends itself readily to ritual. An important facet of all that it means to be human is having a relationship to fire.

In our early history as Homo sapiens, fire was integral to our daily survival. Through its use, we could endure the cold, make appetizing food, keep predators at bay, encourage fertile ground for crops, and forge sophisticated tools and weaponry. Fire is the element, particularly when coupled with water, that has allowed humans to create a developed society.

Socializing around the campfire set the foundation for our development of language and the rich mythology and folklore that define our diverse societies. As early as 200,000 to 40,000 years ago, during the Paleolithic era, we were building primitive hearths from stones, arranged in a circular pattern. This use of the hearth, and celebration of it, continued until the recent development of the gas range, 150 years ago. Until the rise of the stove, every home had a hearth and a fire tender, intimately engaged with the noises, movements, wants, and needs of the household fire. With fire being so useful to our mundane lives, it is no wonder that it rather quickly became involved in our rites. Fire and burning remain at the core of Hoodoo.

Parallel to the hearth and stove is the candle. Knowledge of the language of candles, as well as what makes them most effective, fell into the hands of specialists akin to hearth tenders. Like fire itself, candles were and remain both useful in the mundane lives of humans and enriching to magickal practices like Hoodoo.

Burning, whether controlled burns or spontaneous burns to keep predators at bay or to condition the soil, let us know certain resins and leaves were fragrant when burned. Burning different parts of herbs, from roots to leaves, led to the rise of incense. The use of incense has continued to develop over the years and is helpful to the Hoodoo. It will be explored further this month.

## 63. Raising Energy Through Fire

Getting in the right frame of mind for conjuration is not always easy. As we begin this month, here is a way to help you get your mind right and raise your energy, using fire, in the process.

### Opening the Way

You will hear the term "opening the way" a lot in Hoodoo. There are beings that help do this, and you, as a Hoodoo, can help make things happen by moving psychic obstacles using rites and tricks as well.

1. Find a suitable place to make a fire. This may be your fireplace, a barbecue pit, or a safe outdoor clearing where you will not catch anything on fire. Be very intentional and careful about this first step.

2. Gather dry wood, twigs, and brush grasses.

3. Arrange the wood: brush first, then twigs, and then logs.

4. Make sure air can circulate well through your fire arrangement. Don't make it too tightly fitted.

5. Light the brush at the bottom, and gently fan so the fire spreads to the twigs and logs.

6. Let the fire become stable. This will take about ten minutes. During this time, you may need to add more brush or twigs, or rearrange parts of the wood so the fire gets air.

### Gazing to Open the Way

1. Make yourself comfortable, resting on a blanket, chair, or Earth Mama.

2. Take slow, deep meditative breaths to go into a state of relaxation.

3. Gaze deeply into the fire for at least a half hour.

4. At a safe distance from the fire, close your eyes and reflect on your visions.

5. Now listen to the primordial stories of the fire.

6. Listen until you hear messages that fire sends your way.

7. Put out the fire completely using sand or water.

8. Jot down what you saw, felt, and heard.

## 64. Luck Draw Mojo Bag

You need to always be attentive, resourceful, and engaged with your work. For example, go back to that fire you made. The wood you burned has changed form and is still useful. Here is a mojo bag you can construct out of remnants from the fire.

1. Get yourself into a relaxed meditative state.

2. Close your eyes, if you are comfortable. If not, almost close them and let your vision be soft and unfocused, looking downward.

3. Breathe out while counting to eight, then breathe in while counting to eight.

4. Do this for several minutes until you begin to feel lighter and more relaxed.

5. Open your eyes and lift your gaze slowly.

6. Carefully surveil the remnants of the fire.

7. Is there a piece of charred wood that catches your eye? Pick it up.

8. Search the area for another attractive piece of charred wood. Pick that up.

9. Go to your work area with your wood.

10. Put the charred wood into a red flannel.

11. Draw the string tightly, sealing in the wood.

12. Carry this mojo bag in your top left pocket, so it will be close to your heart.

13. This will draw luck.

## 65. Bird Feather Fix to Unhex

Now you will work over your stove, but first, there's some scavenging to do. You will need different types of feathers for this old-timer's Hoodoo trick.

Find yourself some speckled chicken feathers. (So rather than being all one color, these feathers need to be mottled.) If you or your associates have chickens, this probably isn't so hard to do. If not, and you are an urban dweller, try going to a co-op that sells eggs. Ask if you can have a handful of speckled feathers. Make this even more meaningful than the trick alone through bartering. Bring along something you think the owners might enjoy, such as a nice loaf of quick bread or corn muffins, and offer it in exchange for the feathers. Another option is to go to a shop that sells freshly slaughtered or live chickens. Again, ask if you can have a handful of speckled chicken feathers.

Once you have your feathers, bring them home. Bless the chickens whose feathers enable your work. Say a prayer of gratitude to your other source, if you have one, for your feathers:

*I'm lucky that I have you*
*(or that I found the source named _____ ).*
*I have these colorful and unusual feathers in my gifted hands*
*with which to unhex myself (or my client/friend).*
*As you share your blessings with me, in turn I give my thanks and*
*sincere gratitude to you.*
*Blessed be!*
*Blessed be!*
*Blessed be!*

Heat up two tablespoons of lard in a cast-iron skillet. Add the speckled chicken feathers. Fry the feathers until they are crispy and remove them. Let the fat cool and congeal. Rub yourself (or another victim of evil Hoodoo) with the fat. This should unhex you/them.

## 66. Buzzard Fix

Now that you're used to using feathers for your work, how about doing some true scavenging? Spend a bit of time getting familiar with buzzards if you aren't already. You'll want to learn about their feathers and where the birds live and what they look like.

Next, you need to get yourself in the right state of mind. You can do this through fire gazing again, as you did a few days ago, only this time you may use a candle to make things easier. Gaze at the candle to see what wisdom you can find within the fire for your buzzard hunt.

Dress in a manner that is suitable for feather hunting in your area. You may need to drive farther out if you live in the city, or go to a local forest preserve. Use your ingenuity, something with which all Hoodoos are blessed. Perhaps you'll need to go to a zoo, bird rescue center, or bird conservancy. Do some research to find the best source of buzzard feathers in your area.

Once you have a few feathers, take them home. You're going to need to burn them all the way down to ash in a container of your choice. Once you've burned them and collected the ash, make a little fire in a cauldron. Add the feather ash to the cauldron. Add apple cider (or other available) vinegar, to fill the vessel the rest of the way up. Set your alarm so you can get up for three sunrises in a row. Sprinkle this powerful potion on the path of your enemies before they are up to walk it. Eventually they will walk out of your life.

## 67. Chaos and Luck

Domesticity sets the tone for magick undertaken in Hoodoo. Produce and cooking ingredients, as well as shopping bags, believe it or not, coupled with fire can change the vibe of your living space.

Today, let's experiment. Get your Hoodoo journal or notebook out for this work. You'll want to take notes and reflect on what happens with your different burnt materials.

First, stock up on beautiful red and white onions, with tight, ample skins. Onions in general bring good luck to your home and are good for overall health.

Chaos is sometimes useful as well, and onions play a role in creating chaos, should you need it. This is a simple trick.

Burn the skins of your red and white onions like incense, to create chaos and confusion at home. Why is chaos a good thing? For one, it may buy you time as you are figuring out different things to do, without others getting involved. Chaos also helps others forget about an argument that has been ongoing.

When you want to bring good luck into the picture behind the chaos, burn the red and white skins with a bit of brown paper bag, pepper, and a sprinkling of sugar.

Try these different uses of onion skins, and record the effects of burning in different ways in your Hoodoo journal.

Note: Tomorrow you will need to arise at 6:00 a.m.

## 68. Magick Time

You have been working with Hoodoo for a couple of months now, during which time you may have noticed how frequently we use the number six. For example, 6:00 a.m. and 6:00 p.m. are times we hold dear. They are magickally charged times of the day, roughly dawn and dusk—your magickal working hours.

Yesterday I asked you to awaken today at 6:00 a.m. I invite you to get dressed and grab your favorite shawl or blanket and wrap it around your shoulders. Walk clockwise around your home. What does this special time feel like, sound like, smell like? Now walk counterclockwise pondering the same thought. Collect your information mentally. Go back inside and write it in your Hoodoo journal.

At 6:00 p.m. (preferably at home), do this same exercise. If you are not at home, take a brisk walk and make your observations.

Remember, the six o'clock time periods are your highly powerful hours. You can begin rites at 6:00 a.m. and often are asked to continue them at 6:00 p.m., especially with candle work.

## 69. Candle Use in Hoodoo

Candles go beyond helping one see and setting an atmosphere in Hoodoo. In their way, they help us see, but not in the mundane sense. Candles open an avenue into affecting others by influencing their health, outlook, and attitude. In this regard, candles are psychological tools and can be used for healing. Of course, just as they can be used to heal, some use them in a dark manner to harm or hex. Candles are used to create and set a magickal environment in the home. This can be romantic, as in love draw or other love magick. Creating a peaceful home is another important aspect of candle work in Hoodoo. On the other hand, they can be used in confusion practices and to hex. In Hoodoo, we use candles to augment all sorts of other work as well, from success to prosperity, in blessings and in mourning, to celebrate and for closure.

Candles may be used in ways that jibe with Catholicism and that may or may not have religious intent. Some of the saints who are petitioned are believed to serve dark purposes, while others work through the light. Saints are distinct within themselves, yet it is not a stretch to see their relationship to other types of beings from the African diaspora, including the lwa of Vodoun and the orisha of Santeria. Bringing in an African element even further, candles are believed by Hoodoos to bring the saints back to life.

## 70. Hoodoo's Array of Candles

You will want to have a variety of candles to serve different purposes. You can make some types, if you are so inclined, and I will share some recipes to do so in the coming days. Purchasing candles from sound sources, so that they are of the highest quality possible, is important. It may be possible for you to forge a relationship with artisans who specialize in candle making. That way, you can have your candle made to your specifications. Some religious companies, such as Athenian Candle Company in Chicago's Greektown, have a wide assortment of candles, including those that salute the saints. Here is a breakdown of candles used in Hoodoo.

**Figurative:** This type of candle resembles a human engaged in various actions. The lovers candle is an example of a figurative candle used for love draw. Candles that depict saints for their various qualities are another type.

**Statuary:** This type of candle can lapse over into figurative but may also contain other types of sculptural shapes to depict a certain action, being, or animal.

**Symbolic:** There are many different types of symbolic candles. These candles contain symbols to aid your work, for example horseshoes and four- or five-leaf clovers for luck draw.

**Votive:** These short-statured types are excellent devotional candles for the altar.

**Column:** These may contain various symbolic colors. Their density and thickness allows them to burn for longer periods of time, which is useful when you need to burn them for a specific number of hours and/or days.

**Taper:** These long and slender candles are useful for carving (names and messages), sticking with needles and pins, and anointing with Hoodoo oils and herbs.

## 71. Return to Me Love Trick

Candles are useful for various types of love magick. This trick is for bringing back a wayward lover and comes from an informant from Mobile, Alabama.[26] You should always think long and hard about a breakup before trying to repair the relationship and bring the person back. Once you have decided it is prudent to try again, proceed with this trick.

Get yourself nine pins and a white candle. Stick the pins into the candle, going all the way around the candle. Slant the pins downward by pushing them gently. Roll the candle and pins in sugar. The white of the candle is designed to restore peace in the home. Burn this sort of candle configuration every day until the partner returns. If there is no return, it was not meant to be.

---

26. Hyatt, *Hoodoo, Conjuration, Witchcraft, Rootwork.*

## 72. Luck Draw

You started this month considering ways to engage and work with fire. Candles are a nice and easy portable fire that you can focus in on and make things happen with. This trick invites you to interact with the smoke to control your luck. When you engage with smoke, you are engaging in a very ancient substance. As you do this trick, do it knowing of the ancient nature of smoke and seek to invoke its power.

Get yourself into a nice meditative position. Allow your breathing to fall into a pattern that brings you into a state of peaceful concentration. Try breathing in for a count of eight and then breathing out for a count of eight. Notice your breath, but try to shut out other thoughts. When you are ready, light a white candle at dawn (approximately 5:00–6:00 a.m.). As the candle burns, play with the smoke. Trace your hand over it as you make a wish for your luck to improve. This is an excellent way to draw luck into your life.

## 73. Candle Colors and Symbolism

Candles of specific colors have designated magickal uses and correspondences in Hoodoo:

**White:** This is something of a multipurpose candle, as white candles are widely available and easy to obtain. They have a specific bearing on the peaceful atmosphere in the home and are thought to bring goodness and luck.

**Pink:** These candles support a peaceful environment or friendliness and are useful for love, companionship, and relationship magick.

**Red:** Symbolic of blood and the life forces of vitality and strength, red candles bring energy, which may be used for healing. They are also associated with matters of love, including fidelity, love draw, sensuality, sexuality, and fertility.

**Purple:** These are highly spiritual candles that may add a peaceful quality because many of them contain lavender. They are used in spiritual healing and to clear the way.

**Blue:** A symbol of the Blessed Mother Mary and the ocean, blue is a cleansing, sanctifying, clearing color. It is used in psychic matters and visionary work as well as in spiritual blessings.

**Green:** This is a complex and rich color reminiscent of the verdant Earth Mama. It is useful in fertility work, money and prosperity draw, financial matters, and love magick. Green candles are also popular for luck draw.

**Brown:** Brown is symbolic of the Great Mother and of healing and recovery. It is also the color frequently used to bring someone or something back.

**Black:** A black candle is as versatile as a white one, although black has a bad reputation. Black candles are used in hexing and dark magick but can also be used to banish and absorb hexes and negativity.

## 74. The Magick of Opposites

Things are more alike than they are different—even opposites. We are all familiar with the phenomenon of opposites attracting, and have observed this polar attraction in magnets.

Hoodoos are very observant of the people and things in our lives. We employ the power of opposites in magickal rites such as this candle rite, which utilizes both white and black candles and was inspired by an informant in Hyatt's book from Memphis, Tennessee. There is so much made of the differences between black and white, but here you'll see the polar opposites come together for a good cause.

### Luck of Opposites Rite

For this rite, you will need a white column candle and a black column candle at least four inches tall.

Burn the white candle at dawn (approximately 5:00–6:00 a.m. in most places). Use your hand as a magick wand. Trace over the smoke, with your full power and intent, and wish for luck.

Repeat this ritual at dusk (as the sun goes down), but this time use the black candle.

## 75. Restorative Candle Rite

Pink candles can be used for different purposes, as you learned a few days ago. This unique candle ritual, which was inspired by an informant from Mobile, Alabama, addresses various issues.

### Return to Me Love Rite

Breakups don't happen in a vacuum. Typically, before you split up with your partner, there is a significant amount of discord. This most likely occurs in the home and affects where you live. Arguing brings down the energy of a place, from a high-frequency, energetic, positive zone to a dank, low-energy, negative abode. The original informant said this rite was good for getting your fellah back, but it can be used to bring back a partner of any gender.

You will need a pink and a white taper candle for this work. You will also need about two tablespoons of white cane sugar.

Put your sugar out on some brown kraft paper or newsprint paper (without any print). Recite this over it:

*My materials are humble,*
*my love is real.*
*Lover, come back to me straight; don't dally or stumble.*
*Let my intent come through my breath and touch*
*to seal the deal.*

Be sure to say this with intent, and let your energy and breath exude into the sugar crystals as you say it, as many times as you need to.

Roll the white and then the pink candle in the sugar. Burn them as you reflect on the return of your partner.

## 76. Anointing, Dressing, and the Signs

Anointing has a lot of Christian religiosity attached to it, but it can also be used by pagans, and of course Hoodoos have engaged with this because of our merging of Christianity with our practice. Anointing is the practice of consecrating or conferring a holy substance (typically a holy oil such as olive oil) onto a candle. Dressing a candle consists of adding various magickal and mystically imbued substances (such as herbs or even sugar) to it to enhance its work. Of course, most of the work of the candle comes through the flame, and the flames have much to tell you.

The correspondences between actions and reactions in candlemancy are very logical:

• A candle with a flame that won't burn or burns slowly shows there is a stubborn reaction to your trick or spell. It may take a long time to come to fruition, or it may not be meant to be.

- A fast-burning candle flame shows that either the work will take quickly or it will play out too quickly, so you need to keep watch.

- A candle that flickers shows a reluctance from the spirit realm to accept the work you are undertaking and indicates that something about the work is not quite right.

- A candle that burns with black marks or soot is a warning sign that darkness is afoot and there is resistance and perhaps a counterspell going on elsewhere to block your work.

- If you hear lots of hissing, snappin', and crackling, some messages are trying to come through from the ancestors or spirit realm. Be very attentive, focus, and listen to their messages.

### 77. Create a Candlemancy Chart

Today, create a chart in your Hoodoo journal that is related to your candlemancy. You can take any types of notes you want, but be sure to include these:

- Date of trick/spell
- Type of work
- For whom the work was performed
- Rate of flame burning
- Consistency of flame
- Noises observed
- Color around the flame left on the candleholder (looking for black soot)
- Outcome of the work (Was it effective or not?)

## 78. Candle Care

There's nothing more frustrating than having a good candle that is effective for your work but will not burn properly. Yes, there are spiritual reasons for this at times, but there are also physical, mundane ones. For regular care of your candles, try these fixes.

1. Votive candles can be difficult to keep burning consistently, but a few simple tips will keep them in good condition. It is a good practice to take a burned-out votive and place it in the freezer, upside down, for eight hours or so. This causes the candle to contract, releasing the stuck wax that is preventing a good burn.

2. Sometimes soy candles and novenas especially, but even columns, will get snuffed out due to excess wax. If this happens, trim the candle using a sharp kitchen knife. Take about a half-inch of the entire top off the candle, being careful not to cut into the wick. Do this as often as needed.

3. If your taper doesn't fit into its holder, simply use a sharpened knife as a whittling tool, reducing the sides in a tapered motion until it fits, or use a candle shaver.

4. When a candle is too small to fit into its holder, drip some melted wax into the holder. Place the candle in and hold in place until the wax hardens.

5. When wax has spilled over onto your altar cloths, put them in the freezer overnight. When you remove them from the freezer in the morning, the wax will easily fall away, either through careful folding of the cloth or by scraping it away (quickly) with a dull knife.

## 79. Good Old-Fashioned Teacup Candles

Many old-time Hoodoo recipes call for teacup candles, which are not typically found in shops. It's nice to have a few lovely handmade candles made from natural ingredients. Making candles yourself puts you in the driver's seat in terms of their intent and direction. They become imbued with your energy, desires, hopes, and dreams. Every step of the way, you can breathe your intention into the candle, and you'll end up with a very strong candle indeed.

The candle you will make tomorrow will be an excellent addition to your ancestor altar, for reflection, meditation, and observation. If you can, get a good relationship going with a local beekeeper. If that's not an option, use the internet. You'll also want to use sustainably sourced palm shortening, which is easy to find at health food stores and from soap-making and candle-making suppliers.

Finally, there is the teacup itself. This creates a space to incorporate your ancestors into your work. You can approach your relatives about using a cup or two from the china closet, or you can simply go to a thrift shop, flea market, or resale store and select the cups that call to your spirit.

For each teacup candle you plan to make, have four ounces each of beeswax and palm shortening. You will need #4 cotton wick (square-braided), a scale, pencils with beveled edges (#2 pencils work well), a stainless steel bowl, kraft paper (rags or newspaper), and a four-cup Pyrex measuring cup (with pouring spout).

## 80. Make a Teacup Candle

Keep all the tips from yesterday in mind as you begin this project. Be sure to have some time set aside and a very clear head. Have an intention in mind, and focus on it attentively as you work. This separates this candle from a mundane candle, for this teacup candle has history, intent, and magick steeped into it. Gather the supplies from yesterday.

1. Measure some shredded or cut beeswax. Put into the stainless steel bowl.

2. Add water to the saucepan. Nestle the stainless steel bowl with beeswax into the saucepan. The fit should be relatively tight, so water doesn't get into the wax. Melt the wax over medium heat. (It's very important to keep the heat at medium.)

3. Measure the wicks against the teacups; cut the wicks two inches taller than the top of the cup. Dip the wicks one at a time into the melted beeswax to coat well, all the way around. Set on a covered tabletop or countertop. Carefully pull the wicks taut so they will be straight.

4. When the beeswax is melted, measure four ounces of palm shortening and add to the melted beeswax. Stir with a stick or skewer that is disposable. Pour in enough melted wax mixture to cover the bottom of the cup. Put the end of the waxed wick into the wax in the cup; hold upright so it is straight, as it firms up. Repeat for the other cups.

5. Stir the wax. Put the pencil on top of the teacup. Wrap the waxed wick around the pencil to stabilize it. Pour wax into the cup about ½ inch to the rim. Let cool and set up for a day. Trim the wick ½ inch from the top of the candle.

## 81. Blessed Mother Altar and Rite

Mary, mother of Jesus Christ, is a venerated figure in Christianity, particularly within Catholicism. She is appreciated in her virginal state as the Virgin Mary, when Christ was conceived, and as his Blessed Mother as well.

The Blessed Mother is celebrated in Vodoun of New Orleans, and appreciation of her made its way into Hoodoo as well, being that so many traditional Hoodoo practitioners are also Christian. Here is a ritual to the Virgin Mary and an altar for the Blessed Mother.

For the Virgin Mary's help in any matter at all, here is a traditional Hoodoo candle rite. Get a pink candle, which reflects her gentle qualities and warmth. Burn the candle as you focus on your intent on Monday, Wednesday, and Thursday.

### Blessed Mother New Orleans Altar

The Blessed Mother loves all children. You can tap into her motherly quality and ask for the wishes you desire by setting a beautiful bouquet of flowers on a pink cloth on your bed table, mantel, or regular altar. You'll need a white candle blessed by a priest or consecrated yourself by blessing it with a holy substance such as olive oil or salt. Choose to remain dedicated for three or nine days; burn the candle for that duration of time.[27] Each day, reflect on the flowers as though they are her image and breath. Refresh the flowers as needed.

## 82. St. Peter's Altar

One of the Catholic saints who draws the attention of Hoodoos is St. Peter. He is a remover of obstacles and sometimes stands

---

27. Hyatt, *Hoodoo, Conjuration, Witchcraft, Rootwork*, 818.

at the crossroads and acts as a door opener. In Catholicism, St. Peter is considered the head of the church on earth. People from the African diaspora have noticed that his powers are suggestive of Papa Legba in the Vodoun pantheon, and in Santeria, as well as Lucumi, his image relates somewhat to the orisha Ogun.

St. Peter was imprisoned by King Herod. An angel set him free by removing his arm and leg irons and opening the door. This saint is associated with locksmiths, keys, legal battles, the court system, and laws. Just as doors were unlocked for him, he is believed to be able to do so for you, using his iconic symbol, the key.

### Hoodoo Altar to St. Peter

Purchase a fresh key. Put a St. Peter candle or a simple green candle on your mantel or altar, in a fireproof holder. Put the key over your door on a nail, or rest it on the trim. Add some roses to a vase of water. This is a basic St. Peter's altar.

Be sure to be attentive to this altar: keep the flowers fresh and burn the candle regularly. In Hoodoo, St. Peter can be good or bad, so handle his image and items carefully.

## 83. St. Joseph's Altar

A very popular and grounding ceremony honors St. Joseph, husband to the Virgin Mary. It occurs on March 19 and is called St. Joseph's Day. This is primarily a Roman Catholic celebration, particularly revered and maintained by the Sicilians. It made its way into Hoodoo after Sicilians settled in New Orleans in the late 1800s.

St. Joseph is believed to have brought on the rains that salvaged the much-needed fava bean crops that sustained the Sicilians during a drought in the Middle Ages. He now is considered a fatherly figure who provides food and blessings. The lesson of St. Joseph's Day is of hope and of sharing with family, friends, and those less fortunate. St. Joseph teaches about belief, faith, and making due, and about luck, one of the centerpieces of Hoodoo.

Beans have long been associated with luck, and the fava bean is venerated on St. Joseph's Day as his gift. Bread is something that feeds many, requiring only a few inexpensive ingredients. Lamb and fish are used in feasting in numerous cultures, and the Italians are particularly fond of including fish in celebrations. On your St. Joseph's altar, include a green and brown candle or a St. Joseph novena candle to represent him. Also include an array of seafood, or breads and cookies shaped like fish. A lovely array of flowers, including roses and lilies, can be placed on a shiny silk or satin blue cloth to represent Mary and the sea.

## 84. I Want My Belongings Back! Rite

Nothing is more infuriating than having someone take your belongings or keep them once you've asked for them to be returned. This rite is designed to help you get your things returned, and is inspired by an old-timer's rite by way of Mobile, Alabama.[28] On day 74 I spoke about the magick of opposites. Now here is something you might call cater-cornered, or directional, Hoodoo.

You'll need two black column candles, nine pins, and nine needles.

Write the name of the offender on a black candle nine times. Place this candle in a dark corner and light it. In the opposite corner, stick nine pins and nine needles in the other black candle.

---

28. Hyatt, *Hoodoo, Conjuration, Witchcraft, Rootwork*, 828.

Light this candle. Call the offender's name out loud nine times. Burn the candles for fifteen minutes. Perform this exactly at 6:00 a.m, noon, and 6:00 p.m. Each time, wet your fingers and snuff out the flame when you're finished. Do not touch the candles once they've been set and lit.

## 85.Black Candle Working

You must take black candle workings very seriously and work with them carefully. Black candles are very potent, so your intention should be well considered and you should see if there are alternate ways of sorting out the issue before resorting to black candle working. If there is no other option, you should then proceed with this type of work using caution and respect. Here are some tips for working with black candles:

- After lighting a black candle, don't touch it until it goes out unless you get sick or weak as it burns, in which case you need to put it out and begin again another day when you are stronger.

- Dress the black candle; write on it and then wash your hands with blessed salt water.

- Let the candle do its work, but don't carry its energy in your body by touching it when it's loaded and ready to work or working.

- Put the black candle out by carrying it—in nine circles to the left and nine circles to the right.

- Avoid blowing out a black candle, as that may release bad energy into the living space.

## 86. Wishes Come True

Roses are considered highly spiritual and healing. The mere sight and scent of a rose can perk up the spirits of someone not feeling well. With the mood elevated and the mind turned toward positivity, there's no limit to what kind of positive Hoodoo can be done.

This trick incorporates a purple candle, for a high spiritual charge, and dragon's blood, a natural resin incense that comes from several different species of the palm tree. Without any additives or complicated blends of other herbs, dragon's blood brings energy and vigor to an otherwise stagnant room.

If you want luck to flood your home and grant a wish, try this trick.

You will need the following ingredients:

- ½ cup rose petals
- Charcoal (preferably bamboo)
- Incense burner or fire-safe bowl
- Purple candle
- Candleholder
- Piece of dragon's blood

1. Hold the rose petals in both hands and breathe your request for good luck into them gently.

2. Activate the petals by scrubbing them between your hands, releasing their scent.

3. Thank the roses for sharing their gift with you and for giving themselves to you for your work. Set them aside.

4. Light the bamboo charcoal in your incense burner. Let it get white-hot.

5. Light the purple candle and put it in the holder.

6. Light the dragon's blood and put it in the incense burner, alongside the heated charcoal.

7. Gently and slowly add the rose petals, along with more of your intent for your wish.

8. Let this smolder as you slowly walk clockwise throughout each room of the space you are activating.

## 87. Fire and Ice Reflection Ritual

As the seasons change, it is helpful to play out the drama in your home. To switch gears and begin to focus on spring, use ice combined with the warming energy of candles. Try this work to bring beauty from nature and the elements into your life today. This display is designed for reflection and energy gathering for seasonal Hoodoo.

Bring together the following items:

- A collection of your favorite evergreens and some newly blossomed crocuses and daffodils

- Plastic container, 4 x 8 inches

- Water

- 2 small cans

- A few stones

- Yellow and green column candles, 4–6 inches long

- 2 small candleholders

1. Make a collection of your favorite evergreens. Choose a few cuttings each of holly with berries, juniper with berries, cedar, spruce, and pines. Collect some newly blossomed

crocuses and daffodils, gathered yourself, if possible, or from a local florist.

2. Partially fill the plastic container with water.

3. Add two small cans (which will later hold your candles) to the container.

4. Weigh down the cans with a few stones placed inside them.

5. Place flowers around the edges of the container and evergreens and berries in the middle area.

6. Place in the freezer or outdoors, if it is cold enough, until frozen solid.

7. Remove the cans.

8. Flip the container over to release the ice. Place upright on a fireproof plate or foil-covered cookie sheet.

9. Put the candles in the candleholders and place inside the holes left by the cans.

10. Light the candles.

Gaze on the fire and ice as you think on what you enjoy most about spring and summer. This is a gorgeous reminder of the beauty and mystery of the seasons.

## 88. Hoodoo Gardening: Tobacco

Tobacco has an interesting, if not sordid, history, yet it is requested by the ancestors as payment during petitions. This has been the case traditionally, and thus it is incorporated into Hoodoo and several other paths. Like it or not, we must take heed.

Most African Americans have been touched by enslavement in one way or another. Many of our ancestors, including mine, were slaves on the Southern slave plantations. I keep dried to-bacco leaves hanging in my kitchen, near the hearth, as a tribute to them, and I like burning tobacco from time to time, also as a tribute.

Over the next few days, you will be working with tobacco leaves. Have you ever grown a tomato plant? Well, then you can also grow tobacco. One plant will yield approximately ½ cup of tobacco. Tobacco plants are easy to grow just about anywhere. I grew my own tobacco plant to honor the ancestors, and I live in zone 5, a typically frigid area with a very warm summer, and mine grew as an annual. There are sixty-seven species of to-bacco, some of which are quite lovely night bloomers with an intoxicating fragrance. Ornamental tobacco species include *Nicotiana sylvestris*, *Nicotiana langsdorffii*, and the award-winning *Nicotiana alata* 'Lime Green.' I suggest trying some of these, as well as ordinary tobacco, for their interesting growth, flowers, and moonlight blooming, which will enhance your outdoor Hoodoo activities.

## 89. Growing Tobacco

Start indoors in a growing container with a plastic cover. Starter sets are best, but be careful not to purchase peat pots. They don't work so well. Use organic planting soil. Spread the soil in the container with its little pots. Completely saturate the soil through spritzing with water in a spray bottle. Add the tiny seeds. They will germinate in seven to ten days. Weed out weak growers after about ten days. Continue to water and give plenty of light. When there is no danger of frost, move the seedlings outdoors and let harden a few days before planting directly in the soil. Plant three to four feet apart in the mid-afternoon. So if you have a small garden, you can only plant a few, or use large pots. Water all around the root base when you set them in the ground. They love organic fertilizer and will attract various hungry moths, so have a soap spray or neem on hand to spritz as they grow. In the fall, harvest by respectfully cutting the plants near the base. Tie with twine or ribbon. Hang upside down, away from direct sunlight, to dry. Crumble to use the leaves in the upcoming recipe for kinnikinnick incense.

## 90. Workin' Your Tobacco

There are many stories, recollections, and photographs documenting the ways various Native American groups and African Americans were brought together in early American history. One meeting of the cultures most likely involved tobacco. As we just explored, African Americans grew and harvested tobacco as slaves and afterward as free people. The Algonquin Native Americans celebrated and pleased the ancestors by doing prayer, meditation, and purification rites using various smoldering blends of herbs. Tobacco is a popular herb to smolder. Kinnikinnick is used synonymously with uva-ursi, being a fragrant incense blend of tobacco and bearberry (*Arctostaphylos uva-ursi*) and traditionally many other ingredients as well. Bearberry is commonly called uva-ursi by herbalists.

It is very pleasurable, relaxing, and agreeable to the ancestors to burn kinnikinnick. I find it particularly pleasing to blend uva-ursi leaves with an array of indigenous trees and herbs. You can smoke it, treat it like an incense, or put it in a little medicine pouch and use it as a medicine bag to draw good health.

## 91. Create a Peace Offering

Gather the following ingredients:

- Leaves from entire tobacco plant (dried) or ½ cup smoking tobacco
- 4 ounces uva-ursi leaves, dried
- 2 white oak leaves, dried
- Handful dried, shredded white sage
- 2 ounces pine needles
- ¼ teaspoon juniper leaf essential oil
- ¼ teaspoon pine essential oil
- ¼ teaspoon cedar essential oil
- ¼ teaspoon bergamot essential oil
- A sterile glass container, like a Mason jar

All herbs should be dried first and torn into tiny pieces in a nonreactive bowl. As you tear up the herbs, thank them for giving their life force over to you so the offering will be effective. Clear your mind and concentrate on peaceful and lighthearted thoughts. Fondly remember your ancestors who have passed on. Keep this type of mental mindset and dialogue going the entire time you work.

Once your material is nicely dried and torn, drop in the essential oils through an essential oil dropper. Use a different dropper for each oil to preserve its authentic scent. Breathe your peaceful and commemorative intentions into the blend and inhale the healing aroma as you work.

Let this blend's scents and powers come together in a glass container for four to six weeks. Shake and stir with a stainless steel spoon occasionally. Store away from direct light.

Either burn this purposefully on a bamboo charcoal, once it has matured, or place a pinch or two into a chamois skin and cinch off with twine, to use as a medicine bag, to which you gradually add more items.

## 92. Cigar Magick

Since we're talking about and working with tobacco, we would be remiss to leave out the carefully rolled, dried, and fermented cigar. Cigars are pleasing to various spirits and beings throughout the African-American spiritual pantheon, most notably the lwa in Vodoun. They are also sometimes used in Hoodoo. Their inclusion is most likely due to the importance of tobacco and tobacco products to people with heritage from America's South, African Americans mainly, and our connection with Hoodoo.

### *Make a Wish Cigar*

This rite was adapted from one that was shared with Hyatt by an informant from Fayetteville, North Carolina.[29] It is designed to help the participant gain what they desire. Gather these items:

- Hoyt's Cologne
- Cigar
- Lighter

Pour some Hoyt's Cologne into a spritzer. Spritz a cigar until it is well covered in the cologne. Hang it up and let it dry or place on a cookie sheet to dry.

---

29. Hyatt, *Hoodoo, Conjuration, Witchcraft, Rootwork*, 655.

Once it is completely dried, take several puffs of the cigar as you concentrate with great focus on your desires. This will help you get what you want.

## 93. Curio of Note: Smudge Stick

Here are instructions for making a smudge stick.

- Gather available sprigs and branches in the morning after the dew has evaporated.
- Cut each herb between twelve and eighteen inches long.
- Bundle the herbs, then tie them with hemp string.
- Bring the bundle inside and hang it upside down away from direct sunlight.
- Dry for several days—the bundle should still be pliable.
- Lay the herbs on a natural fiber cloth or newspaper.
- Fold, then roll it until there is a neat six-to eight-inch-long bunch.
- Bundle using natural hemp string or natural (undyed) cotton string.

This takes practice. The more of these you make, the more you'll get the hang of it.

When you feel a need for cleansing, clearing, or banishing, or when you are doing home blessings, light this smudge stick. Blow it out and just let it smoke. Wave this like a magick wand around the area or person to be blessed. Travel in a clockwise direction in each room. Snuff this out when finished in an earthenware bowl.

## 94. Curio of Note: Incense

As we close this chapter, be sure to take time to settle in to the notion of flame, fire, and smoke. Explore these traditional combustibles and practice interpreting patterns and symbols revealed by the smoke.

**Palo Santo** (*Bursera graveolens*). A Hoodoo stimulated by the ancient, woodsy aroma of palo santo can cure and unhex. Akin to the smudge stick and burned the same way, palo santo is used for cleansing and clearing. This incense balances energy, enabling peace and luck to prevail. To use, hold at a 45-degree angle away from your body. Smoke released from its smoldering works healing magick on all in need.

**Frankincense** (*Boswellia sacra* and *Boswellia carterii*, also known as *beyo* and *olibanum*). This healing incense frees objects, spaces, and people from evil spirits. Its gift is purging and purification. In energy healing and vision quest, you most definitely want to employ spiritual frankincense. Quality frankincense readily acts as a conduit for spiritual growth.

**Myrrh** (*Commiphora myrrha* and *Commiphora abyssinica*). From ancient times to the present, this incense has enjoyed reverence. Use myrrh for blessing, clearing, meditation, invocation, cleansing, healing, prayer, and even exorcism. Possessing similar qualities to those of frankincense, their individual strengths are heightened when combined: two parts frankincense to one part myrrh.

Note: Use a mortar and pestle, when needed, to get resin chunks down to a manageable size. Small chunks are preferred for dream quests and energy healing because they release more smoke to reflect upon.

# CHAPTER 4
# FOOT TRACK MAGICK: DAYS 95-123

Humans and animals touch the earth with their feet in so many ways. Imagine the grace of a ballerina coming down to the stage from a breathtakingly high arabesque, the lightning speed of the cheetah's quick-turning footsteps on the hunt, the impact on the rain-soaked earth from a herd of elephant steps, and the delight stirred by the first steps of a child. How about the cautious steps of two lovers on the way to meet each other to carry on their affair? There are so many examples of ways we trod on the Earth Mama that the head spins.

We walk with haste, anger, deceit, intention, happiness, focus, and, at times, joy. Our footsteps vary widely according to the occasion, and they have meaning attached to their purpose. The skillful analysis and manipulation of footsteps can unlock unfathomable power.

Hoodoos have long been attentive to the magickal potential of the foot's imprint. The heel, toes, sole of the foot, and sole of the shoe, as well as shoes themselves, play a role in a fascinating facet of Hoodoo called foot track magick.

Foot track magick addresses love, peace, war, protection, and banishment, among other issues of importance. Through the practice of foot track magick, the warrior spirit of the Hoodoo is sharpened. We learn to sense, observe, predict, and act at just the right time. Footsteps in the sand and soil are real one minute and impressions only captured in our mind's eye the next.

Adding herbal and elemental concoctions to the foot path yields results. Moreover, we can work on others by capturing their foot tracks under the right conditions. Further effects are derived from putting things into the soles of our shoes. The use of foot powders and naturally heated floor washes opens an additional arena. Working with shoes through placement of shoes around and beneath the property, and even making potions from shoes, is an additional way to work intention.

As your imagination opens, I'm sure you can see that this is a fertile area to explore. You can develop your mental acuity and unite actions with purpose more quickly through the practice of working with foot tracks. These practices are deeply of the spirit realm, yet they are also a practical form of Hoodoo. This month is dedicated to working on developing your repertoire of foot track magick. As always, use your best judgment and common sense with all your Hoodoo workings. Things can go very badly if you do not. If you are collecting footprint dust of another person, consider that it could be misunderstood as stalking. For that matter, avoid doing anything stupid or illegal.

## 95. Look at the World Anew

Hoodoo invites you to see the world differently. It asks you to be present and in the moment, through keen awareness. Sometimes, like this month, you will be asked to look at something you may have taken for granted. We are going to be taking note of our daily walks, or travels, this month for a very important reason.

Footsteps help you arrive at a destination and potentially stay there. Your steps also lead you away, sometimes for good. Foot track magick takes steps seriously, seeing them as potentially disruptive or encouraging, depending on their purpose.

The parts of the anatomy involved with walking play a major role in this magick, including the legs, knees, heels, toes, and soles of the feet. What we wear on our feet and legs is also employed. This includes shoes primarily but also socks, or, if you'd prefer, hose or tights.

Someone meaning to cause chaos might put brambleberries (blueberries, blackberries, or other berries) in your path. Your weight makes them splatter, popping and making an alarming plopping sound as well as a surprising sight. You can rest assured that if this happens, bad juju is afoot. Mustard seeds are also used. Their action is gritty, as they create a small but noticeable barrier between your feet and the ground. Being grounded is important for the Hoodoo. You don't want anyone or anything to throw you off or deter your work or daily goings-on.

## 96. Walk the Hoodoo's Way

Today, as you go about your day, be mindful of your environment. What do you see as you move about? What are the constants? What things change from day to day? Notice the ground (sidewalk or soil) especially, and take notes in your Hoodoo journal. These are the questions I want you to ask:

- What is the distance between your sidewalk (pathway) and your front porch or stoop?

- What is the shape of your pathway home?

- How does it smell on your path?

- How do you feel when you reach your pathway home?

- What objects do you encounter there daily, and which objects are only there occasionally?

- What is the color and texture of your landing stair that takes you from outside indoors?

- What have you put on your pathway, porch/stoop, and door to make it home?

- What have you or could you add to the sides of your pathway to personalize your space?

- Have you ever treated/washed your front step? With what? When and for what reason? What were the results?

- Walk around your property and get a feel for what is there.

- Slowly walk (travel) around your neighborhood or the land near you. Take in all the sights and smells. Notice how your legs and feet feel all along the way. Do any spots make you ache or feel drained? Walk (travel) for about one hour.

- As you return home, what do you see that you hadn't seen before? Take notes. Jot down everything you saw and felt that stands out.

## 97. Foot Track Specimens

Equipment used ritualistically will help as you are collecting foot track specimens and with doing your spells and rites. Take some time today to source materials to help with your collection of foot tracks. Here are some ideas:

- Mason jars are easy to sterilize and come in several different sizes.
- Tiny antique jars like vials with corks are useful for smaller specimens.
- Droppers and pipettes help transfer liquids.
- The surgeon type of plastic gloves helps keep your materials from being crossed with your personal energy.

Have fun shopping! Look in your local antique stores and second-hand shops. Find interesting estate sales and block sales to attend, and mark your calendar for sales happening in the future.

For your more standard materials, like droppers, pipettes, and gloves, check out lab suppliers, herbal supply shops, and apothecaries.

Next, stock up on covert clothing and ritual wear. By "covert" I mean hoodies, dark clothing, or plain clothing that is not bright or flamboyant—anything that will help you not call attention to yourself. Clothing that helps you blend in is good for your foot track magick. Take care not to look so covert that you appear suspicious though!

At times you may decide you want to wear ritual wear for certain rituals. This would include long gowns or robes in black, red, or white. There are many good ritual wear suppliers on Etsy and eBay.

## 98. Green Gourd Rite

Gourds have been a constant source of entertainment. They have also served practical purposes and brought good luck to the lives of Africans in the Motherland and the New World for thousands of years. Music made from gourds is a high form of the griot art of the Mandinka people. The instruments created from gourds range from a harp-lute sound to a fiddle sound, which is arresting and beautiful. There are many different folk remedies that incorporate gourds. Having them on your property ensures good luck, and growing them on your fence provides protection. Growing calabash helps fortify your residence from people seeking to plant or drop bad Hoodoo items near your home for you to encounter.

### Green Gourd Rite

Is there a certain person who is getting on your nerves? Here is a good traditional foot track magick rite that incorporates the help of the green gourd. [30]

1. Walk your property or the area where you are living, barefoot.
2. Get the dirt of your foot tracks, just from your right foot.
3. Place this dirt in a green gourd. Fix it well by placing the gourd top firmly on the gourd or by using a cork.
4. Throw the gourd over your left shoulder into a stream or river.

Now you can have the peace you desire.

## 99. Hoodoo Gardening: Green Calabash

*Lagenaria siceraria*, or calabash gourd, is a lovely green gourd that is useful for the following rite. It will also fortify your home against evildoers, just by growing it on your property. To grow, sow directly into soil by your fence, or if you have a small space,

---

30. Hyatt, *Hoodoo, Conjuration, Witchcraft, Rootwork*, 2,845.

use pots and a trellis. The seeds grow quickly and the plant grows vigorously. It prefers well-drained, moist, fertile soil and a sunny location protected from the wind. If the plant gets larger than six to eight feet, trim off the tip of the vine to encourage more gourds and less vine growth.

The gourds are ready to harvest when the stem is shriveled and brown. Cut the stem a good two inches or more from the top of the gourd. Wash the surface with hot, soapy water and set out to dry completely. You can also wipe the surface with grain alcohol, vodka, or gin, to kill bacteria and mold-causing spores. For about one week, let the gourd dry in a well-ventilated area away from direct sunlight. The skin will begin to change color and harden. Move the gourds to a dark area with plenty of air circulation. If you can hang them, do so. If not, a screen will make a sufficient drying rack. Spread them so they do not touch. Check them every few days at first. Turn them for even drying. Then check on them weekly, still turning as needed.

After about six months, when the gourd feels light, the skin is dry, and you can hear the seeds rattle on the inside, it is cured. Cut off the top to use as a water carrier in rites, as needed.

## 100. Hoodoo Gardening: Hot Medicine of Red Pepper

Hoodoo calls for the use of red pepper and Guinea pepper, which are one in the same. Peppers (*Capsicum annuum, Capsicum frutescens*, and other varieties) have been an important component of the herbal healer's remedy chest for centuries. They have been employed by Hoodoos for hundreds of years.

Today, I encourage you to consider the use of peppers in Hoodoo medicinally, since a lot of our other work is built around their magickal qualities. Let's not forget that a lot of their efficacy in Hoodoo is derived from their medicinal qualities.

When Hoodoo strikes in a negative way, there is a general feeling of malaise. Aches and pains accompany the bad vibes and the feeling of being not quite well. Hoodoo used for healing and making war takes all of this into consideration. Here are some of the wonders that peppers can work on the body and mind:

- The counter-irritant elements in peppers ease body aches, including rheumatic pains and arthritis.

- Cayenne's chemical constituents encourage the brain to secrete endorphins. Filled with endorphin energy, we can walk over bad juju and more without feeling ill!

- Red pepper not only relieves pain but also blocks messages of pain before they can be received in the pain center of the brain.

- Cayenne is one of the most effective natural stimulants.

- Peppers strengthen the heart and boost circulation.

- In some cases, a tincture or tea made of one teaspoon of cayenne's powdered seeds added to one cup of hot water will stop a heart attack as it is beginning. (If you suspect a heart attack, call 911.)

- Cayenne facilitates a therapeutic flow of healing actions within nutrients, making them quickly accessible to the body.

**Warning:** Do not use cayenne on broken skin or in mucous membranes, and be careful with exposure to eyes.

## 101. Hoodoo Gardening: Cayenne

As we discussed yesterday, you will find a great need for red cayenne peppers in Hoodoo and specifically in foot track magick. Peppers are super easy to grow in abundance. Typically the fruits and their seeds are used, but some old-style recipes call for their leaves. Growing peppers yields fruits, seeds, and leaves galore. You can then have them not only for magick but also for healing, decorating, and soul food cooking.

### Growing Cayenne from Seed

When growing cayenne from seed, I recommend using a growing kit with a plastic top, although you can use egg cartons if you put a hole in the bottom and cover with plastic to create a little greenhouse.

1. Soak cayenne seeds in a glass overnight in a window, under the light of the waxing moon.

2. Put the seeds on a paper towel in the morning.

3. Place three to four seeds in each cell, spaced evenly.

4. Cover the seeds lightly with a bit of potting soil—do not bury or completely cover them.

5. Moisten the soil, being careful not to move the seeds.

6. Cover.

7. Put on a sunny windowsill.

8. Dampen the soil every week for six weeks.

9. Weed out any weak seedlings.

10. Transplant outside after the last frost, wherever you live. Dig some small holes. Remove the plants from the grow cells and press them firmly into the earth. Water the soil

regularly, and mulch to deter weeds and keep the soil moist longer.

11. To keep away bugs, spray with organic insecticides, such as neem in a spritz bottle or organic soap with water.

## 102. Curio of Note: Sulphur

Sulphur, also known as brimstone, is a component of foot track magick and other forms of Hoodoo. It is inside us and all around us. Sulphur is one of the dozens of elements that make up the foundation of the earth. Moreover, sulphur and other elements come together to form our universe. When you work with sulphur, you are working a dynamic magickal substance indeed.

Elemental sulphur is nontoxic. It is a vital, though infrequently thought of, nutrient. It is no wonder sulphur is so dear to foot track magick. The telltale signs of bad Hoodoo done against you (mental distress, stress, lack of energy, diminished willpower, hair loss, weakness, crumbling nails, and general ill health) can be treated with sulphur. As the eighth most common element in our bodies, sulphur is to be taken seriously, yet we make little effort to directly seek it.

Today, various whole health companies online are dealing in the element as a supplement, called Flowers of Sulphur (FOS), organic elemental sulphur, organosulphur, and simple yellow granulated sulphur.

Sulphur is used to treat the suspicious symptoms of bad juju. It is also used for the following:

• Aches and pains in the body

• Lethargy

• Alzheimer's disease treatment and reversal

- Ulcers

- Hemorrhoids

- Digestive disorders

- A variety of mental issues

- Hair and skin disorders

- As an antiseptic

Now that you know these things about sulphur, tomorrow go ahead and use it.

## 103. Drink and Walk Spell

Walking over an object of ill intent, deliberately put in your path to zap you, buried, or on the ground's surface, can make you ill in a variety of ways. Here is a very potent foot track magick spell. It combines a health fortifier in the form of sulphur with the power of the number nine.

You will be doing this spell at an important time of the day: early morning. Mornings allow you to get a jump on your enemies. The morning is also a great time for renewal work, as the time of new beginnings.

### Nine-Day Drink

1. For nine mornings in a row, add a teaspoon of organic sulphur to hot milk (dairy, lactose-free, nut, organic soy, or hemp). Heat it up until it is quite hot, but don't boil it.

2. Stir and then drink.

This will fortify you and help your spiritual illness pass, if you have one.

### Nine-Day Hot Foot Powder

Now make some hot foot powder, so you can step as freely as you please.

1. Put some red pepper and a bit of sulphur in your shoes. Add a thin barrier over these two ingredients if you'd prefer, like newsprint paper (which has no ink to soil your feet), cut out to conform to the soles of your shoes.

2. Refresh the pepper and sulphur for nine mornings in a row, and your spiritual illness should pass.

## 104. Southern Prosperity Spell

In foot track magick, you can step in shoes with hot foot ingredients so you stay well and protected. You can also use the power of shoes themselves, in various forms, for your benefit. This spell is for prosperity and is derived from an informant's account in Hyatt's research.

1. Obtain and burn to ash a used shoe.

2. Add a cup of fine white sugar to the shoe ash

3. Add a cup of sulphur and mix well

4. Every Thursday set your intent and then sprinkle it in every corner of your home.

5. Set your intent:

> *Spirits and angels gather near.*
> *I say this with willfulness.*
> *I want you to hear.*
> *I open myself to abundance and prosperity.*
> *I know you can see me, and I hold your attention very dear.*

### 105. Should They Stay or Should They Go?

Doing tricks, spells, and rites that affect the natural flow of a relationship is serious business. It's time to do some soul-searching. It is very important to think about whether you want to bring a wayward lover back or encourage someone with a wandering heart to stay. Conjuration helps you do amazing things, but is it in your best interest to pursue such work?

You personally may be settled into your relationship or happy alone; however, your clients, friends, or family may ask for your help in this area. This is where your Hoodooing skills need to be sharp and well developed. You don't want to hurt your clients, friends, or families by interfering and making something happen that wasn't meant to be.

At the same time, you don't want to just stand by if you see someone in pain, knowing full well you could use your Hoodoo repertoire to help. When helping others, you should ask a lot of questions and listen actively for the answers. Jot down what is said and take notes in your Hoodoo journal. Go home, light a white or blue candle to create a peaceful atmosphere, and reflect. The ancestors and spirits should help make things clear to you through your candlemancy, reflection, and dreams.

### 106. Foot Track Nation Sack

At the beginning of the book we explored different types of mojo bags. The bag most often related to women and those who identify as female is the nation sack. This is a Stay with Me nation sack. Before undertaking this foot track work you'll want to be very sure about the reality of your relationship and whether it is good for both of you.

### Step One

Meditate and reflect on the relationship over a red candle's flame. Gaze deeply and try to gain a sense or vision of how to proceed.

### Step Two

If you've made the decision to move forward, gather the following materials:

- 1 tablespoon or so of dust from the track of the person loved
- 1 tablespoon rosin (this is used in gymnastics and in carpentry)
- 1 teaspoon white cane sugar
- 1 tablespoon sulphur

Put these items in a new nation sack (red flannel bag). Carry it in an intimate location under your clothing or in a purse or other personal bag as you go to the nearest source of natural running water. Say your intention so the universe can hear. Throw the nation sack into the water.[31]

### Step Three

Obtain a sock or some tights or hose from your intended. Bury this item that has been worn, under your steps.

The person will be yours or your client's for as long as it is meant to be.

---

31. Hyatt, *Hoodoo, Conjuration, Witchcraft, Rootwork*, 1,449.

## 107. Stay Here Mojo

Is the person you care deeply for wavering? Do you feel a deep connection to them anyway? Perhaps they need guidance to make up their mind and help them stay with you.

Here is further work in the "Stay Here" commanding direction. This is another mojo bag you can create for yourself or a client, friend, or family member.

Begin with the reflection done yesterday before proceeding. You might do this spell and save it.

You will need the following:

- Soil from 9 footprints
- Jar with a top
- Cotton string
- Steel filings
- Mojo bag

1. Footsteps are the most important ingredient. Without them you cannot undertake this work.

2. Take a cotton string to measure the intended party's footsteps.

3. Gather a bit of the foot track dirt from each of the nine footsteps and put in a jar with a top. Close the jar with the top.

4. Return home and cut the cotton string as measured. Tie nine knots in the cotton string, marking the footsteps and thereby binding the traveling foot.

5. Add some steel filings to the foot track dirt. Mix well and put in a mojo bag, fixed tightly.

Tie this mojo around your leg below the knee with the knotted string—all with the intent of keeping someone you love with you.[32]

## 108. New Orleans Come Back to Me Spell

For this spell, you will need:

- 1 white or blue column candle
- The left shoe of your lover
- Compass, if needed

This spell is inspired by a traditional Hoodoo spell of an informant from New Orleans, Louisiana.[33] It is a spell to get the one you've been longing for to return. It utilizes the shoe as a form of foot track magick and candlemancy.

1. Write your loved one's name on the candle nine times.

2. Chant "Come back to me" each time you carve their name into the candle.

3. Burn the candle at sunrise, over the left shoe of the intended (so the candle burns above the shoe's height).

4. Bury the shoe under your doorstep, where this person has lived with you.

5. This is very important: the heel of the shoe must be facing east and the toe pointing west. (The opposite directions will keep the loved one away for good!) Use a compass to identify the directions if you are not sure.

---

32. Hyatt, *Hoodoo, Conjuration, Witchcraft, Rootwork*, 1,060.

33. Hyatt, *Hoodoo, Conjuration, Witchcraft, Rootwork*.

## 109. Candle and Foot Track Rite

Candles come together to help with your foot track magick quite a bit. Here is yet another candle rite with foot track magick to try. The purpose of this one, like the one you just did, is to return someone back to you, so all the precautions and preparations from the previous days should be done before doing this.

You'll find that as you work through the book, certain rites and spells work better than others. That's why it's always good to jot down notes about the conditions in which the rite was done (situation of the moon, sun, and planets; day of the week; time of the day; and so forth). Certain colors of candles may also work for you better than others, as you will find out through trial and error. As you work through these days, keep in mind that this is a time for trying, experimenting, experiencing, and hopefully learning.

For this rite, you'll need the following:

- A left foot (dirty) sock of your lover (or worn hose or tights cut off at the knee)
- Kraft paper and a #2 pencil
- A black column candle
- Matches
- Candleholder (optional)

Bury the article of clothing (sock or other) outside your door.

Write your lover's name nine times on kraft paper with a #2 pencil.

Turn the name-side of paper face down.

Set the lit black candle (in a candleholder, optional) on the paper.

Burn the candle in this arrangement for three days.[34]

## 110. Covert and Careful Foot Track Magick

A few weeks ago, you hopefully started getting some equipment and garb for your Hoodoo. There's more. Your practice of foot track magick is ever-evolving.

There are some additional tools that will be useful:

**Compass:** Many people don't know their directions, but you need to know them in some of the practices you'll undertake. Pointing something or yourself in the wrong direction in these spells or rites can have dire results. Also, for your tracking activities you may go to unfamiliar terrain. There is a good compass app on most cell phones. Make it a point to get your compass app downloaded or located in advance. If you prefer, purchase a good compass from an antique shop, secondhand store, or sporting goods shop. If purchasing, think about where you'll shop for your compass today.

**Timepiece:** A lot of your foot track magick takes place at specific times of the day. Be sure to have a good alarm, be it on your cell phone, an app to wake you up, or a good old-fashioned alarm. Being able to work in accord with the sun and moon is essential to your Hoodoo practice.

**Calendar:** Be sure to have a calendar, whether it's an electronic, hard copy, desk, portable, or wall calendar. Your calendar helps you keep track of the days on which you are doing your

---

34. Hyatt, *Hoodoo, Conjuration, Witchcraft, Rootwork*, 848.

foot track magick, to know when you started and when you ended.

## 111. Success/Job Spell

If you're after a job that seems very well suited to you, try this spell using shoes. This spell is inspired by one collected in 1936 from an informant working successfully at the job he desired at the Chamberlin Hotel in Hampton, Virginia.[35]

1. Carefully and honestly select a pair of shoes that have a very good feeling to them, which you've worn a lot but no longer need to wear. These hold the energy of your intent, hopes, dreams, desires, wants, and needs within them.

2. Burn the shoes entirely, to ash.

3. Put your shoe's ashes in a jar.

4. Put a few of those ashes in a tiny vial or bottle with a cork and take it with you to the job site or interview.

5. Without being noticed, drop a few ashes on the waiting room floor where you are sitting.

6. When your potential hiring manager isn't looking (this is important), sprinkle a few ashes near their feet or near the chair where you are seated.

7. Make your wish known to the spirits around you mentally as you do so.

Feel firm in your belief that you will get the job and that you will be very successful, as successful as the informant who shared this spell. Your wish should be granted!

---

35. Hyatt, *Hoodoo, Conjuration, Witchcraft, Rootwork*, 647.

## 112. Magical Brooms

Brooms hold a lofty place in Hoodoo and other forms of African-American folklore, so much so that couples "jump the broom" to go from their old relationship into the consecrated domain of marriage. You can cleanse domestic and work spaces and disperse psychic energy held in the footsteps using the sweeping motions of the broom. Having a collection of brooms for different purposes is recommended. It is meaningful to make a broom starting from the seed. Here's how:

1. Purchase or trade (with a grower with seed) for sorghum bicolor seeds, otherwise known as multicolored broom corn.

2. Sow the seeds directly into warm soil. This will generally be in May to mid-June in most regions.

3. It is important that this planting occur after all danger of frost has passed.

4. Plant the seeds in three to four rows, six to twelve inches apart, to encourage pollination. The rows will vary depending on the land in which you can plant. If you are in an urban area, try doing this in a co-operative garden where you can get a nice raised bed, or use several very large pots situated closely together at home.

5. Plant the seeds one inch into the soil, three to four inches apart to start, and then weed back to the six to twelve inches.

6. Plants should germinate in a week or two. They are ready to harvest in 100 to 110 days.

7. Harvest in the mid-afternoon. Tie with hemp firmly and hang upside down to dry as straight as possible.

Today, walk the earth in an unspoiled area of nature, such as the woods or your property, to find a piece of felled tree branch about four feet long—a thick, sturdy branch is best. If you begin hunting for the wood after a fierce storm, so much the better, for then you might just find a branch struck by lightning. Having the opportunity to yield some of that force in your Hoodoo is a unique opportunity. Witch hazel and willow are two types of trees from which you might like to harvest, as they have an extensive reputation as metaphysical, spiritual trees.

Don't worry if this doesn't happen immediately. It may take several walks on different days before you find the stick that speaks to your needs.

When you examine your gathered materials, consider the magical lore connected with various trees. I have written extensively about trees in African-American magick in *A Healing Grove: African Tree Rituals and Remedies for Body and Spirit*. One neat thing you can do to tap into the nurturing and forceful energies of the water deva and running water revered in Hoodoo is to use a piece of driftwood for your broom. Remember, this is no ordinary broom. It can be twisted, gnarled, or aged, with or without bark, as you choose. Once you find your branch, whittle down one side (which will be inserted into the herbs to make a broom), not to a point but to a blunted triangular shape.

### 113. Make a Rounded Herbal Broom

1. Gather materials to add to your broom corn. Find fragrant dried stems of purifying herbs (lavender, artemesia, mugwort, thyme, willow, rosemary, peppermint, sage, juniper, or hyssop). Soak these for an hour to soften.

2. Lay out your materials on newspaper or towels on the earth. Let them dry some so they are not dripping as you work. If it is comfortable, sit on the ground. If not, use a cushion or move to a table. Working under sunlight is optimal.

3. Using strong gardening shears, crop only one side of the bundle of herbs so they are roughly even.

4. Poke the whittled side of the broomstick into the middle of the cropped herbs. Hit on Mother Earth several times, to fix the herbs to serve you through nature.

5. Tie on one layer at a time using natural raffia until it is as thick as desired.

6. Use natural hemp string to secure after the last layer.

7. Optional: Wrap thin-gauge wire over the twine as tightly as possible, and tuck in the edges for safety.

8. Decorate the broom by tying cowrie shells (threaded with hemp string) to the wooden handle. Scratch your magickal name into the broomstick, as well as any magickal symbols desired.

9. Lay your handmade whisk broom outside in the grass under the light of the full moon to absorb her power.

10. First thing in the morning, while there is still dew, sprinkle the broom with sea salt. Take the broom inside and disperse the salted dew to spread positive energy throughout your home.

## 114. Reversal Magick

Some people take their lumps in life and let things be as they may. Others want to change things, particularly when they seem manipulated and thrown in their direction rather than being random. For those of you in the latter camp, you'll be interested in learning about reversal magick today.

Reversal magick is particularly important if you've been hexed or Hoodooed in a negative way. It is a powerful type of magick that takes into consideration some of the basic tenets of Hoodoo, such as the power of direction (cater-cornered, walking backward and forward to throw someone or something off, lateral moves, and so forth).

This is another form of magick within foot track magick. As you can see, Hoodoo is multifaceted and layered, and this leads to its efficacy. So in reversal magick you take what someone with ill intent sends your way and send it back. Reversal magick can also be used in retrieval.

- To do this, you first need to be very observant and aware. You must identify whether something negative was sent your way. If it is a war bottle, you'll know straight away, for example. If someone breaks your heart, this is also a negative action taken directly at your person.

- Next, you must release and reverse what was sent or done.

- You must act at just the right time, while the magick is active and hasn't rooted all the way.

- Lastly, you need the wherewithal and internal fortitude to catch this negativity or find the actual object planted against you and then summon the power and intent to return it to the person who sent it.

## 115. Shielding

Now that you are more familiar with foot track magick, consider protecting your foot tracks the way you would your hair and nails. This is particularly important if you know someone is trying to Hoodoo you.

The places where your tracks are the most obvious are typically moist:

- In snow

- In mud

- At the beach

- On a riverbank

- During the rain

Be mindful of these types of places and types of precipitation. Hoodoos use sweeping to get rid of all sorts of tracks. Make sure you have your broom on hand. You can also rake to disrupt your tracks and keep them from being collected. Altering your tracks as they are made helps; scuffing or mussing them and making them indistinct also helps.

## 116. Protect Me Powder

Protection magick is an important aspect of foot track magick. Hoodoo is many things to many people. Some people are more attracted to its potential to wreak havoc and bring about harm. Others use it for healing and other purposes. In some ways, the world of the Hoodoo—a person so deeply connected to the energies of the Earth Mother and other people—can be a minefield.

Since your feet carry your powerful intent with them, some spells, such as this one, reinforce the power of your feet. This powder gets its oomph from using well-known power elements such as red pepper, gunpowder, and sulphur.

Gunpowder incorporates yet another category of magick: sympathetic magick. If your feet become as strong and powerful as guns, you will be very hard to stop. This potent combination obviously will help you step over malicious things put in your path. With Protect Me Powder, you can go about your day stepping freely and feeling empowered.

This traditional formula is short and sweet. You will need only the following four ingredients:

- Red pepper
- Gunpowder
- Sulphur
- Shoes

Mix the first three ingredients. Add the powder to the soles of your shoes and wear them. Be protected from evil spirits.

### 117. Southern Hot Foot Powder

Informants to Harry Hyatt from both Richmond, Virginia, and New Orleans, Louisiana, inspired this recipe.[36] It's a good idea, since we are on the topic of protection, to try this one today.

Sometimes you can feel it in your legs or feet when someone is trying to Hoodoo you through the ground on which you walk. Of course, you must be very aware of your surroundings, your

---

36. Hyatt, *Hoodoo, Conjuration, Witchcraft, Rootwork*, 471.

path, and the energy within all of it to recognize the subtle shifts that occur when someone is warring against you.

Someone meaning to create chaos might put brambleberries in your path. Your weight makes them splatter and pop. You can rest assured, if this happens, that bad juju is afoot. Mustard seeds are also used. They create a small but noticeable gritty barrier between your feet and the ground. Because being grounded is important for the Hoodoo, you don't want anyone or anything to throw you off or deter your work.

An evil-wishing Hoodoo will employ the ground on which you step to make war. Hoodooing through the feet happens when someone puts something loaded with evil in your foot path, like a war bottle.

To deal with this, try the following rite.

1. Take a bit of unsifted cornmeal (fine grade).

2. Sprinkle it in your shoes.

3. Add two pepper leaves to the instep of each shoe.

4. Put two pepper pods in the heel of each shoe.

You've got hot foot powder now. You are shielded and protected from the evil that people put in your path.

## 118. Mississippi Hot Foot Floor Wash

Floor washes are such an important feature of Hoodoo, and they also factor into foot track magick for a good reason: people track so many kinds of vibrations and energies indoors through their feet and shoes.

Performing a protective hot foot floor wash such as this one, inspired by one shared with Harry Hyatt, will help clear and fortify your living space against unwanted psychic intrusions.

Water dissolves more substances than anything else known to humans. Think of what natural rainwater or lightning water (water gathered during a thunderstorm) can do for your home, paired with the scavenging and clearing power of red pepper.

Here is what you will need:

- Ground red pepper (amount depends on the size of the space being empowered and cleared)
- Bucket(s) of rainwater or lightning water for strong work

First, clear the floor of negative vibes, loose dirt, and objects with your handmade broom. Spritz with sea salt water first or a bit of holy water, if you feel the need for strong clearing and banishing.

Mix some of the red pepper with the rain or lightning water using a wooden spoon. Let this sit in the sun for a few days to steep and release some of the pepper into the water. If you're prone to allergies, wear a mask over your nose and goggles while mopping.

Strain any large pods from the water. Scrub the floor with this hot foot floor wash with a mop. This will get rid of bad juju tracked in by the unaware.

## 119. Curio of Note: Red Brick Powder

Red brick powder is used for several purposes in Hoodoo. One of them is its ability to protect. In terms of a definitive rationale for the rise of red brick powder, the jury is still out. There are several working theories:

1. As you will explore next month, a great deal of magick and mystery is cultivated in and around the graveyard. The

graveyards in New Orleans were above ground during the time of prominence of the Voodoo and Hoodoo queens. These queens practiced their work in the Dumaine Street area, near the cemetery, and sometimes brought bits and pieces of their workings home, including the crumbled and powdered brick from certain graves. The powder contained the properties and, in some cases, the power and force of those entombed.

2. Red is one of the key colors in Yoruba medicine, representing the life force, blood, vitality, and the Earth Mother herself. Red in this form of West African medicine includes various shades of red and some shades of orange.

3. Sympathetic magick may also play a role. Brick for homes and tombs is a very strong building material. The strength within bricks, powdered and sprinkled for various purposes, lends formidable strength to the work performed.

## 120. Cut the Bad Juju

Stop the tracking of bad energy and juju into your home with this simple and easy-to-make powder. For this work you'll need red brick, ground to a soft powder. I have a contractor husband, so this is easy for me to get from drilled bricks. Think creatively of how to source this curio. You may know someone, like I do, who works with bricks, like a mason, or you may be able to contact someone who works at a yard and can supply you with brick powder. A construction site on a brick home in your neighborhood is a very good source. Try local first. Otherwise, you can purchase it online from Etsy, eBay, or various Hoodoo suppliers.

For this powder you will need:

- Red brick powder (amount depends on the area you want to cover)
- Chamber lye (sufficient for your stoop)

Pour chamber lye on your front stoop or step. Sprinkle red powder in and around it. Scrub the stoop with the red brick powder, using a steel wool pad or scrubbing sponge.[37] This color and scent will naturally fade with wind and rain.

## 121. Unhex

Few things are as bothersome and dangerous to your health than being hexed. You can get hexed in different ways, including these:

- The powerfully spoken word (against you)
- War bottles
- Walking over something evil planted in your path
- Spells
- Rituals
- Certain forms of Hoodoo
- Eating something tainted

If you are hexed, you will:

- feel lethargic,
- get confused easily,
- be unable to concentrate,
- feel a lack of sexual desire,

---

37. Hyatt, *Hoodoo, Conjuration, Witchcraft, Rootwork*, 470.

- hear, see, smell, and feel things that aren't real,

- lose the desire to do things you once loved,

- feel weak,

- and experience other troubling symptoms.

If you or someone you know feels this way, trace back through the last few weeks and try to identify the source and the moment when this happened. If nothing else, this exercise is empowering. You should do protection work. There are many mojo bags, floor washes, spells, and rites scattered throughout this book to help with this.

Here is some unhexing foot track magick to do:

If someone has done some evil Hoodoo against you, go to your backyard every morning before sunrise. Take nine steps backward and nine steps forward for nine mornings in a row. You are rebooting through your footsteps.

## 122. Watch Your Step

To conclude all the thought, consideration, and practice you've put into foot track magick this month (not that it ever ends), take another walk in your neighborhood. Revisit your thought process and see if you notice anything different or new.

- Is there an area that makes you feel drained?

- Do you feel weak when you approach a certain crossroads, sidewalk, or other area?

- Is there a certain route that makes you angry or agitated?

- Do you see anything out of place?

- Do you smell something acrid or irritating?

Summarize your observations in your Hoodoo journal. Compare notes with the exploration you did earlier. What has changed? Is anything better than it was before? Now redo any one of the suggested practices to make a difference in your daily walks.

## 123. Walkin' Over Evil Unhex

Who doesn't love freedom? You, as a Hoodoo, are empowering yourself. You want and need to go where you want, when you want to. You never know what you will find in your path that is upsetting or something that disturbs you on a soul level. Having freedom and strength means you are more able to help yourself reach your goals in life. You can also help others.

Knowing your desires and right to have the freedom to take the paths you desire, you may be interested in learning about an unhex called Walkin' over Evil. There are many accounts of how to do this by various informants. This unhex shared with Harry Hyatt is from an informant from Brunswick, Georgia.

This involves attentiveness and awareness, steely willpower, and strength from the herbal and curio world. Hoodoos need extra soles on hand. You can do this more easily today by purchasing Dr. Scholl's insoles, or you may cut them out of parchment paper, kraft paper, or newsprint.

Gather these items:

• Red pepper

• Fine kosher salt

• Sulphur

• An extra shoe sole (handmade is fine)

Mix the first three ingredients, and put under the sole of your shoe. You should be prepared now, if need be, to step free by walkin' over evil.

# CHAPTER 5

# Dirt & Dust of the Graveyard & Crossroads: Days 124-155

Location, location, location. It matters in real estate and it matters in Hoodoo. There are several highly important locales specific to Hoodoo: graveyards, crossroads, and forks in the road. The reasons for this are diverse and intriguing. First let's consider the graveyard.

All sorts of folks are buried in the graveyard: mothers and babies, fathers, soldiers and sons, judges, politicians and criminals, those who walk magickal paths like paganism and Hoodoo, and those on religious paths like Santeria, Vodoun, Catholicism, and other denominations of Christianity. You can visit all sorts of famous people's sites of remembrance. A revered one to Hoodoos is the place where Marie Laveau and her namesakes were buried. Once buried, do folks stay in their graves? Now, why would they want to do that? The spirit is made for wandering. At the same time, what if it were possible to skim a little of the essence of the energy of the types of folks you want to engage with in your work? Where would you go? Why, the cemetery of course.

Hoodoo is a special place in the various parishes of Louisiana. Some of these areas are perched on flood zones. The deceased are not buried there. Instead, they are placed above ground in tombs and sepulchers. Those types of cemeteries in Louisiana are very spiritual places to our practice, as are family cemeteries everywhere. Family graveyards can be particularly useful to the individual practitioners related to the deceased or a Hoodoo affecting someone in a family. Some cemeteries, like Bachelor's Grove Cemetery in Midlothian, Illinois, are renowned for having roaming, meddling spirits. With the variety of people buried in these and other cemeteries across the globe, it is no wonder the graveyard is a place from which we can derive inspiration, ideas, energy, and materials for Hoodooing.

The main material we are discussing in this chapter is graveyard dust, also called graveyard dirt and goofer dust. There will be many days this month when I will ask you to visit the graveyard, because as an educator, I believe strongly in learning through doing in a whole-body, kinesthetic manner. This may not be right for you. You may be going through mourning and find going to the graveyard overwhelming. In this case, you can do a different chapter and come back to this one when you're ready. Conversely, you can purchase graveyard dirt. This is an especially useful option if you face restrictions about graveyard entrance and procuring its soil. You may be very busy at work or with family obligations and need to save these days for when you have some free time or combine the gathering of dirt into just a few days. If desired, there is a recipe included for an herbal alternative to graveyard dirt on day 125.

There is another place that is vital to the practice of Hoodoo. The more you learn about Hoodoo, the more you will understand the significance of the crossroads. At the crossroads, we can also obtain a special substance called crossroads dirt.

Undoubtedly, you've noticed the directionality of Hoodoo. We utilize the four directions of north, east, south, and west, but also catty-corner, backward, forward, and circles. Paths are utilized in the foot track magick discussed in chapter 4. Every manner of traveling through the world is of importance to the Hoodoo and is utilized in our magickal practices.

The crossroads is the convergence of the four directions, not necessarily streets. I use the sidewalk adjacent to my street convergence for some of my crossroads work. With a fork in the road, two directions merge into one. Whether you travel to these mystical places forward, backward, or from the side, they are highly potent and mysterious spiritual and metaphysical places. From hence forward, always hold the crossroads and forks in the road in the highest regard as places brimming with potentiality.

The crossroads are nowhere in a sense, as they aren't a direction, and they are everywhere, because they absorb all four directions. This is a place of unimaginable power, and from here, we gather powerful soil, referred to as crossroads dirt or dust, to be employed in magick. Even in urban areas there are crossroads to be found. In the urban suburb where I live, I find these at the edges of roads, on parkways, and near parks.

Let's not forget forks in the road. Here, two paths, with all their intent and purpose, converge into one road. This is a place of choices and decision making. Beyond which direction one may be able to go in, or redirect, there is also the power held in the merge. Forks in the road are significant and powerful places in the world of the Hoodoo. From the fork, you gain wisdom, insights, and the ability to forge change.

## 124. Opening the Gates

Before stepping out to the cemetery, you must pay homage to the proper spirits who own it and who live and mediate the space, every time you visit. In the African diaspora, your heavy-hitting lwa to call upon is Eshu Elegbara, called by many names. He can open the way, unlock the iron gates of the cemetery (metaphysically), open doors, and smooth communications between humans and spirits. Have a discreet altar set up to him behind your front door, built on a Monday. Lay a red cloth over a black one, forming a cross-shape to represent the crossroads. Place candy, hot peppers, cigarettes (tobacco from your garden or candy cigarettes are fine), an opened container of high-quality hot sauce, and a shot of good rum in a shot glass. Keep this topped up after Eshu Elegbara takes it. It should always be fresh, out of respect for him and to keep him happy. Bring several coins with you in the form of magickal pennies (Indian Heads, if possible) or dimes (Mercury dimes preferred) to pay your way into the spirit realm and honor the spirits. Lay them down respectfully near the place where you take your graveyard, crossroads, or sacred space dirt.

## 125. Graveyard Dirt Alternative

There are numerous reasons why you might not be able to work with dirt and dust from the graveyard, some of which were discussed in the introduction to this chapter. As a reminder, they include laws in your area, time, mourning, and your belief system. Though not the same, there is an herbal alternative to use in place of graveyard dirt. You will draw on the magickal qualities of herbs and herbs associated with metaphysical beings associated with the graveyard. Combining the magickal herbs with ritual will greatly enhance the effects of this herbal blend.

You will be harvesting or gathering mullein, cayenne pepper, and tobacco. Before you do this, say this prayer:

> *Earth Mama,*
> *I honor you.*
> *I seek your gifts.*
> *Through them share your knowledge with me.*
> *In the Goddess's name I pray.*
> *Blessed be!*

Preferably go straight outside to obtain a good amount of mullein from your garden or head off to the farmers' market. If this isn't possible, say this prayer before obtaining cut and sifted mullein from an herbal supplier. Repeat the prayer and then harvest or buy at the grocery store five whole pods of cayenne pepper.

Repeat the steps above with tobacco. The idea is to fill a four-cup jar with the blend of the three blessed ingredients.

Get a large wooden bowl and set it on the ground, outdoors or in your kitchen near the stove.

Sit down in a manner that is comfortable for you.

Recite: *In honor of the ancestors and those who have passed.*

Breathe on and crumble the mullein.

Recite: *Open the way.*

Work the red peppers between your two hands until they are as fine as possible.

Recite: *Yield your power to this bowl.*

Breathe deeply and work the tobacco.
Recite:

> *For all you hold, share, and yield,*
> *I honor you.*
> *Blessed be!*

Put the ingredients in a screw-top jar. Bury it outdoors under the waxing moon, if possible. Otherwise, bury it indoors in a pot of organic soil. Place the pot on a windowsill. The blend will be ready to use in one full cycle of the moon.

## 126. Your Relationship with the Cemetery

Today, I want you to take a spiritual inventory. A new beginning is the perfect mental space for taking note and checking in with yourself. This is a time to work in your Hoodoo journal. Many people have dark or even morose feelings about the graveyard. This reflection is designed to go beyond your notions of this space so you can begin to work with it.

On your 126th day of Hoodoo, I would like you to reflect on the following eleven questions:

1. When was the last time you went to the cemetery?

2. For what reason did you go to the graveyard?

3. How were you feeling after returning from your visit to the cemetery?

4. Have you ever gone to the cemetery to meditate, reflect, or find peace?

5. Are you willing to try doing so, if you haven't already? Why or why not?

6. Do you do the upkeep on a person's grave?

7. If so, what tasks are part of your upkeep regimen?

8. Who do you visit the most at the cemetery? What did they mean to you? How do you feel once you've visited?

9. Have you collected anything previously from the grave-yard? Why or why not?

10. What have you collected from the grave or funerals?

11. Do these objects seem to hold power? Please describe.

## 127. Locations

We began this chapter with an introduction on location. Today you are going to do some research on cemeteries from which you can get graveyard dirt, meditate or reflect and conduct some rituals and spells.

Alternatively, find the most sacred and historical places in your area, where you can glean portable power to use at your disposal. Use your imagination. This day is about tuning in, investigation, and discovery.

To start off, like you did yesterday, put your reflection and investigation hat on. Do some reading, online or otherwise. Find out the following:

1. Graveyard locations in your area that you can get to easily.

2. Cemeteries of special note or interest historically.

3. If your family ancestral burial ground is accessible to you.

4. Have you always wanted to visit a specific person's grave? Is this feasible? Start making plans, including exactly when you will go, how much it will cost for the journey, and what you

hope to get out of the experience that will strengthen your Hoodoo practice.

5. Sacred or historical locations that appeal to you.

Next, I would like for you to have a clear and executable plan to go do some reflection at a local cemetery or sacred space. If this is an ancestral burial ground, so much the better. After doing your research, make a more immediate plan to go to this site tomorrow, if possible. If not, set a date for your visit.

## 128. Graveyard Reflection

So you've made your choice between graveyards or other space. That's a step in the right direction. Here's what I'd like you to do next:

1. Head to the cemetery (or sacred space) at dusk or dawn, if permitted. Otherwise, go when you can.

2. Spend some time walking around.

3. For thirty to sixty minutes take in all the sights, smells, scents, and the appearance of the overall graveyard.

4. Find a comfortable place to sit in the mix of things (amongst the graves or in clear view of the sacred area).

Now comes the meditation.

### Meditation

1. Pick a quiet and still time to do this meditation.

2. Lean against an evergreen tree (if available), sitting on the ground or standing up.

3. Close your eyes halfway.

4. Moderate your breathing to take you to a deeply peaceful though observant place. To do so, first take a deep cleansing breath. Exhale hard. Now inhale through your nose, then exhale gently through your mouth, on counts of eight, until you feel very relaxed, for about five to eight minutes.

5. Now open your eyes all the way.

6. Look around.

7. In your relaxed state, is there a place that appeals to you differently than before?

8. Notice everything, including the way the shadows fall, the light coming through the trees, and the sound and direction of the wind.

9. With your heightened senses, you should now be able to commune with spirits of your choice. You may also be able to learn from spirits that pop up seemingly out of nowhere.

10. Use your time wisely, but don't force things. This is your information-gathering session.

## 129. Gathering Graveyard Dirt

Earlier in the year, you gathered bodily fluids, such as chamber lye, saliva, slobber, sweat, and tears. Today you will be gathering graveyard dirt from the cemetery (or sacred soil from an alternate location).

• To prepare, bring a protection mojo with you from chapter 1.

• Refresh your Eshu Elegbara altar.

- You will need some jars, such as the smaller Mason canning jars or bottles with cork caps that you can fix firmly.
- Get some bubble wrap or newspaper to wrap your bottles.
- A small gardening shovel will come in handy for scooping up some soil.
- You will also need some labels and a Sharpie.

Now it is time to gather your graveyard dirt.

1. First, repeat the meditation from yesterday.
2. Find the area that appeals to you first, then take some samplings. (Be respectful and observe the laws in place).
3. Next, go around and deliberately find a baby's grave or the grave of someone highly respected as a nurturing healer in the community.
4. Take other samples of your choice.
5. Label each sample as you go.
6. Wrap the bottles to keep them safe.

When you arrive at home, bring the jars to your kitchen and say the following while holding your hands with spread fingers over the jars:

> *Wisdom and insight inherent,*
> *you are the dust I respect and revere.*
> *Do my biddings.*
> *Hear my prayers.*
> *Know that I am sincere.*

Store your jars or bottles at home in your basement or under the porch, where they can be bathed in the moonlight each night.

## 130. Hoodoo Gardening: Violet

Violets (*Viola sororia*, *Viola papilionacea*) have many interesting mythological associations. The delicate purple flowers emerge each spring, yielding a bluish-purple heart-shaped flower. They are associated with faithfulness, humility, purity, and charm in Greek mythology and virtue throughout Christianity. In Rome, violets were common funerary plants—symbols of remembrance, faithfulness, deep awareness, the subconscious mind's abilities, and spirituality. They represent prosperity, peacefulness, and the ability to tap into mystical insights.

Because violets are associated with Venus, they are used in love potions and spells. In the Victorian Language of Flowers, violets represent modesty and humility. They are believed to have sprung up spontaneously on the graves of virgins and saints. They have a deep relationship to death and mourning in European folklore. The color indicates the love of truth and truth held in love. These are flowers of innocence and love, often seen on the graves of the innocent and children. In Hoodoo, both the flowers and the leaves are used for protection and prosperity.

- Since you are visiting the graveyard, see if you can find violets. Notice if they are at a child's grave or which people's graves they populate, in general.

- Respectfully take a handful of violets, as they keep malevolent spirits at bay.

- Take them home and put them under your pillow for a good night's sleep.

## 131. Violet Working

If you collected the dirt of a baby's grave when you went to the graveyard, try this spell. Otherwise, you have herbal and other alternatives collected. (Use them after they have matured.) Use this dirt to drive away evil spirits. Couple this dirt or herbal blend with other strong deterrents, and you should have a very safe and sound, peaceful home. For example, mix some graveyard dirt from a child's grave (or your alternative) with salt, gunpowder, and violet-perfumed oil.

As a renowned graveyard flower, violets will bring great potency to your work. Gunpowder is a very potent substance, imbued with active power, and the violet perfume not only is sweet and attractive but may well be from the flowers cultivated by spirits for their own interests. If a child picks your violet flowers, they will be even more blessed by innocence and connection to spirit.

Having some handmade ingredients will further fortify your spell blend. Here's a quick violet-perfumed oil you can make:

1. Pick off the petals of seven violets. Squeeze them into a medium-size perfume bottle that is new, clean, and dry.

2. Add a light, scentless oil, such as almond or peach kernel oil, until the bottle is almost full.

3. Add nine drops of attar of roses essential oil.

4. Top this off with eleven drops each of violet leaf absolute essential oil and sandalwood essential oil.

## 132. Curio of Note: Goofer Dust

Graveyard dirt is called by several different names. One such name is goofer, or goofer dust. Goofer dust is dust (dirt or soil) collected right from the cemetery, from under the foot of a grave. If you want luck in gambling, consider making a lucky goofer dust gambling hand.

### Lucky Goofer Dust Gambling Hand

Luck is illusive at times. It is everywhere, but sometimes it does not appear to be with you. For luck draw, you can depend on this traditional Hoodoo mojo, inspired by a traditional rite.[38]

If you want to concentrate your chances of harnessing the powers of luck, you will need a good hand. Using goofer dust fresh from the cemetery, blessed with the sweetness of violet oil, which also brings prosperity, will help things work in your favor.

1. Gather the goofer dust at night. (Midnight or dusk will be effective.)

2. Tie up the dust in a flannel.

3. Cross the hand over running water.

4. Bless it in the water.

5. As you carry this back, concentrate on positivity and good spiritual blessings.

6. Feed it a few drops of your violet-perfumed oil.

7. Caress, stroke, and squeeze this hand during your games of chance.

### 133. Graveyard Offering

Do you have a vexing problem to deal with? Perhaps a matter of the heart? You can utilize this month's graveyard work to help mitigate the problem. Today, deal with your troubling issue by

---

38. Hyatt, *Hoodoo, Conjuration, Witchcraft, Rootwork*, 564.

using an offering. Employing the goodwill of positive spirits can certainly help lift the burden from you. Spirits, particularly those from someone you know and respect, can work wonders on your behalf. Even in Hoodoo, delegating is a useful tool.

For this offering you will need a bundle of tobacco hung up to dry. (Eventually, use the tobacco grown in your Hoodoo garden.) Thank your leaves for sharing their magickal powers with you. Then take enough of the leaves from your bundle to make a cup of dried and shredded tobacco.

Obtain ½ pint of quality liquor of your choice.

Go to the graveyard any time that is convenient for you, trying to avoid funerals of course! Dig up some dirt from near the breast of someone you knew. Put down the offerings you brought, plus half a dozen crumbled white eggshells mixed with whiskey.

Say the name of the person and then state that you're paying them to take care of your specific troubling situation. Go into as much detail as needed. Sit down and make yourself comfortable as you chat with the spirit. When you are finished, just walk away without ever looking back.

## 134. Appeasing the Spirits

Today, I want you to follow a special procedure to appease the spirits. It involves a specific timing, approach, and offering.

Throughout Hoodoo, and in earth-based paganism, particularly Green Witchcraft, you will come to understand that you don't just take; you must approach your magical materials respectfully. You should also give back, through offerings or libations. Coupling these offerings with an incantation is also helpful. The art of give-and-take is a delicate dance that is useful not just in various magickal paths but in life as well.

On the full moon or the first-quarter moon, go to the grave-yard, entering from the left side. Bring a money offering. A silver dime will be perfect! Set it down on the ground and let it sink in a bit (so you'll need loose soil).

Recite:

> *My heart is open; my thoughts are true.*
> *I want to communicate with all of you.*
> *Before I start, know one thing:*
> *I am not a thief.*
> *I give you this Mercury dime as payment.*
> *I mean to be honest, respectful, and brief.*

Take your graveyard dirt or substitute. Walk straight forward; don't look back.

## 135. Spiritual Protection Ritual

Pennies are lucky and make good coins for offerings. With the help of these inexpensive coins, you can get spirits in a good mood and on your side. Their bright, coppery color picks up on the light, and they are appealing to the spirits for many reasons. The ancestors and other spirits can use them in trade on the other side, so they enjoy having them. Bring some pennies with you when you go to the cemetery each time.

Here is a protection rite:

Tonight, you will be going to the cemetery once again. This time, take a penny with you that you like, along with a yellow flannel cloth and some precut twine, about a foot-and-a-half long.

Go to the graveyard with your materials in hand, as you will be making an impromptu mojo bag. Carry your lucky penny with you in your hand, where it can be seen by the unseen. Scoop up some graveyard dirt, and put it in the heart of the yellow flannel cloth. Using your twine, make a tie crosswise. Wear the penny that has accompanied you, in your shoe for three days. At the end of the three days, throw it in a source of running water, such as a river, fall, or brook. [39]

Now there's no way any harm in the world can come to you.

## 136. Dispelling Hants

*Hant* is a term for an entity somewhat akin to a troublesome ghost. This term is more prevalent in the South and mid-Southern regions and isn't found much elsewhere, apart from within the Hoodoo community.

Hants can haunt people, places, and things, and there is a relationship between the two words. Recently, I was in a cabin, and for no apparent reason the Keurig machine came on, as if to make a cup of coffee, although no one was anywhere near and no one had pressed any buttons on the machine in quite a while. So these hants can haunt even modern machines, and their antics can scare the bejesus out of you!

While my experience was frightening in a way, it was also funny, as I had just stopped working on this book, all about the cemetery and crossroads, and closed my laptop down. Afterward, we had a good scare and an interesting conversation about the meaning of the hants' actions. It was decided that they wanted me to refuel and continue my work—and here you have it!

---

39. Hyatt, *Hoodoo, Conjuration, Witchcraft, Rootwork*, 450.

There are some traditional recipes and formulas for getting rid of hants. This is one such formula to try, to restore a peaceful balance to your home, free from inexplicable events such as the one I had with the Keurig.

### Dispel a Hant

Go to the cemetery during your best witching hour. Gather some graveyard dirt and put it in a box. Once you get home, cut a hole in the top of the box. Bury this under your home.[40] Your hants should be dispelled thereafter.

## 137. Paying Your Part Rite with a Nation Sack

You are already familiar with the ways your mojo bags, hands, jacks, and nation sacks are alive. You know they must be fed, tended to, squeezed, engaged with, and listened to. Your Hoodoo practices should be kept lively by going through various types of activation. I love this ritual because it brings so many types of activation techniques together into one rite.

### We Belong Together Rite

Place some hair of the person you love in your breast pocket or bra. Clear your mind by walking briskly to your nearest local cemetery. If there isn't a cemetery in walking distance, take your transportation there and then walk briskly through it, carrying respect for the dead in your heart. Focus on finding just the right spot from within the graveyard to begin this work. Once you have found your spot, set your intent as you gather some graveyard dirt in a jar.

---

40. Hyatt, *Hoodoo, Conjuration, Witchcraft, Rootwork*, 448.

Mix your loved one's hair and a bit of the dirt together with Adam and Eve root powder. Fix tightly in a red flannel. Tuck this nation sack in your bra.

Go home and draw a bath. Sit in the bathwater, facing the sunrise in the morning, if possible. Vacillate between hollering with desire for your intended and singing softly in praise of your helpful spirits. Empty the tub before the sun rises all the way. Do this nine mornings in a row, then get some High John the Conqueror root and add it to your nation sack for durable strength.

When you don your nation sack, you will draw the one you love close to your heart, similar to the way you are wearing your magical helper. You created this sack with the help of spirits and you have cleansed yourself in a ritualistic healing bath, then paid tribute to them through song and hollering. You can wear your nation sack with the freedom of knowing you have done your part.

## 138. Quick Change Mojo

I'm throwing this quick change mojo out to you today, knowing you will most likely make it on another day, out of necessity. You see, it's not every day one walks up on a lightning stone. It could be today, tomorrow, or a few months from now. The important thing is that you begin the process of opening yourself up to finding one. What you can do right away is walk to a tree that has been felled by lightning. Near the tree, you might just get lucky and find a lightning stone. A lightning stone is the essential material you need for this mojo to work.

Lightning stones are created when lightning contacts organic material such as sand or dirt. You want to find one at the base of a tree trunk or near a thick felled branch. They look like glass. Today, hunt for a stone or gather your thoughts in your Hoodoo journal on an approach to obtaining this special stone.

Lightning comes into our consciousness and vision swiftly. It is associated with power and the power to make changes. This is the reason your mojo will be a quick change mojo. After you find a lightning stone, you can do this work.

Take a small lightning stone and tie it in a red flannel. Sprinkle graveyard dirt atop it. Feed this with some luck oil. Add a large, unbroken nugget of frankincense to the bag.[41] Shake to mix the ingredients and also to keep them content together.

Put this mojo in a pocket you can easily reach. Wear it for gambling or other ventures involving chance.

## 139. Success Hot Foot Powder

It's not just those engaged with magick who understand the psychic and psychological workings in our daily lives. Hoodoos however, are particularly aware of one type of psychic and sometimes physical obstacle put on our daily path to foil our attempts at having a good life.

It's a thing of beauty to be able to walk over the obstacles put in our way by ill-meaning Hoodoos or others. Believe you me, those obstacles are always there. Moreover, as you get over one, another appears. So having a good variety of hot foot powders on hand is always a good practice. This hot foot powder combines foot track magick with graveyard dirt to yield very potent results.

---

41. Hyatt, *Hoodoo, Conjuration, Witchcraft, Rootwork*, 655.

### Success Hot Foot Powder

After a heavy rain, set out to the cemetery. Get about a half-cup of soil in your usual manner: at your perfect witching hour, after energizing your body, and while focusing your mind through a brisk walk and meditation.

Once you get back to your home, mix this soil with a bit of white sugar and cayenne pepper. Put this in a cauldron set on a fire outdoors or inside using a small pot placed on medium heat on the stove. The idea is to evaporate into the air the rain that is within the graveyard dirt. Once dry, sprinkle a bit in each of your shoes.

This potion is designed not only to help you hot-foot right over obstacles and find success but also to continuously keep enemies at bay.

## 140. Magick of the Crossroads

The foot track magick that proceeded this month carries over into our current work. Graveyard dirt is also put into shoes to bring various results. It is not just dirt or dust from under foot but is also useful in mojo bags and nation sacks. Within these interrelated practices we are now moving into magick of the crossroads. Interestingly, graveyards and cemeteries are often at the crossroads. This deepens the connection of the spaces for potential Hoodoo magick.

If we can pause here for a moment, let's consider other practices and belief systems from the African diaspora that have some relationship to Hoodoo. Proliferating through the diaspora is an appreciation for, utilization of, and interest in the crossroads, as well as the various entities that reside there. This space is held in high regard by numerous types of practitioners.

Let's continue to delve deeper into this mystical and metaphysical space before you visit it. Armed spiritually with knowledge and some basics of its power, you can proceed there in due time.

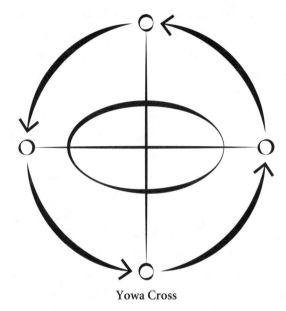

**Yowa Cross**

## 141. Yowa Cross

In the Kongo cosmology, an area from which my matrilineal line is traced, we find the yowa cross. As you can see from the illustration, the yowa cross has a central cross image at the heart of it, along with arrow-like forms, which guide the eye around the cross. These are the energies of the four directions. In the middle of the cross, there is an oval.

The yowa cross beautifully illustrates the energies at the crossroads. We clearly see a vertical line, which could be interpreted as a pathway, and a horizontal line, which creates a boundary. The oval highlights this important meeting place, almost as if circling an item on a document.

There is the crossroads' nexus inside the oval. This is an important meeting place, where spirits, ancestors, the departed, and other spiritual entities congregate. With consideration, tributes, offerings, and a careful approach, you may be able to communicate with beings, usually outside your normal daily life, at the crossroads.

Do some reflection on the crossroads today. Get your Hoodoo journal and a pencil or felt-tip black pen. Sit down comfortably. Use your deep breathing and meditation to go into a trancelike state. Open your eyes softly and copy the illustration of the yowa cross as you consider every aspect of its design, including not just what you've read but also what it means to you.

## 142. Mapping

As you have learned through practice, there is a great deal of power in the soil from the cemetery, as well as from other sacred spaces. Hoodoo taps into the magickal potentiality, or ashe, of the cemetery, yet there are other places equally compelling. One such place is the crossroads. Crossroads are the nexus of converging forces. Influential spirits dwell at the crossroads, including but not limited to tricksters. You need to have your bearings and wits about you when working crossroads dirt. Not only will you want to meditate before setting off, but you may also want to repeat the focusing activity once you get there.

By this point, you most likely have located a cemetery or two with soil and energy to help you work your Hoodoo. Let's continue to build your toolkit and practice by mapping and then experiencing the magick at your local crossroads.

Today is a map-making day. Get yourself some paper, such as graph paper, if you like straight lines and precision. Start with a #2 pencil. Draw your home in the center of the page. This should be simple; the basic A-frame house you drew in second grade is fine. If you feel so inclined, get as elaborate as you'd like, but keep your home relatively small, as there's much more to draw.

Next, draw the streets to mark the directions from your home to the cemetery (or cemeteries) or other spaces you have been working with. A simple asterisk to mark the spot, along with the name of the cemetery, is perfect. Now, for your crossroads—note the crossroads in the four directions around your home. You want to mark a crossroads north, south, east, and west of you. Once that's done, you can go ahead and mark each crossroads with an *X*. Forks in the road can be marked with a *Y*.

Go back to your map and give it some colors derived from nature. You could use brown for the streets, draw in some trees, color in the cemetery, and emphasize the *X* and *Y* areas with a highlighter pen.

## 143. Bargaining at the Crossroads

The crossroads is known as a place to form agreements, make oaths, set pacts, and barter. Traditional blues songs highlight this aspect of crossroads magick in song. One of the most notable bluesmen, with an almost inextricable relationship between his blues and the crossroads, is Robert Johnson. He is said in some quarters to have sold his soul to the devil there to become the great bluesman we so revere.

I shun this belief, because there is plenty of evidence that African-descended people have approached various entities at the crossroads for favors and blessings, including the lwa of Vodoun and the orisha of Santeria. More on this tomorrow.

## 144. Eshu Elegbara of the Crossroads

You already have an altar set up for Eshu Elegbara. Now let's get in deeper with him. He is the most prominent of the crossroads and cemetery beings, also known as Papa Legba in Haiti, Elegua in Cuba, and Exu in Brazil. In fact, he has more than 120 paths and has been syncretized with St. Anthony and St. Peter in Catholicism.[42]

No matter what you call him, he is vital to your interactions with the crossroads. While traditional Hoodoo doesn't speak his name, the way the crossroads is approached as a sacred space bears a striking resemblance to an appreciation for Elegba.

Elegba is important for one because he owns the roads. He can open and close roads, and of course the crossroads is an important metaphysical pathway. He can remove obstacles from your path and stop enemies' evil work in its tracks before it reaches you. He is hell-bent on justice, and since he is such a lover of truth, it is hard for mere mortals to deceive him, though he will play tricks on us. Moreover, he can mediate between the spirit world and humans, and thus he is often petitioned at the crossroads. Musical ability, creative artistry such as sculpture and ironworking, and even the dexterity needed in games like dice can all be enhanced by paying tribute to Elegba at the crossroads.[43]

---

42. Illes, *Encyclopedia of Spirits*, 393–394.
43. Ibid.

## 145. Fulfill My Desires

Getting what you want requires reflection and consideration, so you know all the implications and ramifications of your desires. Grab your Hoodoo journal and make a list of the things you want, randomly. Now redo the list, prioritizing what you want the most and listing your wishes numerically. What is it that you want the most?

Look hard at your map, taking deep cleansing breaths as you do so. Make sure your mind is very clear. Which crossroads is most appealing for you to visit today? Got it? Good. Now dress properly and grab a jar with a top and a small gardening shovel that fits into a backpack or other tote bag. Next, walk to the spot that called out to you. Once there, take a few more deep cleansing breaths, and a big exhale, to release any hidden, stale energies.

Focus on your intent while visualizing the middle of the crossroads. Go to a safe place to dig for a bit of soil in each direction as you make your wish for what you want. Safe and powerful crossroads are found near lakes, beaches, and streams in forest preserves and nature preserves. Breathe your intention into your crossroads dirt as you put it in the jar. Shake it up when you're finished collecting it, to mix thoroughly. Then sprinkle a bit of crossroads dirt in each of your shoes for some foot track magick. Be on your way, assured that very soon you will be getting what it is that you want.

## 146. The Bitter and the Sweet

Sometimes your best efforts may be foiled. Ill will from others may be the culprit, or perhaps you just have bad luck. One of Hyatt's informants from Jacksonville, Florida, inspired this remedy for crossed situations. This will help unhex the bad work of others that has been put on you. If you have bad luck, it's life force will be cut loose so that you are free to go about your business. Ultimately, good luck will be ushered in and you will find the success that is your destiny.

Go to the crossroads that calls out to you today. Thank the Earth Mama and attending spirits of the area for allowing you to find this spot. Ask for permission to take a bit of their blessed soil home. Next, dig deep into the earth. Scoop up some of this soil and put it in a jar. Screw the top on tightly and head back home.

Put some spring water in a pot, along with some fresh-squeezed lemon juice. Add a tiny sprinkling of the crossroads dirt, and stir. Bring this to a boil. Let it cool until it is still warm but not too hot. Drink this and it will cut off your bad luck.

### 147. Luck Reflection

Today we're back to your Hoodoo journal. This is a day for taking a personal inventory. Get in touch with how your luck is running, and try to identify the possible culprits by asking yourself the following questions and then writing down the answers:

1. Do you feel lucky? Why or why not?

2. Have you found anything suspect in your path, which may indicate someone has put bad Hoodoo on you?

3. If you feel this is true, walk back to the spot and see if the substance is still there. If nothing is there, see how you feel walking over it.

4. What were your observations and feelings? Go into as much detail as possible.

5. Have you received something suspicious in the mail? If you have an article that doesn't make you feel good and you don't need it for anything, burn it.

6. Did anyone give you the evil eye when you were out and about during the day? Write down all the details about the situation on a piece of brown kraft paper with a #2 pencil. Read it over once and then take it outside and burn it.

7. Was something given to you that doesn't make you feel good, such as an article of clothing, some prepared food, or a book? Go find it right now. Hold it in your hands and close your eyes. How does it make you feel? Write it down in your journal, then dispose of this and any other similar objects in your house. Burning is spiritually cleansing, or you can return objects to Earth Mama by burying them.

8. Inhale. Hold your breath as long as possible, then exhale hard, making a sound of release.

9. Evaluate your luck over the next few days. If it doesn't change, there is more luck-reversal work to do.

## 148. House Blessing

Much of your work at the crossroads is built around cleansing, purging, and removing bad juju. You'd be surprised at how many times you and your personal objects and interior spaces have come into contact with hexes and negative vibes in general. Yesterday you tapped into these situations, their sources, and contaminated objects.

Today, it is time to head back out to the crossroads. At the crossroads, your goal is to gather material to remove chaos and discord from your home, so you can have a peaceful home. This is inspired by a traditional rite from New Orleans, Louisiana.[44]

Walk to the crossroads, saying your favorite prayer, incantation, or affirmation. Keep it simple, and repeat it until you get there. Once at the crossroads, do the following:

Take four steps east and scoop up some dirt; put it in your jar.

Go back to the center of the crossroads, and then four steps west, scoop up some dirt; put it in your jar.

Return to the center of the crossroads. Now take four steps north and scoop up some dirt; put it in your jar.

From the center of the crossroads, take four steps south; scoop up some dirt and put it in your jar.

Gently shake the jar to mix the ingredients.

When you return home, lay the crossroads dirt in the four corners of your house. This will bring peace to your home.

## 149. Crossroads Altar

Today, you are going to head back out to the crossroads. Consult your drawing, and feel in your soul the best location to go. A place deep within nature is advised, such as a forest preserve or near a natural body of water. Bring a sturdy bag, purse, tote, or backpack with you. Wear the powerful color red to increase the efficacy of your work.

Once at the crossroads, perform the following rite to prepare for what is to come.

Stomp your feet and clap your hands while moving clockwise in a tight circle. Say:

---

44. Hyatt, *Hoodoo, Conjuration, Witchcraft, Rootwork*, 432.

> *Crossroads spirits, awaken.*
> *I am here to receive your messages in the form of*
> *objects for my altar.*

Repeat until you have moved clockwise nine times.

Stop and let any dizziness subside.

Take nine steps north and look around you. What objects call out to you to fetch? Thank them for appearing to you, and put them in your bag.

Go back to the center and take nine steps south and repeat the previous steps. Repeat all actions to the east and west as well.

In closing, say the following incantation:

> *Crossroads spirits, thank you for my precious gifts.*
> *I will treasure them in your honor*
> *and keep your wisdom close to my heart.*
> *In peace and with graciousness I depart.*
> *Blessed be!*

## 150. Forks in the Road

At a fork in the road, you typically have a couple of choices about which direction to travel, each heading in an opposite direction. Forks present a conundrum, and they can be puzzling when you are unsure of yourself. Luckily, just as with their more complex counterparts, the crossroads, which gives you four choices, there are supernatural helpers residing at the forks.

A fork in the road is a beautiful place. It asks you to challenge the status quo and be very clear with how you move through the world. Sometimes you may catch yourself moving robotically out of habit. You will do something a certain way because that is how you've come to think it should be done.

In Hoodoo, there is a lot of thought about how one travels through the world. This was brought deeply into your consciousness during your intensive work with foot track magick, and it continues in our current explorations.

A fork in the road is also a mysterious and mystical place. Otherworldly energies converge there, and if approached in just the right manner, it can help you strengthen all that you do.

## 151. Forks in the Road Meditation

Today you are heading to the nearest fork in the road, with your Hoodoo journal and a pen, as well as something comfortable to sit on, if you so choose. For privacy, use the cloak of darkness, and you can wear a hoodie or cape to make yourself even more difficult to distinguish from your environs.

Find a comfortable place to sit near or alongside the fork. Spread out your blanket or whatever you have brought with you to sit upon. Take off your shoes, if weather permits. Fold your legs in the lotus position. Place your hands on your legs in a relaxed manner, with palms upward and open, in a receptive gesture.

Take deep breaths, in through your nose and out through your mouth, in counts of six or eight. The longer you take between breaths, the quicker you will reach a deep stage of relaxation. Close your eyes partially, but don't get so comfortable that you fall asleep. Awareness is critical.

Let your eyes focus now on the third eye, which reacts with and sees into the unknown. Try not to think at all. Every time a thought arises, sponge it out, like words on a blackboard. Continue to simply focus on your third eye and your breathing pattern: inhale for six counts and hold, then exhale for six counts, and so forth.

After about ten minutes, stretch your body gently, and gradually open your eyes fully. Keeping yourself relaxed and unhurried, notice what new thoughts begin to fill your head. What do you see that wasn't there before? What do you hear or smell? Are you being guided to a nearby location? What is spirit telling you?

You can write down the answers to each of these questions in your journal. Jotting things down keeps your thoughts in a more permanent and useful form than the mind alone can achieve. When you have learned your lessons of the day or night, whatever the case may be, head back home, with your head filled with fresh thoughts and the possibility of new directions.

## 152. Jack at the Forks

Metaphors abound in forks in the road and crossroads magick. After all, when you come to these unique spaces, practical decisions are to be made, such as which direction you will take. Spiritually, the same thing happens. You come to these loaded, magickal spaces especially when you need direction from the spirit realm. This is where your Jack can come in handy. Remember him from the first month of this work, when you devoted yourself to creating and using various types of mojo bags and similar objects?

Today, grab your Jack and head out to another fork in the road that calls to you. Use the map you drew a few days ago for ideas of where to go. Once there, do some soul-searching deep within. What is it that you wish to know? Be sure it can be answered with a simple yes or no. Is it love matters that perplex you, or a career decision, or something involving your financial situation? For some, it may be issues around the legal system and justice.

## 153. Forks in the Road Divination

Whatever it is that troubles you, bring it with you in your heart to the forks. Now, with your Jack at your disposal, make sure that he is attached from a strong and intact string. You can ask Jack your question out loud, using clear language. Then, with him hanging from his string, notice his direction of choice. Is he headed right, for an affirmative answer, or left, to say no?

Is the answer what you suspected or is it a complete surprise? Thank Jack for his wisdom. Give him a squeeze and replenish his energy with a spritz of Hoyt's Cologne. Put him away for safekeeping in your pocket, near your heart.

As you walk back home, decide what first steps you can take to move onto this pathway laid out before you by the meeting of Jack and the fork.

## 154. Forks in the Road Rite

It is time for you to do a conjuring rite at a fork in the road. You should wear all red or black for this work. Look at your map. Decide in which direction you will head out to your most promising fork. Walk with power and purpose. Once you get there, draw a circle in the dirt. Within the circle lay out two chicken bones to make a cross suggestive of the crossroads.

Raise your palms upward toward the sky and tilt your head upward. Recite:

> *Spirits of the forks in the road,*
> *I call to you!*

> *Spirits of the north, I welcome you!*
> *Spirits of the east, I respect you!*
> *Spirits of the south, I honor you!*
> *Spirits of the west, I acknowledge you!*
> *What messages do you bring me today?*
> *How can I strengthen my path?*
> *Spirits of the forks in the road,*
> *I call on you to speak your truths.*

Turn 360 degrees, slowly and observantly.

What do you see, hear, or smell? What sparks awaken within you? What must you do? Things should come readily into your head, for these are the spirits of the forks speaking to you.

With palms facing outward, away from your body, recite:

> *Spirits of the north, I am grateful to you.*
> *Spirits of the east, I thank you.*
> *Spirits of the south, I appreciate your wisdom.*
> *Spirits of the west, I am moved by you.*
> *Return as you were.*
> *Blessed be!*

## 155. Cleansing Sitz Bath

You have experienced such rich and delightful things over this past month and visited places mentally, physically, and metaphysically that you had not known. Now it is time to close this chapter and the circle on this work, for now, with a cleansing sitz bath and holy oil treatment.

Salt is one of the most cleansing, purifying, and blessed substances on earth. Begin this work by cleansing your bath. Sprinkle medium-grind kosher salt onto a sea sponge and then wet it with rainwater. Use the salted sponge to cleanse and bless your tub and then rinse it with clean rainwater.

Now add a jug of warmed spring water to your tub. Add a few drops of rose oil (attar of roses) to the water, and swirl to mix. Soak in the rose-scented water. Immerse a clean sea sponge in the water and squeeze it atop your head. Let the water drain down your body, and along with it, your worries and cares. Step out of the tub onto a rug or towel. Anoint your body with your St. John's wort anointing oil. Pat yourself dry gently, letting the water and oil sink into your skin.

Say the following incantation:

*I am cleansed.*
*I am whole.*
*I am sound in body,*
*Pure of mind and of spirit.*
*I move forward with knowledge and light.*
*So mote it be!*

# SECTION II
# TRICKS OF THE HOODOO'S TRADE: SPELLS, RITES & MORE

Whereas in the five chapters of section 1 you were learning about the basic elements of Hoodoo, in section 2 we'll be putting those elements together into usable form. Moreover, these elements will be combined to address those issues that are vital to traditional Hoodoo and continue to be important in our daily lives: love, luck, abundance, prosperity, career, traveling, moving, and success. In Hoodoo, we use the elements of Hoodoo through spells (also called tricks), rites, rituals, ceremonies, prayer and incantation, candle and incense work, and specific formulas. We begin this section with the magick of love, one of the most compelling, driving forces of life.

# CHAPTER 6
# ATTRACTION, LOVE & RELATIONSHIP TRICKS: DAYS 156-185

One of the most amazing feelings we can experience as humans is love. Love can be tantalizing, sweet, tender, eye-opening, energizing, mysterious, and life-changing. Societies have been forged, shaped, built, and destroyed in reaction to matters of the heart. As the song goes, there's a thin line between love and hate. Reactions to illicit affairs or being jilted have brought down highly developed societies and great leaders.

Love, and matters of concern to the heart, are of central concern to the Hoodoo. You will need to know all about love magick to practice Hoodoo. Many are attracted to this path because it contains numerous ways of addressing love's concerns. These concerns include attracting love, or what Hoodoos call love draw. Keeping a lover faithful and bringing back a wayward lover are matters we also address. Protection and luck in love also play a role. In short, every aspect of love is considered in Hoodoo. This month, your sixth month of work, you will develop a handy love magick repertoire. In these next thirty days, let's build on what you explored previously in section 1, from mojo bags and nation sacks to washes, baths, candlemancy, and foot track magick. All these components of Hoodoo can enhance your love life.

We begin this section with a focus on love because of its significance to our lives. Love comes in many shapes and forms. It can be romantic and aimed outward, or it can be about acceptance and more inner-directed, manifesting as self-love.

As with your other work, be sure to stay grounded as you pursue this work. When it comes to inserting your magick into changing the natural state of things, you must have powerful motivation and stick-to-it-tive-ness. Bringing back someone who has left a relationship, for example, requires discretion and a strong enough will to change what has been done. Moves and changes in love relationships require great thought and careful consideration.

Love magick using Hoodoo can be rewarding and can change your life forever. That is why you must proceed with this type of Hoodoo with gravitas and highly sharpened skills. Love magick requires patience and is a great teacher. You will learn to do your part, but beware, for love magick as an act is loaded. It can be finessed but never forced—as it should be!

## 156. Lovin' It Up

For your first day focused entirely on love, I invite you to do some self-exploration. For this, grab your Hoodoo journal and a pen. That's all you need—that and a clear head.

Sit down, preferably with your back to a strong, old tree. If this is not possible, due to weather or other challenges, a wooden chair would be ideal. This will put you in touch with nature in-doors, and the hard quality of the chair will keep you focused.

### Reflection

Love means different things, depending on where you are in your life and the lens through which you view life. Today is a day of reflection, visualization, and planning. Get yourself relaxed in the way that works best for you—through a walk, meditation as I've guided you previously, or deep, cleansing breaths.

1. Close your eyes and think about what love means to you, in this very moment. For example, do you seek love, do you want to assure a faithful partner, are you more concerned with self-love, or are you focused on the concerns of others?

2. See what your concern related to love looks like. Visualize the best-case scenario.

3. Open your eyes and write down what it is you have thought about and visualized.

## 157. A Week of Floral Love Draw Oils

Smells are a part of the way we attract or repel others. The topic we will explore this week is essential oils and fragrance oils, which have long been a part of Hoodoo, particularly in love draw. Here are four relatively easy-to-obtain types of oils, along with their qualities.

### Rose

If you seek love, are in love, or want to show someone you love them, then typically the rose (*Rosa spp.*) is going to play a part. Roses are deeply sensual flowers. They are suggestive of female genitalia and the flush of color on your body that is precipitated by being near someone to whom you feel an attraction. Rose comes in various ways to apply to the body, one of which is rose oil. You can make this flower useful in your brews and potions by employing attar of roses and rose absolute.

### Musk

Musk has been used as an attraction oil since ancient times. This deeply earthy scent is traditionally created by the scent glands of certain kinds of deer. With musk oil, you are accentuating your natural ability to attract with the power of animal spirit.

### Neroli

Neroli (*Citrus aurantium* or *Citrus bigaradia*) is an expensive and intensely sweet oil made from orange flowers. It is high-frequency and hypnotic. Neroli helps you love yourself when you've been jilted. This is a great confidence-boosting oil for dating and new relationships. It is also calming.

### Lotus

Lotus (*Nymphaea lotus*) is another ancient type of oil beloved in Egypt. It has a very sweet scent, with a hint of musk. There are obvious correlations between the pink and plump lotus flower's behavior in spring when it blooms to welcome pollination and that of a woman at the height of attraction to her partner. There are many different types of lotus with distinctive oils. With the colors, the scents and uses change.

Metaphorically and symbolically, white lotus oil would be fitting for your love magick, as it only blooms at night. Blue lotus, like that depicted in Egyptian art, particularly in creation stories, can be used for fertility and attraction as well.

## 158. Hoodoo Gardening: Lesser Periwinkle

Lesser periwinkle (*Vinca minor*) is a plant closely tied to magick in many spots across the globe. For example, in France, lesser periwinkle's name translates to "flower of the sorcerer," as no witch or sorcerer would have been caught without its vines trailing across their property. It is a fast-growing plant and ground cover. If you want to add it to your garden, do so in a place where other plants will not grow or where you haven't planted, as it needs lots of space.

Not many plants' blooms are blue, but this one comes close. The perky little flowers can be seen during some of the special days on the pagan calendar, including Beltane (May Day), which is dear to Hoodoos and a time of fertility and love. Litha (the summer solstice), another time of intense passion and sensuality, comes just as we're celebrating the sun on the longest day of the year.

Lesser periwinkle has various medicinal uses. It is a relaxing sedative and also works on the brain as a cerebral stimulant. In terms of love magick, Hoodoo informants report that chewing the flowers deepens the love between a committed couple by softening their hearts. Top a salad with fresh spring/early summer periwinkle flowers. Eat this together and feel the love-expanding effects.

In terms of your garden, lesser periwinkle can grow in zones 4–8, in any sun condition, from full shade to full sun. It will also do well in highly varied soil conditions, from light and loamy to heavy clay. Seeds and plants are an excellent way to get them started quickly and are widely available.

## 159. Love Draw Powder

This formula features calamus root (*Acorus calamus*), an herb used to create holy anointing oil, mentioned in the Bible. Different types of sage are used for magical purposes by people of a variety of paths and beliefs. Calamus is both sacred and symbolic of love. Sage is a very sacred multipurpose herb. This is an easy-to-make powder, with wide-ranging implications and uses.

Gather the following ingredients:

- 1 cup calamus powder
- Several white sage leaves
- Airtight container
- Red flannel

At 6:00 a.m., put the calamus powder in a large bowl. Crumble the sage into the powder. Breathe your intention into the sage, and crumble it powerfully between your palms over the powder. Now mix the powder, being careful not to stir up any dust or inhale it. Put this in an airtight container, such as a jar with a spring top, and let steep for a full cycle of the moon.

### How to Use Love Draw Powder

1. Add it to other potent love ingredients in a mojo bag to draw love.
2. Sprinkle some into a mailed package or letter.
3. Sweep it down the front steps to pave the way for a loving interlude.

## 160. Rose Sachets

We have explored the ashe of four love oils. For the next four days in a row, let's play with imaginative ways of using them, so they become a part of your love draw magical work.

To make some rose sachets, gather the following items:

- ½ pound pink or red dried rose petals
- ¼ cup Queen Elizabeth (orris) root powder
- ⅛ ounce rose oil or rose absolute
- Solid sachet bags with a drawstring

In a bowl, crumble the rose petals, all the while focusing intently on their ability to draw love to you—love of yourself, of others, of a potential partner, and for the world. Really imbue your roses with an extra infusion of love. Sprinkle on the Queen Elizabeth root powder, which will not only preserve your botanical mix but will also amp up the ashe of it. Smell the rose oil or rose absolute and visualize your goal. What or whom do you want drawn to you in a loving way? Meditate on your desire and then add the elixir to the botanicals. Crumble with your hands further, encouraging the mix to serve your purposes. Put as much of the rose mixture as desired into the sachet bags. Place these under your bed pillows, in the chairs and behind the pillows in the living room, and in your drawers, so that key factors of your life are powered by the rose.

## 161. Musky Hot Oil Treatment

Locs or locks; tresses, mane, crown—we refer to our head, hair, and scalp in various ways. Stroking and touching the hair is a surefire way to let your intended partner know, while on a date, that you want them and are interested. This touching of the hair also releases a scent, when you are strategic about it. Let's use some animal attraction to make a musky hot oil treatment.

You will need these items:

- 1 teaspoon musk oil
- ⅓–½ cup shea butter or Moroccan oil (This will depend on the thickness of your hair, your taste, and availability of the oil.)
- Basting brush or paintbrush
- Scent-free shampoo (if desired)

Put the musk oil in a bowl. Swirl to mix. Think about the possibilities. Let your mind expand with the excitement of what is to come. Relax and let the aroma penetrate your mind. In a separate microwave-safe bowl, add the oil/butter. Microwave until melted/ warmed. Don't burn this or let it overflow. Start with shorter heating times and watch carefully. Now add the musk oil. Bring these nurturing and sexy substances together to create a hot oil treatment. Stir well with a disposable wooden chopstick or metal spoon. Set aside. Now break your hair into sections and apply this warm treatment to your scalp with the brush. When completed, treat the ends of your hair. Shampoo with scent-free shampoo, if desired. Towel dry. Watch out! You will be hot to trot!

## 162. Neroli Luffa Soap

All that is sweet, tender, and arousing you can find in your little bottle of neroli. Layering is always a good way to add to the staying power of your aromatherapy scent. Today we are working neroli into your personal care in two related but different ways, starting with a neroli luffa soap.

Making your own soap is a pleasure. This pleasurable feeling is amped up by working in the heavenly scent of neroli. The idea of the luffa is that you are literally peeling off the old layer of yourself, opening the way for something new to occur. You will use this soap as a gentle exfoliator. Don't work it too hard; do it just enough to suit the purpose described, so as not to irritate your skin.

Gather these items:

- 1 pound melt-and-pour soap (I suggest either an olive oil, shea butter, or buttermilk base.)
- A microwave-safe bowl or a double boiler
- 1 large luffa sponge
- 1 loaf pan
- ¼ ounce neroli essential oil

Melt your soap base in a microwave-safe bowl or a double boiler. Do this slowly so the soap doesn't overflow. Put the luffa in a loaf pan, or cut a large luffa in half and put into two pans. Mix in the neroli essential oil (into the soap base). Pour the neroli soap over the luffa, covering well. Allow the soap to harden overnight. The more you wash and prepare yourself to love, the more the luffa and its deep-cleansing and purifying ability will be revealed.

## 163. Lotus Oil Massage

Love and lovely oils go together, as you learned over the past few days. To extend your practice, today reach out for the oil utilized by Black folks for centuries, tracing back to ancient Egypt and Kush. Always quite a rare oil, lotus is mentioned in traditional

Hoodoo by various practitioners. For this massage, you will use it judiciously, along with the silky-smooth, virtually scentless sweet almond oil. Gather the following:

- 1 dram (⅛ ounce) pure lotus oil
- 8 ounces sweet almond oil

Add the lotus oil to the almond oil. Swirl gently to mix, avoiding bubbling. To use, warm this erotic oil in your hands with your breath and hands, lovingly and with intention. Apply liberally, working on arousal and pleasure. Make sure both of you (or all of you) are massaged, so this isn't one-sided.

## 164. Listening and Experimenting with Flowers

Every flower has a story, and a language it speaks to the soul. During the early to mid-twentieth century, Hoodoos had preferred floral scents, as noted in the various catalogs such as *King Novelty Company Curio Catalog* out of Chicago. These scents are captivating and old-fashioned to the modern nose, but you can still find them in the form of perfumed oil, cologne, or perfume. Who knows, you might like them. You probably have your own attributes that you lend to these flowers when you smell them. They will work on different people in different ways. Here are some of those found in the King Novelty catalog:

- Narcissus
- Lavender
- White rose
- Lilac
- Lily of the valley

- Orange blossom
- Honeysuckle
- Jasmine
- Sweet pea
- Violet

See all that empty space next to each flower? Well, how about you fill it in? This is your day to go out to the shops and explore these scents from flowers. Take your Hoodoo journal with you and report on what you think of each one. Answer the following questions: Would you like to use this scent in your romantic and dating repertoire? Why or why not? How will you utilize it (hair, skin, massage, etc.)?

### 165. Wrap-Up: Exploring Love's Best Flowers

You've spent the past week devoted to flowers, exploring them and their uses. Now, to wrap up the week, let's brainstorm ways to use these flowers so closely associated with love, in the home.

1. Narcissus (white narcissus, for example) is a good flower to grow from bulbs in the home. Let its intoxicating scent spread through the room, affecting all within smelling range. These flowers will bring on a happy, peaceful, and sensual feeling if you are patient and open yourself to their possibilities.

2. Lavender is a great multipurpose flower in all its forms (incense, oil, cologne, soap, water, fresh, dried, honey, and so forth). I particularly enjoy washing the home with a lavender spiritual floor wash, which is created simply by

blessing the essential oil with your intent and then adding it to some spring water, and washing the floors.

3. White rose, lilac, lily of the valley, and violet are all sexy perfumes, which will aid in your attraction work.

4. Orange blossom comes in the form of a water, which works wonders when paired on the altar with loving entities, such as the goddess Venus or the lwa Oshun.

5. Try growing sweet pea or jasmine near your front or back door. These gentle, pretty, enticing climbing flowers will draw in good, loving vibes to your home and hearth.

But don't stop there. What are your ideas for using these flowers? Which ones are you going to grow in your Hoodoo garden? Where are you going to source them?

## 166. Controlling a Lover

Let's face it, sometimes lovers get out of line. This is when, as a Hoodoo, you can take control. You are a very powerful person, growing more so every day. But we all need assistance. Enter devil's shoestring, the Hoodoo's special herb. We've had this discussion before. You know that you need to do control work judiciously on behalf of others or yourself. Think about whether you want to do this trick before taking the time to get into it.

Once you've decided, you will need these items:

• Devil's shoestring

• Knife or scissors

• Jar with a screw top

• Whiskey

Do this work on a full moon, if possible, during a waxing moon. Take some strands of dried devil's shoestring and cut them into 1½-inch pieces. Place in the jar. Now pray your intention into the jar. Think only of the party you want to be controlled. Don't mix anyone else up in this work. Breathe your intention and fix it with a long, hard stare. Add the whiskey as you continue to reflect on your desire, breathing and fixing as you work. Put a cap on this jar and let it steep for a fortnight. After this time has passed, rub the devil's shoestring and some of the whiskey on your hands.[45] This is what is in store for you:

1. Lay it in the path of your desired and they will yield.

2. Draw prosperity by putting it in your pocket.

3. Add it to your gambling hand for the same purpose as #2.

## 167. Love and Fertility Mojo

Adam and Eve root is referred to by several names, including putty root, because of its ability to bind clay vessels with the substance created from its roots. You'll grow to depend on it as an essential love root.

Adam and Eve plant belongs in the oeuvre of sympathetic root magick. As I mentioned, a putty or binding material can be created from the root. Some of the roots look female, while others are more phallic and manlike, and they couple up and proliferate under the cover of soil.

Today, get yourself a female (rounded) Adam and Eve root and a male (phallic) one. Place them in a red flannel. Sprinkle this with some rose water at first, and then in a few days with whiskey, for a sustained feed. Use this mojo bag to have a positive effect on

---

45. Hyatt, *Hoodoo, Conjuration, Witchcraft, Rootwork.*

your sexual organs, particularly if a child is desired. This will also enable you to win at love and have financial success as a couple. Your roots must be pure, fresh, and clean at the start to be effective.

## 168. Loving Couple Hand

Today is the day you can take matters of the heart quite literally into your own two hands. You know that hand is another name for mojo, yet they each have their idiosyncrasies. I equate hands with extensions of our hands and notice that in many of the traditional formulas, manipulation of the hand is suggested. That is the case with this loving couple hand inspired by one of Harry Hyatt's many informants.[46]

1. Take an Adam and Eve root and wear it close to your body, in a mojo bag, for three mornings in a row. You may want to put this in an upper pocket near your heart, if possible, or in your bra.

2. Then take this to running water, such as a brook or stream.

3. Place Eve (your feminine-appearing root) in the water, and quickly put Adam (the masculine-appearing root) on top.

4. Tell them what is wanted, out loud.

5. Sit down and stay there for three hours.

6. Contemplate your request.

7. The person you've been pining away for is open and waiting for you.

---

46. Hyatt, *Hoodoo, Conjuration, Witchcraft, Rootwork.*

## 169. Hoodoo Gardening: Sampson's Snakeroot

There are several different families of herbs to which the name Sampson's snakeroot is ascribed. Today we are going to explore one that you might want in your Hoodoo garden, as it is common and easy to grow. I'm talking about echinacea (*Echinacea pallida, Echinacea angustifolia,* and more. For our purposes, I suggest growing *Echinacea purpurea.*

In the 1920s, when herbal remedies and Hoodoo were as popular as they are now, echinacea was the most widely used patented plant medicine. It lost favor for a time but had a renaissance from the 1990s onward, when it was considered a potential wonder drug. There are however, serious considerations and contraindications, as well as conflicts with many pharmaceuticals, including things as common as Advil and Motrin. Here we will be growing them as stock for the Hoodoo garden, for Hoodoo magick rather than as a physical medicine.

*Echinacea purpurea* is also called hedgehog. It is of the genus Echinacea and in the family Asteraceae, to which daisies also belong. *Echinacea purpurea* is native to the eastern United States, though it is now grown elsewhere.

You're in luck with this plant, with such a wide growth zone—it grows well in zones 3–10. It can grow to five feet, but different cultivars grow to varying heights. If you have fresh seeds from another gardener or a shop, they will germinate in five to twenty days, following the package directions. You can sew them in the spring in deep pots, to permit root growth. They can be grown from root cuttings during the fall or early winter. They prefer deep, rich, well-drained, and possibly sandy soil, in a sunny location. This prairie plant, beloved in the area in which I live, is also drought-tolerant.

- There are several different preparations and uses in Hoodoo for this magical and medicinal herb. I suggest you begin by chewing a carefully sliced-off bit of fresh root to soften your or your potential lover's heart.

- Second, soak a bit of the root in whiskey for seven days. Let it dry off for a couple of hours and then add it to your hand, along with a High John the Conqueror root. This is used to restore vitality and virility, particularly in men. It will also make you more appealing to potential partners, if you are a man. When the hand weakens, feed it more whiskey.

## 170. New Orleans Fire and Ice Love Spell

Love is a fickle thing. It can fill us with mental aches and longing, wishing and dreaming. This may be happening to you, someone you care for, or a client. If you want to capture the heart of a seemingly out-of-reach person, this is the Hoodoo spell for you to try. It is described by the informant who shared it originally as being foolproof.[47]

This spell is simple and beautiful and is built around Hoodoo's attention to the power of opposites. In this work, we harvest the power of bringing together ice and fire. Opposite magick is strong magick.

Gather these items:

- 1 yellow column candle
- 1 white column candle
- 1 blue column candle

---

47. Hyatt, *Hoodoo, Conjuration, Witchcraft, Rootwork*, 823.

- A very large bowl (like a decorative glass, Pyrex, or ceramic serving bowl)
- Kraft paper
- Pencil
- 25 pounds of ice cubes
- Matches or lighter

Put the candles in a bowl in the bedroom in a fire-safe and sturdy place, like on a side table. Write the names of the intended lover nine times on nine little sheets of paper. Put the papers upside down in the bottom of the bowl. Pour enough ice around the candles to fill the large bowl. Burn the candles for one hour, nine days in a row. Give the ice back to Earth Mama after use, and use fresh ice each day.

## 171. Love-Drawing Ledge from Mobile, Alabama

This trick employs numerology and the power of horseshoes and sulphur. You're going to work your entryway as well, because this is the portal through which you want your love to enter. Doors have magical ashe, whether they are mundane and practical or magical doors.

1. Get nine horseshoe nails and some sulphur and lard.

2. Heat the lard in a cast-iron pot until it is fully melted.

3. Put the nails in the lard with the sulphur at 6:00 a.m.

4. Cover.

5. Leave the mix on the stove without heat until 6:00 p.m.

6. Call your love's name as you look at the mixture in the pot.

7. Lay nails across the ledge at the top of your entryway door.

Your love will come.

## 172. Love's Candle Altar

An altar kept close to where you sleep allows you to use your mental power, when in the liminal state between sleep and wakefulness, to gain the object of your desire. This simple bedside altar provides a sensual focal point for your love draw work.

Your love altar involves candle dressing. By dressing your candles, you are releasing scent into the air that works on the senses and can touch the ancestors, spirit guides, and ascended ones so they'll be happy to work on your behalf. You are also enhancing the power of the color selected and any other work (such as writing) done to the candle.

Here is a traditional candle dressing, updated with herbs selected for their well-known magical ability to bring love. You will need the following, in addition to your bedside table:

- Lemon-scented oil or water-based organic spray cleanser
- A small, pretty pink cloth
- Silver candleholders
- 1 pink candle
- 2 red candles
- Geranium essential oil
- Rose petals
- Orange flower water
- A small white dish
- Match or lighter

Cleanse your bedside table with a lemon-scented oil or water-based organic spray cleanser. This depends on whether it is made of wood (lemon-scented oil) or another material (water-based organic spray). Let dry and then lay out the cloth atop the table. Arrange the silver candleholders to face south, east, and west. Roll the candles in a small amount of geranium essential oil and place in the holders. Crumble the rose petals around the arrangement. Put some orange flower water in a small white dish. Light the candles and reflect on your heart's desire.

### 173. Love's Egg Magick

Eggs are magical, mystical, and spiritual. Stories abound about eggs because they are strong yet fragile. They are also handy little tools for your Hoodoo work. They feature prominently in many magical forms and different types of folklore. If someone leaves you (or your client) and you want them to return, bury an egg on your (or the intended party's) property. Wait nine days and the person will return.

### 174. Anna's Coffeepot Ritual and Prayer

Sometimes you do lots of work in a relationship and then find it just plain doesn't work—but you still want it to. Here is an old-school rite and prayer to help the two of you get along and cement your relationship. Be sure this is the right thing to do, however. Sometimes when there isn't chemistry or there are other problems, like a wandering eye, the relationship might not be meant to be.

If you decide to do this for yourself or someone you're working with, after taking time to meditate and reflect, here's what to do.

You'll need the following:

• Access to a cemetery (or space that is special to you)

• 2 pennies

- Coffee pot
- Kraft paper
- Salt and pepper
- Matches or lighter

Go to the cemetery (or other space) at 11:30 p.m. with your equipment. Put the two pennies and some graveyard dirt from your shoe in the coffee pot. Pray your most sincere prayer over the pot. Write the person's name on the kraft paper at midnight. Put salt and pepper in the coffee pot.

Go home. Next, three times a day, heat the pot at 6:00 a.m., noon, and 6:00 p.m., nine days in a row, but on the third day write him a letter in the morning and put it under the coffee maker. You should get back together in three days to three months if it is meant to be.

## 175. Love Mojo

White lodestone is known as a stabilizing curio that will help keep a couple faithful while also making their love secure. Seek out a pair of white lodestones in the ways you have learned so far in the book. You will want a reputable seller, and it is optimal that you get the stones on your own so you can select what you want for your work.

Add these male and female white lodestones to your mojo bag. Feed with Hoyt's Cologne.

## 176. Counting on Love

One of the special features of Hoodoo is its incorporation of numbers. Here are some candle spells in which you are asked to use a specific number of items.

### Spell to Bring Back a Lost Love

Candle work employing the inherent power of specific numbers is the focus of this spell to bring back a lost love, from an informant of Hyatt who hailed from New Orleans, Louisiana.[48]

1. Take a nice and thick or long taper candle.

2. Sign the person's name on the candle.

3. Hold the candle upside down and burn for a few minutes.

This should encourage them to change their ways and return to you.

### Spell to Turn Your Luck Around in Love

If you feel unlucky in love, this is the perfect spell for you. Get six red candles that are either very long or quite thick. Put them on a fireproof silver or white plate (if pillars) to accentuate the candle's ability to reflect upward and outward—catching the ancestors' interest. Stick sixty pins around the one candle (thirty on each side). Burn this candle along with the other five plain ones, reflecting on your wish to turn your luck around. Repeat with a different (single) candle stuck with the pins for six nights in a row.

## 177. Curio of Note: Chamois

Chamois is a soft, comforting, seductive material made from animal skin. You can use it to carry your luck draw materials, herbs, roots, and oils. It will bring love, as well as the peace, abundance, happiness, and success you want to go along with it. Create a simple mojo bag and stuff it with a lodestone pair. Hang it from your neck on a soft though durable, wearable string.

---

48. Hyatt, *Hoodoo, Conjuration, Witchcraft, Rootwork.*

You can step up your use of chamois, directing it at matters of love in the following way, reported by way of New Orleans, Louisiana. Cut out two pieces of heart-shaped chamois of the same size, and sew together. Fill with a lovely sachet powder such as Queen Elizabeth root, if you want to attract a woman (see day 184). This root is well known for its attraction powers. Ladies, wear this over your heart.

### 178. Come Back Here! Spell

Do you or someone you know pine away for a lost love? Well, today you're going to learn a way to put a fix on that. You will need the following:

- A piece of white parchment paper, 3 x 6 inches
- A fountain pen
- Dragon's blood ink (enough to fill the pen)
- A glass bottle with a large mouth and a cork or screw on top
- 2 teaspoons rose water
- 1 teaspoon orange flower water
- Holy water (if desired)
- 1 teaspoon Jockey Club cologne
- 3 teaspoons honey
- 3 lumps of sugar
- Lodestone pair (your he and she)
- ½ teaspoon steel dust
- A light blue or white candle

Take your piece of white parchment paper and some dragon's blood ink and the pen. Load some of the ink into the pen. Now write the desired person's name three times. Write the other name (the name of the one who wants the lover to return) three times on top of that first name. Put the paper in a glass bottle with a cork. Add the rose water, orange water, holy water (optional), and Jockey Club cologne. (You'll probably have to order this classic scent from online unless you have an old-fashioned perfumer nearby.) Now add the lumps of sugar and the honey. Put a white he and she lodestone inside, with steel dust. Stir to mix.

Lay the candle in the potent mix you just created, making sure the wick doesn't get wet. Stand the candle upright and light for an hour at 6:00 a.m. and an hour at noon for nine days while focusing on your intent.

### 179. Lover, Come Back to Me Spell

Sometimes it takes experimentation with different spells and tricks to get your lover (or your clients' lover) to return, so here's another one to try.

Dirt daubers are little devils that are hard to get rid of. They love warm climates and have a role in Hoodoo, often darker work but not always. This is a dirt dauber's trick.

You'll need these items:

- The underwear of the person you want to return

- Scissors

- A dirt dauber's nest (I had a friend of mine who lives in Texas send one to me, as dirt daubers don't live in my area. You can try to get someone who lives in a warm place to mail one to you as well.)

1. Cut a hole out of the crotch of the underwear, one big enough to stop up with the nest.

2. Insert the dirt dauber's nest in the hole.

3. Bury this under your steps.

This will bring your partner back and keep them there.

## 180. Hoodoo Gardening: Lovage Root

Lovage (*Levisticum officinale*) is a useful plant, both magickally in Hoodoo and as a culinary plant. It has a long history as a medicinal herb as well. In medicine, it is used for stomach upsets, gas, colic, and fever and to extract stuck objects and substances. It is a complex herb, with celery-like stalks, cilantro-like leaves, and the strongly earthy aroma of carrots or parsnips. In some parts of the world it is used to flavor broths and soups, as well as a cordial drink, but we are concentrating more on its use in magical herbal Hoodoo, where it is used to inspire steadfast love, luck, finding a steady and loving partner, and returning love. Sometimes referred to as bo' hog, this plant aids in love and sexuality, particularly when paired with sympathetic herbs and roots.

Since this is such an easy plant to grow and so useful to you and your friends, family, and clients, let's have it be a part of your Hoodoo garden.

The plant can grow in a wide variety of climates, in zones 2–8. All you really need is rich soil, which can be amended with your compost, good draining ability, and a sunny location. All this will help lovage flourish.

## 181. Stay with Me Spell

Faithfulness is a big concern in relationships, and rightfully so. This binding spell, using various elements of nature, will help secure your relationship and get your love to stay close by.[49] For this work you will need these items:

- An apple
- A knife
- A scoop or spoon
- Rose water
- Honey
- Parchment paper and pencil
- A pink or red taper candle

Set your apple on a secure and stable surface. Cut the top off and hollow out the inside with a spoon or scoop. Fill with rose water. Add a bit of honey. Write the person's name nine times on parchment paper using a pencil. Put this parchment inside the apple. Stop it up with the top you cut off.

Get your candle and burn it in front of the apple, concentrating on your intent. Do this at 6:00 a.m., 6:00 p.m., and midnight for seven days.

## 182. Lucky in Love Hand

This is a hand that combines a lot of the tools and tricks discussed thus far in this chapter. It brings together some very strong herbs. In combination, their individual powers are accentuated and enhanced. The roots and herbs are brought together for a difficult

---

49. Hyatt, *Hoodoo, Conjuration, Witchcraft, Rootwork.*

task. They are designed to turn your luck around so you can find just the right partner. You will want to do deep, relaxing breathing and focus on a red or pink candle as you work.

Gather these items:

- Lovage root (for drawing love and aiding with sexuality once you've met your goal)
- High John the Conqueror root (to attract a man)
- Queen Elizabeth root (to attract a woman)
- Hoyt's Cologne
- A red or pink candle
- Matches or lighter
- Sampson's snakeroot
- A small red flannel drawstring bag

Soak the roots in some Hoyt's Cologne. Remove and set them on a paper towel. Focus every fiber of your being on your goal. Use creative visualization to conjure up just the right person for you in your mind. Light the candle with strong intention. Heat up each of the roots with the flame. (Hold the roots up high so they don't put out the candle or catch fire.) Put each root in the hand. With this hand (kept activated through squeezing it, talking to it about your desire, and refreshing the Hoyt's Cologne by spraying the bag), your wishes will come true if they are meant to.

## 183. Curio of Note: Divination Stone

The moon is feminine energy, correlated with many female goddesses, lwa, and spirits, including the very familiar Isis and even Mother Mary. Here is a way to utilize the moon's mystical powers and sensual, feminine energy to boost affections. You can also add a moonstone to the love hand that you made yesterday, if you'd like. This stone is thought to arouse tender passion and give lovers the power to be super in tune with each other. Moonstone is a visionary divination stone.

Select a moonstone from a trusted source, in person if possible.

Hold the moonstone in your hand and bless it with your intention. Feel its vibration and then charge it by burying it outdoors in sea salt or the soil, under a waxing moon. After seven days, hold the stone in your hand and see if it feels like it is of a higher vibration than when you put it there. Most likely it will be; if not, bury it for another few days and then check it again. Repeat until you are satisfied with its vibration. A carefully selected moonstone grants you and your lover good fortune and the ability to read each other's thoughts when needed.

## 184. Hoodoo Gardening: Queen Elizabeth Root

Queen Elizabeth root (*Iris florentina* or *Iris germanica*), also called orris root, is frequently used in Hoodoo in powder form to draw love from a potential lover who is female, female-identified, or feminine in spirit. It is also useful as a fixative in handmade potpourri incenses and as a powder on its own. The flowers are the typical bearded iris, which are white, with the edges of the petals tinged with purple. They give off a delightful violet scent and can bloom twice in one season, making them a boon to the perennial garden. The root in question is a rhizome, meaning it is a bulbous rootlike plant part that grows at a right angle from the foliage.

A variety of garden centers and catalogs sell this plant under the names of reblooming bearded iris and German iris. I have a nice bank of them in my parkway garden and they grow beautifully, returning year after year. You'll need to be super-patient with your harvest, but all the while you'll get to enjoy the beauty and fragrance of the flowers. After about five years there should be sufficient rhizome growth to spare, in which case you can cut some off and then dry it. After drying it, you will grind it down to a fine powder using a food processor or a mortar and pestle. While you can easily buy orris root powder/Queen Elizabeth powder, there is an immeasurable feeling of satisfaction and pride that comes from using herbs from your Hoodoo garden.

## 185. Leaving Love Behind Rite

Don't suffer needlessly from unrequited love. When it's time to move on, get yourself going in a new and positive direction. This way, you are being proactive in terms of taking control of your love life. This rite utilizes two things that are surefire ways of making things you desire happen: lightning water and a green candle.

You will need the following:

• A bucket of lightning water

• A green candle

• A tub

• A sea sponge

• Sea salt

• A basin

• Neroli luffa soap (from day 162)

• A nice big seashell

First, there is the lightning water. Lightning water helps forge powerful and dramatic changes. On a stormy day when there is both thunder and lightning, gather a bucket of water. Bring this inside and save it for the rite.

At sunrise, embark on this work.

Concentrating on your intention of severing old ties, light your green candle. In this rite, green symbolizes action and motion. Place the lit candle on a stable surface on the side of the tub, where it won't fall or catch anything on fire. Using a sea sponge and sea salt, cleanse your tub for the work to come, remembering what a sacred substance you have in sea salt. Rinse the tub with water from the tap. Now set your basin to the side of the tub. Pour ⅓ of the lightning water into the tub. Wash yourself with some of the neroli luffa soap you recently made. In this case, this soap is used for self-love. Cleanse your body, from the head down. Take a seashell and pour the lightning water over your head to rinse nine times. Do this once a day for three days, using a third of the lightning water each day.

To complete this rite, remove the water from the bathtub, putting it in the basin. Take it outside and throw it toward the sunrise. With it, you are tossing away the vibrations and feelings your body has been carrying for that nonexistent but pesky would-be love.

# CHAPTER 7

# LUCK, ABUNDANCE & PROSPERITY WORK: DAYS 186-215

There is truth to most sayings, for example, "You can never be too rich." We could discuss what is meant by this saying for hours because being rich has varied meanings. Wealth seems wonderful from what I hear, but it doesn't necessarily make you happy. Be that as it may, to get rich—or, as I prefer to call it, prosperous—you need luck. Luck is one of those elements of life that helps us attain goals and fulfill our desires. It seems elusive, yet it is available to us if we make a conscious effort to obtain and harness it, which is what this chapter is all about.

Luck is one of those topics that runs rivers straight through the corpus of Hoodoo. You'll notice that some of your love draw work is also blended with luck draw, for the two can work together. Everywhere you look, whether it is a bath, incense, spiritual wash, or mojo bag, there will most likely be a way to use these substances and objects that is connected to drawing luck.

This month we will begin by exploring luck and its symbols, colors, and workings, and then in the coming weeks we will get into some of the issues and concerns some may have that are connected to luck. The two areas we'll focus on are abundance and prosperity. I don't use the word *money* as a part of this spiritual work very often because abundance and prosperity supersede money. Money runs out, but abundance and prosperity are full, rich, and endless, if you treat them right. They keep the cash and goodwill flowing—abundance is having all you want, and then some. Prosperity is sustainable abundance.

Belief, faith, worship, talismans, prayer, power objects, the ancestors, and culture all play a role in luck. This is going to be a fun and useful 31-day period spent helping you conceive, cultivate, and manage conditions so that luck, abundance, and prosperity can be yours to use however you see fit.

### 186. Are You Lucky?

Luck is highly valued, much sought after, and often in seemingly short supply. Today is a good day to start assessing the status of the important aspects of your life. Take out your Hoodoo journal and write down the following areas of your life. If there are others you feel should be added and examined, go ahead and add those to the list. Remember, this work is for you!

1. Health
2. Family and friends
3. Love
4. Home life
5. Community
6. Career/success

7. Financial security

8. Happiness

9. Abundance/prosperity

Now, starting with the first word on the list, write down the current state of affairs in that area of your life. Be sure to state whether you feel fortunate in that area. Why or why not? Next, rate the aspect from one to five, with five indicating you feel very lucky and one, not so much. This is your baseline. As we work this seventh month of your work, we are going to be trying to improve how you feel in each of these nine areas through Hoodoo's many luck workings. We will revisit this list before moving on to the next month's work. Take your time with this and be candid. You will recognize some of these elements of Hoodoo, but hopefully you will work them with fresh eyes and the power of intent.

## 187. Horseshoe

Horseshoes hold a high place in Hoodoo as a lucky charm. This is due, at least in part, to the fact that they are made of iron and involve metallurgy. In Africa and especially in early African-American culture, metalsmithing was a celebrated profession and activity. The entire process of metal work, from beginning to end, casts an energizing vibration on the psyche. This magickal viewpoint, which appears to be an Africanism, is active still in Hoodoo.

### How to Use Horseshoes

There are contrasting views on the best way to hang the horseshoe. Some believe that hanging it with the prongs up catches luck. Others believe that by hanging it with the prongs facing down, the inherit magick of the shoe and the luck it has drawn can flow out into the environment.

The luckiest type of horseshoe is one that is found. I hunted for mine in a large Antique Barn and found one there.

The nails are also considered lucky. You will notice their use in some Hoodoo rites and altars. They can also be bent, using jeweler's tools, and shaped to make a lucky ring.

## 188. Lucky Horn Nut

I like things that aren't perfect, cute, or too sweet. This is probably what has drawn me to the lucky horn nut. *Trapa bicornis* is an odd-looking pod, which I find quite beautiful, in the way of a gargoyle. It has many names, including devil pod, devil nut, and bat nut. We know that the early Hoodoos bought some of their materials from catalogs that sold items from China, which attests to the multicultural and intercultural nature of Hoodoo.

This Asian aquatic plant is used in China, where people carry it with them to bring good luck. The luck sought is typically against drought and starving, and if you look at it closely, your mind might wander in the direction of a sacred cow, which is also saluted for such purposes.

Dried and polished up nicely, lucky horn nut will have a long life. It makes a perfect addition to your luck draw mojo bags.

## 189. Charming

Throughout this month, you will be introduced to or reminded about charms that are known to bring luck. Are there charms that you possess in your home? Think about them. Go look for them right now. Take your time.

Once you have your charms on hand, I want you to recharge them. If it is a mojo bag, feed it. To do this, you can spritz it with Hoyt's Cologne or take some of the key items out of it—for example, the lodestones or High John the Conqueror root—and soak them in whiskey for the next week. Make sure the jar is exposed to the moon, to absorb some positive moon vibrations.

What else do you have? Perhaps a piece of lucky charm jewelry, such as a four-leaf clover pendant, horseshoe earrings, or a mixed charm bracelet filled with objects that have brought you luck in the past. Spend some time cleansing your jewelry with materials appropriate to the metal or material. Let it dry fully in the sun. After it is dry and feels charged with sun energy, smudge it. A bayberry taper candle will do the trick. This type of candle brings luck, wealth, happiness, food to the pantry, and gold to the pocket.

## 190. Rabbit Lore and Magick

There are many intriguing aspects to rabbits. They are fertile; thus, they frequently replenish their stock. They are fast and savvy, making them survivors. Rabbits are believed to be able to shapeshift into forms that best suit their purposes. Br'er Rabbit is a tricky character whose story has been told through the ages in African-American folklore. As a trickster, Br'er Rabbit is respected, yet we can still have our suspicions about his motivations. There is mystery and power in the trickster, particularly if you can harvest some of that power and get them to be on your side.

When I was a girl, many people had rabbit's foot pendants and keychains. This is growing less popular, but in Hoodoo the use of the rabbit's foot remains a lucky emblem. Rabbit's feet are considered lucky for bringing about happiness and improved overall health.

## 191. Mrs. L. Acker's Lucky Mojo Bag

This bag utilizes tree magick, foot track magick, and the power of the graveyard. It is a mojo inspired by Mrs. L. Acker's bag, as recorded in *Folk Beliefs of the Southern Negro.*[50]

You will need the following items:

- Left back foot of a rabbit (from a butcher shop)
- Buckeye
- Horse chestnut
- Ham bone (luck bone from a pig)
- Red flannel bag
- Hoyt's Cologne
- Spritzer bottle

The mojo you're making today is imbued with animal magnetism and plant energy. It is sure to improve your chances at whatever it is you desire and bring better fortune into your life. Let the rabbit foot dry out completely before putting it in a bag. Carefully select your buckeye and horse chestnut, and thank them for the magick they hold before adding them to the bag. Boil the luck bone to get all the meat off and soak it in bleach so that it is clean and will maintain its integrity without rotting. After drying it in the sun for a few days, put it in the red mojo bag, remembering the full significance of red in Hoodoo (vitality, strength, heart, beauty, love). Add some Hoyt's Cologne to

---

50. Puckett, 316.

a spritzer bottle. Saturate the bag well, realizing you are feeding the soul of your mojo. Repeat this spray treatment about once a fortnight.

## 192. Good Luck Big Outfit

Big outfits once were popular ways of having a large toolbox or toolkit for Hoodoo workings. These comprehensive collections are wonderful ways of having accumulative power on hand for any event, concern, or issue that arises. This box is inspired by a King Novelty Company Curio Catalog from the late 1930s. It was called Mo-Jo Brand Curio Luck Box. This box promises luck in gambling, games of chance, love, and financial matters.

You'll need these items:

- A sturdy box
- Piece of green silk fabric
- Your he and she (matching pair of lodestones)
- Lodestone powder
- Adam and Eve root
- Jockey Club cologne (gambling)/Hoyt's Cologne (general draw)
- Red flannel bag

Lay a piece of green silk fabric in the box. Put the items listed here in your box. Keep this under your bed until you are ready for the work, or give it to someone you care about, along with the following instructions:

Soak the lodestone in whiskey for a good week, during a full moon. Soak the Adam and Eve root in Jockey Club cologne or Hoyt's Cologne, depending on your purpose, for the same amount of time. Keep your jars capped tightly to keep the energy inside working in a compressed manner. Swirl your two jars gently each day to accelerate the luck infusion magick. Take most of the liquid off the stones and root by blotting with a paper towel. Spritz with the Jockey Club cologne and place inside the bag—along with your vision for the luck that is about to come your way.

## 193. Lucky Egg

Eggs have many different applications for Hoodoos. Today you'll be learning about the Lucky Egg, although you might not use it right away. When you're involved in the right game of chance or gambling and need it, you'll know just what to do.

All you need is a Sharpie, a fresh egg, and a strong will to make things go your way. You can also do this on behalf of a client or friend.

Without being obvious, observe everyone who is playing the game. Note their appearance and style of play. Make an excuse so you can leave the game for a while. Write everyone's name down with a Sharpie on the egg. Put it in your pocket or someone else's pocket (to lend them luck). As you write their name, focus on having your friend and yourself come out as the winners of the game. Take your time. With every letter you write, focus. Strong intention and focus will lead you to victory as you gamble or otherwise play other sorts of games.

## 194. NOLA Fast Luck Mojo

Today is the day you will create a mojo bag to improve your luck quickly. This is a traditional bag inspired by one of Hyatt's Hoodoo informants.[51] I am partial to this bag because of the numerous different qualities of Hoodoo it utilizes and for its obvious ties to African beliefs. It uses a needle for activation, a powerful herb that fits the doctrine of signatures for this work, a luck stone, and a potent feeding solution. You can't go wrong when you skillfully and purposely combine these items with belief and intent.

Here is what you will need:

- A brand-new sewing needle
- A leather or chamois pouch
- Some dried five-finger grass
- Your he and she (male and female lodestones)
- Steel dust
- Whiskey or Hoyt's Cologne

Pierce the pouch with your intentions, wishes, and desires by using a new sewing needle to accentuate your thoughts. Sprinkle in about a tablespoon of the five-finger grass. Sprinkle the he and she with steel dust and add to the pouch. Put the needle in the bag. Spritz with whiskey or Hoyt's Cologne today and every two to three weeks afterward to keep your bag alive. When you reckon it needs renewing, you can also add more steel dust to your he and she.

## 195. Conqueror's Spiritual Floor Wash

Floor washes are potent. They are a comprehensive way of covering large swaths of space with the herbal and spiritual vibration desired. Over the months of this year, you have become

---

51. Hyatt, *Hoodoo, Conjuration, Witchcraft, Rootwork*.

familiar with the might power of High John the Conqueror root. Today, let's make a High John the Conqueror root floor wash to empower you to change your fate while opening the way to better fortune.

Obtain a High John the Conqueror root from one of your most trusted suppliers. Select a root that calls to you for its protective power and ability to work with your spirit energy. Once you have your root, enliven it with some whiskey, as a feed. Take your root and put it in a Mason jar. Fill this jar with whiskey as you focus on your intent to tap the energy of your powerful root. Screw on the top and let it steep for nine days. Each day at 6:00 a.m., connect with your root by swirling the whiskey in the jar while focusing in on your intent. This will also help extract some of its medicine into the spirit.

On the ninth day at 6:00 a.m. or at sunrise (if that's earlier), open the jar. Observe how smelling this potion makes you feel. Let yourself feel empowered and open. Add the brew in the jar to a bucket of spring water. Enhance its brightening ability by adding about a half-dram of Van Van oil. With this addition, breathe your intention into the bucket of spiritual wash. Stir to mix with a stainless steel whisk. Mop the floors of your home. Wipe down countertops and other spaces where you desire this energy. Be sure to work deeply in a psychical and spiritual sense, moving furniture and getting into corners and especially into dark spaces.

## 196. Week of Reflection (Day 1):
## The Power of Stones and Minerals

Stones and minerals are two extremely potent sources of magick and are utilized in Hoodoo. We are made up of minerals, and they are elemental—in us and all around. Stones are ancient and timeless. They contain history and are the essence of history. Employing them in our work can enhance its efficacy. In African-American culture, birthstones, for example, have been important sources of inspiration and power, worn as jewelry. There are several stones that you'll see used in different ways, particularly to draw luck. Minerals, too, have an important role. For the next few days, we will reflect solely on the power of stones and the minerals connected with luck.

### Beauty Pebble

Crystals have been called "beauty pebbles" in African-American folklore for good reason: they are gorgeous, with all their nooks and multi-leveled surfaces. They present a new way to see that is indeed quite beautiful.

## 197. Week of Reflection (Day 2): Working Smoky Quartz

Smoky quartz ranges in color from grayish-brown to deep black. It can be transparent or translucent. This is a wonderful crystal for meeting your financial goals in pursuit of wealth. With it, you can ground and center, remove negativity, and be protected. These important steps open the way for having your dreams come true. Smoky quartz is excellent for your overall well-being. Incorporating it into your Hoodoo practice will help make your wishes come true and bring abundance and prosperity and, of course, good luck. Today, I will lay out three ways of using this important crystal.[52]

---

52. *King Novelty Company Curio Catalog*, 1938.

Clear nine smoky quartz crystals of various sizes by soaking them in whiskey for nine days under a waxing moon. Pat to dry.

1. Get in a very comfortable position, with the crystals in your hands. Breathe in the meditative and deeply relaxing way in which we have been working.

2. Vision quest: Gaze intently at your handful of crystals. Now that they are charged, what do you feel and what do you see for your future?

3. Setting intent: Bring your hand to your mouth and whisper your wish to the stones. Place them around yourself, using a counterclockwise motion. Now take your time and reflect for at least a half hour on obtaining your wish.

## 198. Week of Reflection (Day 3): Luck Stone Powder

Any stone with luck in its name is obviously worth investigating during your stone and mineral reflection week. Luck stone[53] is also called lodestone, an ancient magickal conglomerate used in all manner of Hoodoo drawing work—luck draw being one of its ultimate results. When you obtain your he and she (male and female lodestones), you'll notice they have powder or crystal clinging to them. Steel powder that clings to lodestone is valuable on its own. It will help you draw success in games of chance and money matters and generally help you become luckier. Sprinkle steel powder or anvil dust on your mated he and she and let your luck grow, expand, and become sustainable.

---

53. *King Novelty Company Curio Catalog*, n.d.

## 199. Week of Reflection (Day 4): Golden Tiger's Eye Stone

Tiger's eye is an attractive stone that is utilized in Hoodoo for numerous magickal purposes, including attracting good luck, money, love, and winning numbers.[54]

To have good luck you need to have lots of positive energy around you—golden tiger's eye can make that happen. This stone opens a window into psychic perception, letting you see the world in a very clear way. It goes further by warding off darkness that either lurks naturally or is put in your path by someone with ill intent. Having this stone in your life permits light to flood into your environment and your body. Healed and sound, you can pursue your heart's desire, courageously and with confidence.

Clear your tiger's eye by either soaking it in whiskey or burying it in the earth or sea salt for about a week. Check on it periodically to see if it feels different (heavier, lighter, or has an energetic effect on your hand). Once it has the desired feel, you are ready to work with it.

Tiger's eye is a great aid in building prosperity:

• Add it to a green mojo bag to invite the good luck necessary to usher in abundance in the form of increased income leading to financial wealth.

• Put it inside a red mojo bag to capitalize on the strength, vitality, and confidence-building power inherent in the color red.

---

54. Ibid.

## 200. Week of Reflection (Day 5): Moonstone

As you've discovered, the moon is an important component of magickal workings and is incorporated in Hoodoo. Moon energy is sympathetic, reflexive, nurturing, sensitive, and intuitive. It is also connected to deity, lwa, and certain orisha. The moon offers a deep opening into the mysteries of our daily lives.

Moonstone is so named because it resembles the moon physically and spiritually. Through its use, you can open your psychic abilities, which allows you to be shielded from negativity. It is your stone for the good medicine and holistic health necessary to have good fortune. This is the stone of new beginnings, cooling energy, and peacefulness.

Today, begin the process of seeking out moonstone for your Hoodoo practice. Obtain the perfect stone for you, one whose energy has a good vibe. Take it home and clear it using one of the methods you've tried during this work.

### Moonstone Potion

Soak your moonstone in a bottle of rainwater, in a window or outside, under the waxing moon. Let it continue to soak for the full lunar cycle, until the moon is full and most powerful. Meditate every day for at least ten minutes while your moonstone is steeping. Take note of your dreams in your Hoodoo journal. On the full moon, at sunrise, bring your potion into your workspace. Dip in a sea sponge and press the elixir from the stone onto your third eye (ajna). Next, dab the crown of your head (the very top of your scalp). This very act will bring strong energy in the direction of good luck and abundance. Let it soak into your life.

## 201. Week of Reflection (Day 6):
## Blow Out

Today, let's revisit the element sulphur, which is ever so import-ant in Hoodoo. You might need to bookmark this spell because it must be done on a Friday.

Get up early on a Friday morning, preferably right around sunrise. Traveling clockwise, set out four fireproof plates or censers in the four main corners of your house, facing north, south, east, and west. Place some sulphur on each of the surfaces while you concentrate on drawing luck. Set each pile of sulphur on fire, one at a time. Let the sulphur burn and then, traveling counterclockwise, blow out the flames. The smoke will continue your luck draw work for you long after the fire is extinguished.

## 202. Week of Reflection (Day 7):
## Gift Yourself

When we started this week of stone and mineral work, I men-tioned the significance of birthstones. Let's complete this week of work by spending some time dedicated to these special stones, combining them with your birthday month. Bringing earth and fire together with the intensity and purpose of color is an excel-lent way to bring energy and purpose to your celebration. Bless your birthstone jewelry by smudging and clearing it first with a sage smudge stick and then setting it on your bed table, along with the two important candles for your sign (see the list below), and reflect on bringing your wishes to life this year. This rite, if done purposefully, should bring you luck in obtaining abun-dance as you perceive it.

*January:* Birthstone: garnet; candle colors: red and black

*February:* Birthstone: amethyst; candles colors: yellow and blue

*March:* Birthstone: aquamarine; candle colors: blue and green

*April:* Birthstone: diamond; candle colors: green and yellow

*May:* Birthstone: emerald; candle colors: blue and antique gold

*June:* Birthstones: pearl, alexandrite, ruby; candle colors: red and blue

*July:* Birthstone: ruby; candle colors: green and black

*August:* Birthstones: peridot, spinel, sardonyx; candle colors: red and yellow

*September:* Birthstone: sapphire; candle colors: antique gold and black

*October:* Birthstones: tourmaline, opal; candle colors: green and antique gold

*November:* Birthstones: topaz, citrine; candle colors: yellow and black

*December:* Birthstones: tanzanite, zircon, turquoise; candle colors: red and yellow

## 203. Lucky Hand Root

Ever wonder how certain herbs became connected to Hoodoo? Well, the answer is complex. Hoodoo is a collection of folkloric practices, some of which are Africanisms, and others which are from a wide range of magickal beliefs from around the world.

Lucky hand root, also called salep root, is one of those roots that couldn't help but land in Hoodoo. Its appearance and bearing speaks to our sensibility, stirring thoughts of how to use it. This significant herb in rootwork is growing increasingly rare. It is one of those orchids that has been overused, so you might like to find a substitute for it or content yourself with chips from it, from which you can make magickal oils and spiritual baths or washes. Getting an intact root is challenging, but it can be done, particularly if you forage for it yourself or purchase one on eBay, Etsy, or a similar website that has some of the feel of a yard sale. People grow tired of things, even roots, and will resell an intact, fully fingered lucky hand root from time to time.

- Lucky hand root can be infused in oil, which is then used to feed your mo' money type of mojo bag.

- This oil can be applied judiciously to your money to attract more.

- It can also be added to a bucket of water, along with brewed five-finger grass and ginger, for a prosperity-building floor wash.

- If you are lucky enough to get a fully intact lucky hand root, make a money-attracting pendant or pair of earrings from it.

## 204. Mo' Money

In many different forms of folklore around the world, money is important. Not only is it a way of showing appreciation for a reader or healer, but it is also used to acknowledge the ancestors and those in the spirit realm.

### Money Magick to Draw Prosperity

1. Coins can act as talismans, for example the Mercury dime. You can use your Mercury (or silver) dime in your mojo bags, on your altar, and as power jewelry. To wear it, pierce a hole into the dime, then string or wire it with fittings for earrings or as a pendant.

2. Another way of using money for luck is burying it in your Hoodoo garden. Caress the coins with your hands and visualize them bringing you more money—see it coming toward you. Breathe this vision into the coins. Bury them in a vibrant garden that is being used. When you dig them back up next season, more money should be there than what you originally planted.

3. Finally, here is a simple but lovely and effective way to draw prosperity. All you need is your wallet, some paper money, and Hoyt's Cologne. Follow the directions for the previous project, using paper money this time. Now spray the money with Hoyt's Cologne and put it back in your wallet. Your blessed and happy money will draw more money to it because it is rich in spirit.

## 205. Lucky Pocket Piece

Sometimes you need a good strong shield for protection. Shielding and protection from evil allows room for goodness, light, and luck to flow into your life. This unique pocket piece, inspired by one of Hyatt's informants, is designed for such a purpose.[55]

You will need these ingredients:

- Your he and she (lodestone pair)
- Queen Elizabeth powder
- A Mercury dime
- High John the Conqueror root
- A straight pin
- White thread

---

55. Hyatt, *Hoodoo, Conjuration, Witchcraft, Rootwork*, 246.

- A sewing needle
- Red flannel fabric

Organize all items, except for the white thread and the sewing needle, on the red flannel. Create a mojo using the needle and thread, but start with only nine stitches, pulling the thread toward you. Then on the other side do nine more stitches, with the thread going away from you. Do not cut the thread or knot it. To tie off the stitches, stitch twice in the same place, but do not pull the thread all the way through. Pass the needle through the loop twice. Pull the thread to tighten it down to the fabric. This should keep the stitches sound. Stick the straight pin deep down inside the mojo. Tie this up to create a bag. Wear it in your left pocket when you need luck and protection.

## 206. Hoodoo Gardening: Five-Finger Grass

*Potentilla spp.* is the botanical name for cinquefoil, also called five-finger blossom, five fingers, hand of Mary, five-leaf grass, crampweed, silverweed, goose grass, goose tansy, and bloodroot. In Hoodoo it is commonly known as five-finger grass and is a very useful magickal plant in our work. Its five prominent attributes are wisdom, power, health, money, and love.

Depending on where you live, you can sow these seeds in spring, late summer, or early fall. It will grow in zones 4–8. Five-finger grass is easy to germinate from seed. It may also be growing wild near you, as it thrives in dry open areas, such as pastures, roadsides, and open fields. The sulphur-yellow flowers are pretty and this is a perennial plant, so you can enjoy it and its magick for many years to come.

It reacts especially well with the third eye, or ajna. Five-finger grass, simmered in your cauldron for about five minutes in a cup of water, can be strained and used to bathe the third eye and open the way to having the luck to obtain what it is you desire.

To go in a different direction, get yourself a bucket (about four cups) of rainwater or spring water. Simmer a cup of the dried herb for five minutes, covered. Strain over a large mesh strainer. Scent with the energizing ginger essential oil by adding a teaspoon and then amp it up even further, engaging the power of the Earth Mama by adding a half teaspoon of vetiver essential oil. Stir well. Head over to the sink and let your hair loose, if it is pinned up or braided. Leaning over the sink, rinse your crown with this brew while making your wish to have luck in any of the five areas of five-finger grass work.

## 207. Hoodoo Gardening: Sweet Plant of Good Luck

*Galium odoratum*, from the family Rubiaceae, has a bevy of colorful names, including sweet-scented bedstraw, sweet woodruff and woodruff, wild baby's breath, and the one more familiar to Hoodoos, master of the woods. This last name is a literal translation of the German *Waldmeister*.

Why all the sweet references? This is largely due to its chief aromatic constituent: coumarin. Further, its sweetness confers good luck in a variety of different ways. This plant not only carries luck with it in obtaining a job or in various types of battles, but also makes a very nice garden plant in certain conditions.

Master of the woods has festive star-shaped leaves that are pointed at the ends and small, white, delicately perky flowers. It grows in zones 4–8 in partial to full shade, making it a nice addition to urban gardens with lots of shade-producing buildings.

It prefers rich soil (an opportunity to use your compost), and while it will grow in dry soil, it should be watered frequently in such conditions. It makes an excellent ground cover, thriving in acidic soils.

This herb's scent intensifies as it dries. Dried master of the woods can be pulverized using a mortar and pestle and then added to sachets. In a sachet, it will attract luck and deter moths at the same time. Its dried flowers can be used in potpourri. Primarily it is known to be added to May wine in Germany, called *Maibowle* or *Maitrank*. It is considered a good luck talisman and has a lengthy history. It was carried into battle by the Teutons. You can add it to your favorite wine. Steep for three hours, then strain. Drink it before undertaking challenging and difficult matters for which you need good luck.

## 208.–209. Steadfast Love

Next you will be creating a lucky love charm. This will be done over the next two days (perhaps it will take longer). Take your time because this is very important work. When we finally find someone to love and it is mutual, we want that love to last. Keeping love strong and alive is a lot of work and something we should do everything we can to sustain. This is an old-fashioned Hoodoo charm that promises steadfast love. Of course, it should be done in combination with a variety of different types of holistic work to make its work long-lasting.

The first charm used in this mojo is the four-leaf clover, which is a rare variation on the more common three-leaf clover. Clover is quite invasive, so if you have a lawn, you probably also have some clover. Sorting through a clover patch and finding the rare type needed will take dedication and persistence. This persistence will pay off because there are two ways the leaves bring luck. Each leaf symbolizes hope, faith, love, and luck, or fame, wealth, love, and health. Either way of seeing the clover is useful for this work because love figures prominently in both. The luck of the clover is believed by some to be traced back to Eve, who carried this lucky charm with her when she left paradise.

I recommend preserving your clover before adding it to the mojo bag. To do so, press it between two heavy books until it is flat and dry. Then take two small pieces of waxed paper and sandwich the clover between them. Press lightly with an iron, on a low setting, to stick the wax paper together so you are still able to see the clover.

Next you need a wishing bean. Wishing beans are called by many names, including fava beans, broad beans, and African wishing beans. Fava beans are easy to obtain from an Italian grocer. There is no need to go out of your way ordering a special bean with an interesting-sounding name; just go to the shops and pick your own, or better yet, grow it in your Hoodoo garden. Fava beans were mentioned in the St. Joseph's Altar entry on day 83 of this work. In short, this bean of St. Joseph promises peace and safety in the home, faithfulness, and persistent love, no matter the circumstance.

Add the pressed clover and the wishing bean to a red mojo bag with your intentions and desires at the fore of your mind. Hang this mojo behind your bed, as it is believed to bring all the attributes described.

## 210. Curio of Note: Wishbones

Bones play an important role in luck, as charms, and in ritual. One that immediately comes to mind that you can work with any day of the year is the V-shaped clavicle bone, the *furcular*. The furcular has come to be called the wish, wishing bone, or merry thought. Wishing bones are for wishing because of the symbolism and folklore connected to their ritualistic use.

The belief in using the bones is thought to have begun with using hen's as oracles. This practice of divination was recorded in ancient Etruscan practices. There, fowl were considered magical creatures, and their body parts were used to foretell the future. The Romans took this belief closer to what we do today. They had a tug of war with the bone, like we do on Thanksgiving. Inspired by the Romans, the British adopted and adapted this practice, calling it a merry thought, around the seventeenth century.

I find it helpful to have several of the bones dried and prepared to use. The Etruscans dried the bones in the sun for several days, and I suggest three days since it is such a potent number due to its relationship to several trilogies. Begin this work the next time you eat chicken or turkey from the whole bird. You can make this a community affair by asking family, friends, and coworkers to save these bones for you.

For your wish to come true in a rite, gently stroke the bone. In a ritual for two, the pair of you hold the wishbone using your dominant hand with only your pinkie. You both make a wish. The person with the largest piece of the bone after pulling it apart and breaking it on the count of three gets their wish granted. For the ritual to work fully, the wish must be kept secret.

## 211. Wishing Sticks

Pine is a magical tree in many different belief systems. Its evergreen quality speaks of its strength and enduring spirit. It is a useful tree for building shelter but also for spiritual cleansing. This is an old-timer's wish rite that uses what are called pine splinters, sometimes called *lightere* in Georgia, or longleaf pine. You are going to go to a wooded place or perhaps your yard to find bits and pieces of longleaf pine (*Pinus palustris*) and collect them for later use.

Draw a 9 on the ground using a stick. Dig a hole eighteen inches deep right next to it. Make your wish. Carve nine notches into each of your two strong sticks. Cross the splinters so they make an X shape. Make your wish again.

## 212. Holy Wood

Sandalwood (*Santalum album*) is a mellow, earthy incense that is also called holy wood, as it is held in such high esteem as a high-frequency healing herb. The heart of the sandalwood tree has divine status in India, hence the name holy wood. This special wood was mentioned in the oldest India Vedic scriptures, the Nirukta, where it is called *Chandan* in Hindi.

There is not much holy wood cannot do. It is a broad-spectrum wood that opens the way to well-being. It eases mourning and inhibitions, induces a meditative sense of calm, and is an aphrodisiac that builds confidence.

The wonderful qualities of holy wood can work together to help you with a variety of different kinds of luck, from luck obtaining a job to luck in romance. One of the enveloping and soothing ways to engage sandalwood is as an incense. Baieido, a Japanese incense company that was established in 1657, is where I obtain mine. This type is so mellow and is cut perfectly for incense making.

### Holy Wood Luck Incense

Gather these ingredients:

- 2 tablespoons sandalwood
- 1 tablespoon cedarwood
- 3 chunks frankincense
- 1 chunk myrrh
- 1 piece cinnamon bark
- 5 lemon verbena leaves (dried)
- 1 tablespoon balsam poplar leaves (cut and sifted)

This is a woodsy blend that will remind you of the forest. It should also move your spirit to the upper echelons, enabling you to see your way clear to catch the luck life holds for you.

Relax through modulated breathing, as we have been doing throughout the book. Take off your shoes so you can ground yourself well in Mama Earth as you work. Using a mortar and pestle, grind all the ingredients a little at a time until you have a very fine blend. Before a date, interview, performance, or other event where you need good luck, add a pinch of this to a white-hot charcoal. Reach out and pull the smoke over your head as you reflect on its many qualities to serve as a divine wood.

## 213. Mojo Workin'

Blessing your mojo bag, or workin' it, is today's project. This is a simple but effective mojo bag combining candlemancy with curio work.

You will need these items:

- A bay-scented, green votive candle (handmade preferred but store-bought is fine)

• Dragon's blood sticks

• Green flannel

Green candles are about life, action, and attracting prosperity. The bay scent calls out to spirits of fortune and is pleasing to the ancestors. Dragon's blood is a lucky curio. The green flannel connects your wishes with your actions.

Light the bay candle. Close your eyes and focus in on the prosperity pouring into your life. Call your spirit helpers, or if you're Christian or another religion, say an appropriate prayer. Gently smudge the dragon's blood sticks and green flannel well atop the flame so as not to start a fire. Feel the warming energy in your hands. Keep this warmth in your soul as you load the flannel bag with the dragon's blood sticks. Luck and prosperity are bound to come your way through carrying this bag in your pocket and focusing in on your desires.

## 214. Devil's Shoestring Charm
## from Waycross, Georgia

Devil's shoestring sounds dark, but it has some very nice and attractive qualities that are useful in changing your luck. This charm is especially useful for gambling, playing games of chance, gaming, and simply having fun.

Bring together these items:

• Devil's shoestring

• A penknife or kitchen scissors

• Red flannel

• A deep glass bowl

• Hoyt's Cologne

Cut your devil's shoestring while focusing only on your desire. Clear your mind of all other thoughts. You need pieces that are approximately one inch long.

Soak the herb in a deep glass bowl of Hoyt's Cologne. Be sure to also have a good deep whiff of the cologne. It is mind-opening and brings about changes in situations, in addition to being pleasing to the spirits and ancestors. Blot the herb lightly with a paper towel. (The pieces shouldn't be all the way dry, just not dripping.) Put inside of the red flannel. Carry this with you during your gaming.

## 215. Hoodoo Gardening: Life Everlasting

As we wrap up this month, let's turn our attention to life everlasting. This is a plant you can wildcraft (forage) or grow in your garden. It has many names. The botanical name is *Gnaphalium polycephalum*. It and its relatives are referred to as Indian posy, sweet-scented life everlasting, sweet balsam, chafeweed, rabbit tobacco, and more. The name tells the story. To have everlasting life, or a life full of vim and vigor, is very lucky.

The entire plant is useful. The dried flowers and leaves are the primary part of interest for our work, starting today. This is an aromatic herb that grows in most locations as an annual. Its habit is erect. The branched, white, fuzzy stem grows from 1–3 feet. The leaves are alternate, lanceolate, and sessile; dark green on top and white and wooly-textured underneath. You can find it growing in arid fields to piney woods, as well as clear spots, along the Atlantic coastal areas all the way west to Kansas and south to Texas. Either wildcraft this treasure through foraging, bring it home, fix it together with hemp string and hang upside down to dry, or grow it according to your seed package directions.

Once you have your mature, dried flowers ready to use, what I'd like you to do is crumble some leaves between your palms and then mix a teaspoon of the leaves plus the flowers in a cup of spring water. Simmer, but do not boil, for five minutes, covered. Take a few deep breaths of this medicinal wonder through deep inhalations before straining. Strain and drink a cup of tea once a week for the next month and then jot down in your Hoodoo journal how it has made you feel. If you like the results, keep going!

# CHAPTER 8
# THE HOME:
# DAYS 216-244

The topic this month is home. Home is a complex place and concept. It means different things depending on where you are in life and your mindspace. This is a very full chapter. In it we will explore moving, renting a room, obtaining your dream home, ridding your living space of nuisances, and creating a peaceful environment.

The home and hearth can be beautiful conceptually—peaceful, loving spaces from which we go out into the world on our way to meet our goals. We make love primarily at home, and some give birth to their children and then we raise them there. Others have animals as companions, and still others are solitary. Whatever the case, we want this space to be sound and nurturing, a safe space from which we can create a charmed life.

Unfortunately, for some, life is drained or even lost in the home. Domestic violence remains a prevalent problem, arguments abound between roommates, and discord can become pervasive between family members. In these types of situations, we can find as many answers in Hoodoo's herbs, curios, invocations, prayers, spells, and tricks as from other sources.

Objects and substances that you may have looked upon as mundane, like salt and the broom for example, serve an important role in Hoodoo. Therefore, a great deal of space is devoted to them and how they are used traditionally, as well as how those traditions can be updated for modern living.

Home is a complete environment. It encompasses the yard, entryway, gates, threshold, and doorstep. As you move through this month, you'll notice that domestic spaces are addressed in your daily work. You might not have a yard, in which case you'll need to improvise. Your memory will also be tapped from earlier work in the year. You'll notice that some of the activities center around foot track magick, while other areas are empowered through candlemancy.

Hopefully, the highly valued traditions done on the next few days, which have been useful throughout the ages, will be of use to you as you move through life, whatever stage you are in: moving, looking for a place to live, trying to rent out a space, setting up a new home, recharging your home magickally, clearing and banishing unwanted entities or people from your home, and so forth.

Take your time as you go. Take out a good ink pen and your Hoodoo journal. Make some notes using sticky notes so you can refer later to the most significant works for where you are and what matters most to you. Roll up your sleeves, mentally and figuratively. Rest assured that the home is going to be a very important area of your Hoodoo practice.

## 216. Assessment #1:
## What You Want from Your Home

Do you ever dream of a place that's vastly different from where you are living now? I know I have had these dreams repeatedly over the years. One was of a secret garden that I'd hardly ever water, but when I went back to it, it was hanging on—barely. After a while I figured out that the garden represented something in my life that was being neglected. It was writing, because at that time I wasn't writing at all. That was the time before my books materialized. Once I started tending this imaginary garden—my writing—the nagging dream subsided and then went away altogether. Now, however, I dream of a new house in a different location.

Today is the day you are going to go through your dream inventory regarding home and garden. Grab your Hoodoo journal and jot down the basic shape of your dream. What are the outstanding features? Is it telling you to move or to do something with where you currently live?

Don't have dreams about home or garden? Well, keep your Hoodoo journal handy because you are going to take an inventory too. Are you living the way you wish? Is your home peaceful? Every home is in a constant state of flux and needs improvement. Make a list of the things you could do to improve your domestic life. What role do the Hoodoo exercises you've done play? How about Hoodoo gardening and curios—how can you use them? Make a commitment to do something positive today to change the charge of your home's energy.

## 217. Assessment #2: Your Living Situation

Today you are going to take an inventory of your living situation. This will enable you to get a clear picture of your living situation and, hopefully, what it needs to be more suitable and happier. Again, have your Hoodoo journal handy and write down the responses to the following questions:

1. Start outdoors as you approach your abode. In one word, write down how your pathway home feels.

2. What would you like to change about your path?

3. Have a look at your door. Is it fortified with good luck symbols you've worked with in the previous chapter? If not, now is a good time to consider which talismans, charms, and symbols you would like to add and figure out where to get them.

4. Take a deep breath now. This one is going to take a while. Go from room to room, taking your time to assess the feeling and energy vibration in each one. Write down your assessments in your Hoodoo journal.

5. Color, candles, incense, specific herbs, and live plants help change the charge of the room. Go back through the book and decide which of these elements you want to employ for each room. Take your time over the next thirty days and accomplish your goals for each room.

## 218. Dream House Trick #1

Have you, a friend, or a family member been pining away for a certain place to call home? We all do this at one time or another. There is a certain apartment, dream house, or condo that strikes our fancy. If you are doing this trick on behalf of someone, be sure to spend time hearing them talk about the place and why they want to live there. Absorb this information and then carry out the following trick in accord with the type of home they are seeking.

This is a contemporary trick inspired by traditional Hoodoo informants. If your dream home is a house, apartment, or condo, take a photo of it with your smartphone or use a photo from online and print it out (when you get home, if taken on-site). Draw nine circles around the location using a stick of charcoal. Draw the first circle going clockwise, the second going counterclockwise, and so forth. Go back to the house (or apartment or condo building) with wet shoe soles and walk around (where it's legal to do so). Change shoes, putting the ones you've worn with wet soles into a plastic bag. Then seal the bag with a knot. At home, pin the photograph or printout of your dream home to a door. Take some dirt from the heels of the soles and throw it at the photo's door. If the home, apartment, or condo is surrounded by concrete, discreetly scoop up some dirt and dust from the sidewalk or parkway as an adaptation and proceed with the spell.

## 219. Dream House Trick #2: Lodestone Mojo

Financial constraints create roadblocks to obtaining your dream abode, but there's a way to use Hoodoo to get at your goal. All throughout this book, you've been working with lodestone. Lodestone is a very important and potent Hoodoo tool. By now you already know how and where to obtain a good he and she to accomplish your goals. Go to this source and obtain another pair of well-matched lodestones, then create an aromatic magnetic sand to feed the lodestones' souls.

Gather these items:

- A bowl or surface covered with parchment paper
- Magnetic sand
- Hoyt's Cologne
- Your he and she (male and female lodestones)
- Red flannel

Sprinkle some Hoyt's Cologne atop the magnetic sand in the bowl or on the surface covered with parchment. Sprinkle this aromatic feed on the lodestones. Add the lodestones to a red flannel bag. Fix tightly. Whenever the scent is too faint to smell, recharge the stones with fresh aromatic sand.

Make your wishes concerning your dream home. Ask specifically for enough money so you can afford it. This will work best with a request you consider reasonable for your financial situation.

## 220. Broom Week (Day 1): Africa and the Diaspora

By now I'm hoping you've made your own personal broom or obtained one that speaks to you. Many paths use the broom in ritual, ceremony, spells, and so forth. Hoodoo is one such path. In fact, brooms and broomlike tools are visible throughout the African diaspora, attesting to their importance.

If you've been growing your own broom corn, you'll notice its wild appearance. Though it has been domesticated for decades, its wild behavior ties it to the bush or wilderness. There are many examples of this wild aspect of broom and broomlike materials being utilized in annual rites in Africa for cleansing and banishing negative spirits.

The Bomo clan in Nigeria has a tradition that highlights this example. There, a figure clad in grassy, strawlike materials cleanses the village annually of the spiritual, psychic, and physical buildup of refuse that would otherwise clutter the area. At the appointed time of the year, a performer covered in grassy materials moves rhythmically from one area to the next, brushing the areas clean.

In Benin, devotees of Obaluaye, a fierce orisha who heals or brings epidemics, carries a gorgeous but feared broom, called *shashara* by Cuban devotees, to accentuate his work. In Bahia, Brazil, it is a *ja*, whereas Dahomean speakers call it *ha*. This object of ritual and ceremony, which is small like our whisk brooms, is the focus of power. It is an emblem of might that can either raise or sweep away the disease agents capable of afflicting the populace with one fell swoop of its regal bristles.

These examples are but a few of the ways brooms and similar objects inspire awe and command respect in the African diaspora.

## 221. Brooms (Day 2): Jumping the Broom

From the dark past of slavery, enlightened practices persist. One such practice that you may either utilize or help others employ is called jumping the broom. In the Antebellum South during enslavement, black people were not allowed to marry, but like everyone else, they wanted to and deserved to carry out their wishes.

Knowing the power of the broom and seeing that it is representative of going from one area (wild, unfettered) to another (cultivated, domestic), the broom was the perfect tool to use to symbolize marriage. Our commitment was sealed, utilizing a tool that is not only symbolic of the home and domesticity but also an implement that inspires awe in many and is even feared.

You can use the broom you made on day 113 of this work or purchase an interesting and preferably handmade one for a jumping the broom ceremonial rite. Tie off some cowrie shells, which are used for divination and were once so revered that they were used as currency in parts of Africa. Make a spiral of holy white ribbons and peaceful blue ribbons, and tie them onto the handle in the way you desire.

In a bowl, mix together holy water, which is either blessed by a priest or, if you are pagan, created from sea salt and water mixed thoroughly together. To this add some rose oil and sandalwood essential oil to your taste. Spray this holy oil onto the entire broom, from handle to straws.

Now you have a broom, dressed, blessed, and ready for the jumping the broom ceremony to begin. Ashe!

## 222. Brooms (Day 3): Etiquette and Lore

There is a great deal of lore connected to brooms and broom straw, some of which was collected in Harry Hyatt's *Folk-lore from Adams County, Illinois*. There are other sources of stories and lore as well, such as Lafcadio Hearn's "New Orleans Superstitions" and Harold Courlander's *A Treasury of Afro-American Folklore*. Here are some tidbits from Courlander's book:

- First and foremost, you must respect your broom. This means keeping it clean and not letting it touch the ground when not in use. Either hang the broom up by adding a little hemp tie to the top of the handle, or simply rest it on the wall upside down.

- You mustn't sweep refuse outside the door of your home unless you have further rituals to do besides just the sweeping. This is because in West Africa and in African-American beliefs, eager and sometimes ill-meaning spirits hang about outside your doors. By sweeping bits of crumbs and so forth outside the door, you are encouraging and feeding them so they can carry on their mischief. Furthermore, if you sweep outside, your luck goes with it.

- Do not sweep by anyone's feet or even sweep when they are visiting. This is telling them you want them to leave.

- Sweeping after the sun goes down will bring sorrow, discord, and bad luck to your home.

- When a broom falls across your doorway, it indicates that you will go to a distant area or foreign land. If this happens, do not approach the broom directly; instead, walk backward to it (like a spirit) and then pick it up.

Here is an idea from Hearn's work:

- To chase someone's bad vibes from your home, throw salt on the pathway they took to the door and sweep behind them. They won't return.

### 223. Brooms (Day 4): Moving and Settling In

A broom should play an important role in your moving and settling in rites. Who enters the home first? Why, the broom, of course! Now you can do this in several different ways. Just be sure to do so.

1. Tuck your long-handled broom under your arm, bristles facing forward. Be sure the broom enters the threshold before you.

2. Alternately, throw the broom into the house through a window or door before you enter.

Through these actions, you are engaging the broom's abilities as an arbiter of peace and good fortune.

These rites are not stagnant. You must keep them alive. For example, if there are arguments in your home, carry the broom outside and wait a few minutes. Reenter after having thrown it in through a door or window first or by carrying it under your arm so it enters first.

## 224. Brooms (Day 5): Potions

Over the last few days you've delved into the power and mystical symbolism of the broom. Today we'll explore ways to charge up the broom using various easy-to-create potions to enhance its inherent abilities. These potions can be sprayed onto the broom straw, or you can dip the broom into a bowl containing them.

**Rose Water:** Roses act as a nervine. They calm your nerves and make the environment energized yet peaceful. Roses are one of the most highly touted flowers for their ability to tap into the spirit and address matters of the mind. Easy to obtain and possible to create yourself, rose water should be your first potion to reach for if you desire a peaceful and blessed home.

**Lavender Water:** Lavender gives off a gender-neutral scent that is uplifting to either sex. Well known as an antidepressant, this type of potion is useful for changing the charge in your home. Dip your broom into lavender water if you want to move the mood in your home from dark to light. This is especially nice as the seasons change and when someone moves out.

**Holy Water:** This is a heavy-duty spiritual potion that is best reserved for serious illness, hauntings, and seemingly immovable situations. You can either use water blessed by a priest, which is now growing easier to get your hands on, or, if you are pagan, create a saline solution using sea salt and a water of your choice.

**Lemongrass:** Lemongrass brings the spirit of nature into your home. It is brightening and light in spirit. This would be another solution to reach for to improve the mood in your home. I recommend it as a "moving in" potion, as you clear the vibes of previous tenants/owners from the space.

**Orange Flower Water:** Sweet and bright, orange flower water is beloved in Africa and the diaspora. It is appreciated for being pleasing to the ancestors and spirits. Use this potion when you need help from the spiritual realm and for confidence-building on a date or at a special event in your home.

**Florida Water:** Florida Water is another water renowned for its ability to please the spiritual realm. This potion will entice spirits, deities, orisha, and ancestors and yield a pleasant environment.

## 225. Brooms (Day 6): Spiritual Cleansing Ritual

Begin this work bright and early in the morning. Set your alarm early so you can awaken at sunrise. This will be a busy day.

1. Begin my dabbing your pulse points and third eye with Van Van oil. Your Van Van oil is there to open the way and help you envision the ways that you want the atmosphere in your home to change.

2. Meditate while the sun is rising and your Van Van oil is fresh and fragrant. The power of the sun will have a re-markable effect on your body, mind, and spirit as you work. Meditate for ten to fifteen minutes, or longer if you are practiced.

3. Light Nag Champa incense in the first room where you will work. This room should be either the living room or the bathroom. As you move from room to room, carry the incense and censer with you. Let the sweet fragrance bless the space in each room as you work.

4. Turn on mood music to set the tone and energize you as you work.

5. Close your eyes. Breathe in a calming manner. Focus on your third eye. See which broom potion your spirit gravi-tates toward and dip your broom in it. Walking backward, clear the floor of any debris and vibes in the room where you are working. Repeat this step in each room.

6. Set out bright, fresh flowers, such as sunflowers, white roses, or peaceful carnations.

## 226. Brooms (Day 7): Disposal of Broom Waste

Hopefully you've made really good use of your broom this week. But what about all the waste? In Hoodoo, running water—that is, moving bodies of water such as streams, rivers, or brooks—is a good place for disposing of spiritual waste. This doesn't mean you should bring large bits of physical waste there, but rather you can dispose of the dust you collect in this manner. If you have a multi-ethnic grocer nearby, you can buy a large banana leaf, put the dust inside, and tie it off. Take the waste to a body of running water, open your parcel, and mindfully send it along its way, being careful not to have any of it blow back in your face.

**Tip:** If you think you've been Hoodooed, go to someone's house and take a single broom straw. Put this in your hair in a cross shape. Wear it for twenty-one days and the bad Hoodoo will end.

## 227. Van Van Blessing

An Africanism alive and well in NOLA is bringing small amounts of wild substances into the house to impart a new and vigorous energy. This energy is typically refreshing and vibrant, encapsulated in a liquid substance. The traditional oil used for cleansing and blessing the threshold, door, and floors is Van Van oil. Van Van contains lemongrass, a very uplifting and bright formula. Lemongrass can shift a negative vibration to a positive one. With a small infusion of pyrite added to the bottle, it will not only lift and brighten but also bring good fortune.

You should have a nice collection of rainwater and lightning water gathered from showers and thunderstorms, respectively. These types of water make a nice addition to your blessing formula, but if you don't have any, use spring water. The moving water from fresh springs is also powerful. It is traditionally used in Hoodoo for multiple purposes.

### Van Van Home Cleansing Ritual

Take your dram of Van Van oil imbued with pyrite and add three pieces of your broom corn to it. Let this steep for nine days. On the following day, swirl it, gazing at it and realizing the potency of its contents. Concentrate on breathing your wish for an energized and spiritually cleansed home into the oil as you drop each drop into the bucket of water. The number of drops will depend on the size of your bucket and your desire, tolerance, and wishes. Stir the mixture with a stainless steel spoon. (Stainless steel will not absorb the scent of the oil or contaminate other projects or formulas.)

Use the mixture to cleanse your space, chanting your wishes as you go in a clockwise circle. Sprinkle some of the wash around your doorstep and on garments you're wearing. Dispose of the water on soil if possible. Refill the bucket with more water, without the oil. Then rinse, going counterclockwise to seal the circle and intent of your work.

Use this Van Van oil wash to shake off jinxes, drive away bad luck, and help rent out rooms.

## 228. Hoodoo Gardening: Plant of Peace

In Hoodoo, Jack-in-the-pulpit (*Arisaema triphyllum*) is called plant of peace. This beautiful and rather exotic plant is easy to grow and is also native to forty-eight states. Its flowers are unisexual, and having both male and female energy makes it a plant that can deliver a great deal of impact.

This plant's appearance is captivating. It has a tall stalk inside a hooded cup. The plant varies in height from one to two feet. The flowers are very small, green or yellow, with dots lining the spadix. Plant of peace has large three-lobed leaves that shroud the spathe from view. In the late summer or fall, the spathe comes off and the flowers become decorative magickal wands bearing intensely red berries. Inside the berries are one to five seeds.

Plant of peace is easy to grow. It favors woodland environments and shade. The soil must be moist or slightly wet, acidic, and richly composted.

Planting the bare root (corm) six inches deep in the fall will bear flowers in the spring perennially. It should be mulched with organic materials, and though it resists bugs, slugs find it attractive. Slug baits, which you can buy at your local home and garden center, are suggested.

In Hoodoo lore, you are directed to wipe your hands on the leaves before coming indoors. This act promises to keep your home safe and secure, tranquil and peaceful.

## 229. Bluing the Way

Today, let's engage in an age-old Hoodoo cleansing and blessing rite called bluing. Some formulas, like Van Van oil for example, open the way. On this day, you'll be bluing the way, employing all the peace-bringing, serene influences of the color blue as you work, which you also learned about in your work with candlemancy.

Mrs. Stewart's liquid bluing, Mexican anil balls, and Reckitt's Crown Blue squares are materials used both to add a blue tinge to whites in the laundry and to create your mystical floor and pathway wash.

Once you have followed the directions and dissolved your bluing smoothly in a bucket of spring water, river water, or rainwater, it is almost ready to use. Before using, set your intent. What is it you desire from your blue spiritual wash? Do you need protection, security, peace, or good fortune, or a mixture of all four? Begin your work at 6:00 a.m. Ask for what it is you desire, sincerely and directly.

Prepare your surface by sweeping with your magick broom treated with rose water. Rose water is a high-frequency water that sweetens your work. After you have swept counterclockwise, it is time to mop your room in a clockwise direction. When your cleansing is complete, dig a hole in the backyard (if you have one) and dispose of the water at sunrise the next morning.

## 230. Dishwater Foot Track Rite

If you suspect someone is doing foot track magick against you, use your yard and housecleaning fluid to set things right.

You will need these items:

- A basin full of used dishwater
- A gourd to use as a ladle
- Shoes, sneakers, or boots with soles that can hold soil

Gather fresh foot track dirt from the bottom of your shoes that comes from your yard. Fill your ladle with dishwater. Wash down the soles with some of the dishwater and pour some of it on your foot tracks on your property. Pour the rest over your fence, entryway, or entry gate. Do this for three mornings in a row, using fresh dishwater each time.[56]

The person will let go of your foot track for their negative work.

## 231. Making a Bottle Tree

There is a unique way to fortify your home and garden: with a bottle tree. The bottle tree may have several origins, but its relationship to Africa—the Congo, specifically—has been documented as early as 1776. There, Bantu speakers combine various vessels with tree branches to ensure protection over the property on which it is created. Its relationship to African beliefs is quite clear in that glass represents the spirit world and the water from

---

56. Hyatt, *Hoodoo, Conjuration, Witchcraft, Rootwork.*

which the spirits arise. Blue is the preferred color for the bottles used, which is another reference to the cleansing, protective, and nurturing power of water and the gods, goddesses, lwa, orisha, and spirits that reside there.

Hoodoo, however, is multicultural. Yes, it encapsulates Africanisms, but it also embraces European, Native American, and Asian belief systems. The European aspect of the bottle tree exists in the preference for the crepe myrtle tree as the tree from which to hang the bottles, among other aspects. Crepe myrtle grows readily in the southern United States and is akin to Aphrodite's love and attraction energy. When you create your bottle tree to prevent hants (spirits) from invading your property, your first choice of tree should be crepe myrtle. If that type of tree isn't available, use oak or ash.

Today, begin working toward building a bottle tree. Start by collecting various blue bottles from yard sales, flea markets, and estate sales, or search for some on eBay.

## 232. Funky Bottle Tree Rite

Lore and legends suggest that hants are attracted to the way the sun and moon hit the bottles, causing dazzling reflections. They are also attracted to pretty colors generally. You can use your power as a Hoodoo to enhance the bottles' magnetism so that once the hants are attracted, they can't get outside the small hole of the bottle. Trapped at night, when they are typically about, they flourish under the moonlight. Much Hoodoo work is done at sunrise, and it is then that the hants in the bottles get destroyed. They are destroyed by the piercing power of the sun.

### Making Your Bottle Tree

Gather the following items:

- Piece of parchment paper
- A waterproof marker (Sharpie)
- A crepe myrtle, oak, or ash tree that is not too tall, with strong branches
- A large collection of blue bottles, cleansed thoroughly and allowed to dry completely

On a piece of parchment paper, write down a list of your wishes. Copy each single sentence (each of which contains a protection wish) in a spiral motion around a bottle. Say your intent aloud and place the bottle upside down on your work table.

Outside, on the night of a full moon, go outside dressed in your favorite ceremonial robe. A dark color is preferable so as not to attract spirits to your person. Stand in front of your tree, facing south. Hold your arms straight and slightly away from your body. Stretch your fingers wide to summon the power of the full moon. Let it bathe you in its full power. Speak the following invocation:

> *Mother Moon, with your glimmering light,*
> *Make my bottles a beautiful sight.*
> *Draw wandering spirits and hants*
> *Coming into my home; they have no chance.*

Turn to face your tree. Lift your outstretched arms and hands to the sky and tilt your head up toward the moon. Then say:

> *All that I've said, so mote it be!*
> *I say this thrice, capturing all the powers of three!*

Repeat all of this twice more.

## 233. Hoodoo Gardening: Sage with Smudging Ritual

Day 93 offers guidance to help create your own smudge stick. Try to use homegrown plants or sprigs from trees on your property, bearing in mind that part of the spirituality of using smudging herbs is that the herbs should not be bought or sold but rather traded, bartered for, or harvested on your own in a respectful manner, thanking the plant for each part taken. If you do not have any trees or herbs available, you might try bartering with a family member or friend. Here are some items in various types of smudge sticks and their qualities:

**Sagebrush** (*Artemisia tridentata* and *Artemisia spp.*), also known as wild sage, is preferred over culinary sage (*Salvia officinalis* or *Salvia apiana*) as a smudging herb. Sagebrush has been used traditionally by Western groups to treat colds. Spiritually, sage is considered protective of the spirit. It is also known to have antiseptic and tonic qualities to aid our energy levels.

**Mugwort** (*Artemisia vulgaris*) is a very useful, easy-to-grow alternative to the types of sage just listed and is conducive to burning as a smudging incense.

In addition to these traditional native herbs, many people use lavender, hyssop, and rosemary because they are also holy plants that are widely available, easy to grow, and very fragrant.

To smudge, open the doors and windows for good ventilation. Light the smudge stick. Tamp out the flame. Carry the smoking wand north, east, south, and then west through each room. Smoke the corners well. Some people enjoy using a found bird feather to spread the smoke as they travel, but your cupped hands also work well.

### Palo Santo

This is a modern adaptation on incense for the contemporary practitioner. You will not find palo santo (*Bursera graveolens*) in the older Hoodoo lore, yet it is from the family of trees beloved by Hoodoos that includes frankincense and myrrh.

Many people in need of energy healing have fallen under the influence of misfortune. Incense from the mystical palo santo tree is useful for those individuals. Traced back to the Inca, it encourages deep relaxation. An energy healer whose third eye is opened and then stimulated by the ancient, woodsy smell of palo santo can cure those who suffer.

This incense is typically used in South America, growing readily on the coasts and in the forests of Peru. Healers use it in a practice called *sahumerio* (fumigation), which goes back to the rites and ceremonies of the Inca. Containing age-old wisdom from thousands of years ago, its fumes and smoke capture and ground negative energy. It is returned to the universe transformed into healing light. Even unlit, as a sacred object placed in your home wherever you choose, aromatic palo santo activates the astral body. Its scent opens up your physical and spiritual space. With these portals open, gifts of prosperity and good fortune flood in and healing energy takes hold.

### Using Your Palo Santo Incense

Akin to the Native American smudge stick, palo santo incense is used primarily for cleansing and clearing. By working on all the physical and astral components of the body, this incense balances chakra energy, enabling peace and luck to prevail.

You'll burn it like a Native American smudge stick: smoldering, not burning. Hold it at a 45-degree angle away from your body. Ignite it, then let the fire die out.

## 234. Pennies

Do pennies get on your nerves? For many, they are a minor nuisance, filling up their change purse and offering little opportunity to be used. Hoodoo looks upon pennies differently. In this tradition, they are beautiful—the more, the better, as they are good luck charms.

To make sure you always have plenty of pennies on hand for your Hoodoo work, not only for yourself but also for those with whom you share it, start a collection of pennies today. You may first need to obtain a few large vessels in which to hold them. Glass works wonderfully. Once you have your containers, fill them with any pennies you have in your car, wallet, or purse. Every time you get pennies as change, quickly deposit them in your glass jars. While they are waiting to be used further, their copper energy will add a positive charge to your home.

Bright, shiny pennies are pleasing to the ancestors and spirits in the home. They can use them even when you think you can't. To break in a new living space, pour some pennies from your jars into your hands and toss them high in the air, catching the eye of the spirits. Let them hit the ground and stay where they are. This is an old-fashioned way of blessing new spaces that is still useful today.

## 235. Landlord Rite

Let's face it, a landlord—someone directly involved with your abode—can make you miserable. That's not to say all landlords are evil or high-strung, but if you come across a difficult one, look out! Hoodoo helps you take care of yourself with magick and rites of your hand, using easily obtainable materials. Here is a rite that utilizes the cleansing power of sacred salt.

You will need the following:

- A white ceramic plate
- A new box of fine kosher salt
- A window

In the center of the plate add a tablespoon of the salt. Carry this to the window just before sunrise on a sunny day. Let your salt's inherent magical powers become enhanced by the strength and vitality of the sun by bathing it in the sun. After the sun has risen completely, throw the salt out the window off the plate. Now turn the plate upside down. Henceforward, your landlord will soften toward you. If that's not the case, repeat this rite until they do.

## 236. Ancestral Altar

You will need these items:

- Mudcloth or kente cloth
- A blue plate
- Cowrie shells

- Tobacco
- Shot glass
- Whiskey
- Pennies
- Crystal bowl
- A wooden charger plate
- A white candle

Your ancestors are with you for your entire life. Feting them and feeding them ensures they will stay around. Ancestors are helpful in many ways, and they can help you by being a protective influence in your home. This altar is beautiful and meaningful. It is sure to be enticing and satisfying to your folks.

Lay out your mudcloth (or kente cloth) on a small table. These cloths from Africa remind us of our African heritage (all of us). On the blue plate of peace, make a circle around the circumference using the cowrie shells. Fill in this circle with tobacco as you recall enslavement and the will, strength, and endless desire it took to come out of it. Fill the shot glass with whiskey, which is pleasing to the spirits around you, including your ancestral spirits. Put this on the south side of the blue plate. Put some shiny, new pennies in the crystal bowl. Ancestors need currency and this will work nicely. Place this bowl of pennies atop the wooden charger plate to represent the rural areas from which we come.

Light a white candle on this space once a week and remember from whence you came and reflect on where you and your family need to go.

## 237. Curio of Note: Salt

As was mentioned a couple of days ago, salt is a humble yet useful material found in most homes. It is also used for diverse reasons in Hoodoo. This substance is so celebrated that it can stand in the place of holy water when mixed with water. Water is a reminder of our life in utero. It is also the home of many deities, such as gods and goddesses, as well as orisha and lwa. Notice that these beings share qualities of being nurturing yet fierce and highly protective. I'm speaking of Yemaya, Oshun, Venus, and Aphrodite, among others.

Salt holds a high place on multiple paths, including eclectic paganism and various forms of African spirituality, as well as in Hoodoo. This lofty position is quite likely the result of its connection to the sea and survival. For the next two days we will work with salt in ways inspired by traditional Hoodoo recipes and rites. Notice the duality in its use. Salt can be used to bring peace and to welcome or deter guests from ever returning.

## 238. Magickal Salt

Today I'm sharing a few salt spells and rites related to domesticity. This is just the tip of the iceberg in Hoodoo salt lore, yet this work is fun and useful nonetheless.

1. Let's start this work with some advice from a Hyatt informant from Waycross, Georgia. Go outside, and starting in the north, go to each of the four directions and leave one tablespoon of salt. Inside your home, do the same thing in every room. This will make the other occupants besides you feel compelled to move.

2. To be able to rent out a room, put salt water in the center of the room. Dress several white taper candles with bergamot essential oil. Burn the candles next to the salt water. This is an old-fashioned New Orleans Hoodoo good luck charm.

3. If someone tries to break up your home, throw salt in the four corners and invoke either the Father, Son, and Holy Ghost or the trinity of your path.

4. Sprinkle salt on the doorstep to prevent quarrels and bring domestic peace and a quiet atmosphere to the home.

5. If some people come to your home whom you don't like, put your magickal broom upside down in the corner. Then get three handfuls of Epsom or regular salt and place it in the four corners of the house by throwing it, bit by bit. They won't come back. [57]

6. A Hyatt informant from Jacksonville, Florida, advises how to get the things you want. In each of the four corners of your house, going from north, south, east, to west, make a small pile of money. To encourage your angels, beings, or spirits to hear your request, as you lay each pile down, say "money," "prosperity," "love," and "success," respectively. Say these four things with strong intent and they should be granted. [58]

7. At sunrise, sweep up the debris in each room and burn it in the center of the room in a Dutch oven, cauldron, or large can set on a heat-resistant holder such as a trivet. Put salt in the four corners of each room, moving clockwise. In

57. Hyatt, *Hoodoo, Conjuration, Witchcraft, Rootwork*.

58. Ibid.

the name of your highest deity (traditional Hoodoo calls for invoking the Father, Son, and Holy Ghost), lay out salt until there are no more corners left. This rite is from a Hoodoo from Fayetteville, North Carolina.[59]

8. For peace and love, sprinkle salt in the four corners of the house and the side of the bed where your lover sleeps. This is a hope charm to replace arguments with good lovin'.

## 239. High John the Conqueror Root Spiritual Wash

Here are some ways to use High John the Conqueror root. We know by now that High John the Conqueror represents the essence of willpower and the desire for freedom. If you can capture some of that essence mindfully, you will have a powerful spiritual wash that can be used to cleanse many things, from your clothing to your floors or hands. This wash is said to attract good luck and drive away the jinx. It also brings prosperity and success in business and gaming.

Gather these items:

- High John the Conqueror root, cut and sifted (chips)
- A cauldron of rainwater (a Dutch oven or soup pot is fine)
- Castile or unscented organic dish soap
- 2 Meyer lemons
- Lemon essential oil
- Vetiver essential oil

Add the root chips to water that is just about to come to a boil. Bring to a boil and then immediately reduce to medium-high.

---

59. Hyatt, *Hoodoo, Conjuration, Witchcraft, Rootwork.*

Let simmer this way, covered, for thirty minutes. Let cool, covered, for another twenty to thirty minutes. Strain. Add some Castile or unscented organic dish soap, and stir to mix. Squeeze the juice of two Meyer lemons through your hands, or use a lemon press to avoid seeds. Add lemon essential oil and vetiver essential oil to your scent-level preference. Remember, a little vetiver goes a long way.

Cleanse your floors, hands, or clothing by hand with this balanced herbal mix rich with the power of the earth, sun, and sky.

## 240. Hoodoo Gardening: Bay Laurel

Bay laurel (*Laurus nobilis*) is one of those culinary herbs you're probably accustomed to purchasing already dried. It is a wonderful plant to add to your herb garden. When it is at the shops as a culinary herb, the leaves have typically been around for a while. When you grow them, you know they're fresh and thus potent. They're also pliable enough to use in various magickal projects, rites, and ceremonies.

First, here are some growing directions. I received my plant bare-root from Richters Herbs (www.richters.com). You may find that someone is growing it closer to you. If so, start with that bay plant. Alternately, you can start it from seed, following the package directions.

Bay is one of the easiest perennials to grow, and it will grow readily anywhere to zone 8. It prefers full sun, when grown outdoors, and well-drained soil. If you are growing it indoors, avoid terracotta pots. The potting soil should contain moisture-retentive material, such as vermiculite or water balls. Allow room for the roots to grow, and you may still need to replant it in larger pots as it grows. Avoid blazing sun and hot spots indoors. Keep moist.

Outdoors, water your bay plant only as needed, about every week to a week and a half. Allow to grow for a full year, and then the second year, when it is well established, you may harvest the leaves by laying them out on a dry surface and allowing them to dry flat for two to three days.

Bay is a plant that is protective and healing, adds blessings, and clears spaces of bad vibes when burned. It invites good fortune and is good to use when moving into a new space.

## 241. Bay Clearing and Blessings

Once you have your bay dried flat and ready to use, there are several ways you can use it. Bay is a deeply spiritual, cleansing herb. If you have moved to a new space, or someone (like a roommate) has moved out and you want to purge the space of their energy, try using bay. Simply burn it on a very hot charcoal placed on a censer. Carry this throughout the space counterclockwise and fumigate to reset the energy and clear any residue from the old tenants.

Another charming way of using bay leaves is as a garland. Get some thick filament thread or thin hemp string and measure the area you want to cover. This may be an entryway, a doorway, or a wooden trim lining any wall—particularly in a living room/great room type of space. It can also be used in your bedroom in the same manner. I like to also dry some orange slices and cayenne pepper to go along with the bay.

Thread the filament thread with a needle and use it to puncture the bay, then slide it to the end, which has been knotted. Slide on a dried orange slice and a cayenne pepper. These are added for their protective and energy-enhancing properties. Keep going, alternating as you go; this will take you quite a while. Focus on clearing, blessing, and healing energy rising in the space wherein you hang your garland.

### 242. You Can't Harm Me in My Home
### Foot Track Magick (Waycross, Georgia)

Your home is your domain, the space where you should feel comfortable and free. If you find that you have someone coming into your space with unwanted negative energy or bad intentions toward you, it is time to act by fortifying your home using Hoodoo. This is foot track magick inspired by a traditional trick recorded by Harry Hyatt. The informant is from Waycross, Georgia.[60]

Here is what you'll need:

• Saltpeter

• Sea salt

• Freshly ground or pulverized (with a mortar and pestle) black pepper

• Magickal broom

Mix equal parts saltpeter, sea salt, and black pepper as described in a bowl using a spoon. If you know the path the person typically takes or the place where they spend the most time in your home, go there with your bowl. Spread this mixture all over the floor where they walk. After they leave, sweep it outside and their negativity will go with the dust.

---

60. Hyatt, *Hoodoo, Conjuration, Witchcraft, Rootwork*.

## 243. Buckeye Hand from Mobile, Alabama

This old-style hand reported by a Hyatt informant from Mobile, Alabama,[61] centers around the use of a buckeye. Buckeye (*Aesculus spp.)* and Ohio buckeye *(Aesculus glabra)* are attractive trees, native to the United States that grow mostly in the eastern half of the country, north to Ohio and south to Alabama. Buckeye is a nut-like seed that is shiny and dark brown, with a light-colored spot that makes it resemble a deer's eye. It is a useful seed medicinally and cosmetically and has been used in soap making. It is used in hands and mojos, in accord with its American folklore, as a good luck charm and to bring good fortune.

Obtain a buckeye from a tree in your area (if possible). It must be taken from the north side of the tree and it should be male (he). The he will have two eyes, whereas the she will have a single eye. Spritz the male buckeye every other day with Hoyt's Cologne. Put this in a flannel and wear it. Then spread peanuts in the shell out in front of your house. This not only will bring luck to the home and wearer of the hand but will also bring good luck in gambling.

## 244. Peaceful Home Spell

We conclude this chapter with a spell that is designed to bring a good vibe to the home. It will probably require a little work to obtain the ingredients to create the formula, but that can be half the fun of it.

Back in the day, it wasn't really a problem to find chicken feathers of a specific type and color, but it may prove more challenging today, depending on your living situation. People are doing more urban homesteading, raising chickens for their eggs,

---

61. Hyatt, *Hoodoo, Conjuration, Witchcraft, Rootwork*, 534.

so you may be in luck, particularly if you have chickens in your yard. Luckily, you will not need a specific color of feather for this trick.

To create peace in your home, get three chicken feathers and put them in a bowl. Completely coat them with sulphur. Let these mature and strengthen overnight outdoors. Put them under a clear cloche. At sunrise, bury them under your doorstep and watch the vibration of your home change.

# CHAPTER 9
# THE ROAD TO SUCCESS: DAYS 245-277

Success—it comes in many different forms, as its meaning varies from one person to the next. The simple fact is as humans, we want it, whether it is in business, entrepreneurial projects, relationships, or the feeling of satisfaction within ourselves or the environment.

While success comes in various packages and looks different depending on the viewer, for the next month we are going to view it through the lens of the Hoodoo. In this light, success is concerned with interviews, career development, businesses, roadblocks, and sabotage, as well as jobs and an attractive environment. These standard components of success resonate with many, and they will be our focus.

As a writer and artist, I know that the road to success is unpredictable. You may have your life and its work all planned out, only to find yourself wanting something different at some time or another. The road to success is winding. It has forks, crossroads, stumbling blocks, and challenges. The rewards may seem unattainable and may come in unexpected forms. As someone who has had to find various means of support along the way, I have had my fair share of experiences with job hunting, temporary gigs, and, well, let's face it—having the door slammed in my face.

Between my personal experiences and the archived advice from Hoodoos collected by Harry Hyatt and other folklorists, there is much for you to investigate.

In this chapter you will find a dense compilation of advice, work, spells, tricks, rites, and jobs. This magickal work is all related to success in its many manifestations. It ranges from simple to complex—some things even require a few tools. If you're not in search of success currently, use your daily practices to benefit friends or family. Trust me, it won't be hard to find someone in need of work toward success in their career, business, or relationships, or in creating a vibrant and attractive environment.

## 245. A Week of Exploration: Lucky Pennies

These days, there doesn't seem to be much reason to use dollar bills, let alone coins. In the high days of Hoodoo, from whence traditional practices hail, cash ruled. One of the interesting facets of abundance and luck magick is that money is used to yield mo' money.

Earlier on in the first month of this work, which is concerned with mojo bags, you had a good chance to explore and work with dimes. If you are familiar with my other books, you know how fond I am of utilizing pennies in luck draw rites and mojo bags. Pennies—especially specific types of pennies—bring luck and are useful to the ancestors as they trade and barter in their world.

It's your turn now to tuck into an entire week devoted to pennies that yield luck and bring success. This type of amulet is derived from the report of a Hyatt informant who lived in St. Petersburg, Florida, but has been updated for contemporary use.

Gather these ingredients:

- A regular penny
- Tin snips
- Protective eyewear
- A tight-fitting headband
- Eyeglasses or a magnifying glass (optional)

Cut your penny in four equal parts using the tin snips. Wear protective eyewear in case a piece goes shooting off. Use glasses or a magnifying glass if need be. Take the two parts of the head and put them in your hair or on your head if you're bald. Hold it there with a headband. Wear it with confidence that you will have good luck! (You may discard the lower two parts of the penny).

## 246. Keep 'Em Coming Trick

This Hoodoo trick is for those who work from home or have a business in the home. Back in the day, this might have been a distillery or a supper club. Today, there are many different variations on working in the home, from remote work on a computer in a variety of fields to breeding and selling animals to running an e-commerce company.

Basically, if you want to keep em' coming back for more, try this rite shared by an informant from St. Petersburg, Florida.[62] You'll notice it is powered by the magickal number nine.

---

62. Hyatt, *Hoodoo, Conjuration, Witchcraft, Rootwork*, 612–616.

You will need:

- Nine pennies
- Home or business

Take your pennies and put them at the front of the home or business. Alternately, bury them outside the front door. This will attract positivity and good spirits. It will also attract customers and more business.

## 247. Indian Head Job

Today's work was also shared by a Hyatt informant from St. Petersburg, Florida.[63] It entails the Indian Head penny. These are pennies with Native American chiefs on the coin, as the "heads" are perceived as bringing the luck, power, and insight of the figure depicted. You might be lucky enough to own one, or you may need to ferret one out. Whatever the case, once you get your hands on one, you'll use those same tin snips as before to cut the coin carefully into four equal parts. Using only the two parts of the head, place one in the left pocket and the other in the home or business. This will bring you more money and should increase business.

If you can't cut the special penny or don't care to do so, do a rubbing on parchment paper. Put the penny under the paper and then rub a #2 pencil vigorously over the penny. Having captured the image, proceed to cut it into two parts and continue with the job as described.

---

63. Hyatt, *Hoodoo, Conjuration, Witchcraft, Rootwork*, 612–616.

## 248. Indian Head Business Drawin' Magick

Again, you will hunt for an Indian Head penny to use to draw trade to your business. Try your usual avenues and ones I've suggested, such as eBay or Etsy. Have fun in your search and treasure your special aged and very lucky currency once it arrives. Think about this day's work broadly and practically. How will you use it? What are your expected results? Whether you own your business or not is immaterial.

If you work for a company, nonprofit organization, studio, gym, or other similar type of business, you need there to be a steady demand for the work or service provided. You'll want to use your knowledge and prowess with Hoodoo to draw trade to make this happen. This trick brings together your newfound friend, the Indian Head penny, with one we've explored quite a bit—a horseshoe.

Hold the Indian Head penny in the palm of your dominant hand. Look at it carefully. Place it outside the business near the street. Make sure it is facing the street, not toward you. Next, hang a horseshoe over your door. Do these actions with purpose and a powerful sense of intent. Make sure your nerves are calm before embarking on what seems to be simple magick.

Be prepared. These lucky charms work. Are you prepared for ample new opportunities in your current business?

## 249. Indian Head Success Job

There is beauty, mystique, and a wealth of knowledge that comes with age. Aged objects also lend the ability to harness power that can come through a lengthy existence. We hope that with age comes wisdom, and through that wisdom there is the opportunity to come through the gateway of success.

Age and aged objects should be revered, celebrated, and utilized. They frequently come in handy in your Hoodoo practice. This is a wonderful aspect of this path. Think about it. How many times do you wonder what to do with this or that crusty old object? In our times of constantly chasing after what is new, your first idea might be to toss it in the trash—but hold on. I suggest considering ways to use these goodies in your magick.

Here is a trick shared last century by a Hoodoo from Waycross, Georgia. It is designed to increase trade in the home—a perfect spell for the self-employed, telecommuter, or entrepreneur. What you do is get hold of two rusty pennies. Drill a hole in each of them and nail one to the left and one to the right of your doorsill. This talisman will bring luck that leads to prosperity.

## 250. Bringing Money Home

Copper is healing. It eases pain and brings warmth into the home. Using copper-colored pennies with a Hoodoo's intent is a surefire way of helping to create an engaging, soulful, spiritual home. You can do this in several ways, as you've discovered in days 1–5. Here are a couple of additional methods that work in tandem.

### A Personalized Fountain

Purchase a portable fountain. The water element brings flow and energy into your home. When you feel that you have some lucky pennies, toss them into your personal fountain. Be sure to be selective so there is balance between your metal and water elements. Let the energy of the two come together alchemically to enliven your home.

*Coin Toss*

Tossing coins is an ancient tradition encapsulated in various forms of folklore, including Hoodoo. Rather than randomly throwing your pennies in your home, why not capitalize on their relationship with numerology—they are currency, after all.

Today, gather together a collection of Indian Head and regular pennies of different ages, all with a positive energy charge you can feel in your hand. This will take some time because I want you to select eleven pennies. Once you have the pennies that feel heavy because they are so laden with promise, put them in the palm of your dominant hand. Toss them toward Father Sky. Let them scatter where they will. This trick is very useful after you move into a new home when you want luck or as a general success blessing for your abode.

## 251. Abundance Necklace

You may recall seeing ancient sculptures with the subject wearing a coin necklace. This adds a regal bearing and an air of mystery. Since very early in human history, folks have been aware that coins are useful not just on the physical plane but also on the astral one. The ancestors and spirits delight in currency, and those who surround themselves with it daily are looked upon favorably.

This spell capitalizes on the power of numerology. You will see the Hoodoo's love for using odd numbers. For this day's work, you'll engage the lucky number seven. You will need seven pennies and a gold necklace, along with a drill with a tiny drill bit.

1. Arrange your seven pennies in a way that you find alluring.
2. Listen to them. See which penny wants to be first, second, third, and so forth. This might take some time and

meditation, and since it's so important, you might want to sleep on it.

3. Once you've arranged the pennies the way you want them, drill a hole at the top of each one. This should be just large enough to string.

4. According to the Hoodoo informant from Florence, South Carolina, that inspired this spell, your coin necklace will imbue your life with abundance, prosperity, and good luck.

## 252. Money Attraction Magick

This updated version of a traditional rite could be called mo' money equals mo' money, which brings mo' money. This rite is useful for your interviewing process. Every time you go in for an interview for a job you really are sure you want, follow these steps. Refeeding the coins each time will help keep your amulet fresh and alive with drawing power.

Here's what to do:

1. To a half pint of high-quality gin, add a thimbleful of Hoyt's Cologne.

2. Add to this strong brew a carefully selected dime, quarter, fifty-cent piece, and silver dollar.

3. Soak this under Mama Moon overnight, allowing the spirits and the spirit of the moon to soak into each coin.

4. Allow the coins to air-dry in the morning at sunrise.

5. Put the coins in your right pocket, in a piece of green cloth, if you'd like, or a red flannel.

6. You need to make three separate trips to the potential employer. Be creative and make sure you can go this number of times.

7. After the third trip, you should get the job, if it was meant to be.

### 253. Key to Success Mojo

Doors and the keys that open them have high significance in Hoodoo. Keys can open the door to your luck, letting success into your life.

For this mojo, you need an elaborate-looking image of a key, such as the skeleton key shown here.

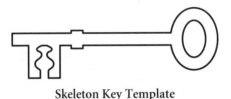

**Skeleton Key Template**

Gather these materials:

• High John the Conqueror root (soaked outdoors in Hoyt's Cologne overnight)

• Paper towel

• Tracing paper

• Key image

• 4 x 5-inch sheet of parchment paper

• Fountain pen

• Dragon's blood ink

- Lodestone

- Flannel (a green one, if available, otherwise red will be fine)

The combination of images and curios in this mojo bag will help you access luck, and through it you'll open the way for success to find you.

Take the soaked High John the Conqueror root out of its container of cologne and set it on the paper towel to dry a bit. Trace the key image onto parchment paper with a fountain pen loaded with dragon's blood ink. Turn the High John root over so the other side can dry off. Once the drawn key image is fully dry to the touch, fold it into quarters. Add your lodestone and High John the Conqueror root to the flannel.

Carry this on your person all the time. Squeeze it. Talk to it. Tell it your wishes. And every fortnight, resoak the High John the Conqueror root to keep it powered up and alive.

## 254.–255. Psalm Success Rite

Like keys, roots, and stones, the Psalms of David are important to traditional Hoodoo. You must recite them with faith and high intention and in a meaningful manner to connect them to your desire. Here are two different psalms associated with success, business, and social transactions. I'm setting aside the next day as well for you to go deep into the meaning and personal messages within these psalms, so this is a two-day reflection. Do this before and after work or when you awaken and at bedtime.

### Directions

Set out a censer, fossil, flat stone, or ceramic plate.

Grind some frankincense finely, about two teaspoons.

Put a charcoal atop the censer or other flat symbolic surface used in prayer.

Light a charcoal and let burn for a few minutes.

With a silver or silver-colored spoon, sprinkle the incense onto the charcoal.

Early in the morning and late at night, go back and forth between these following two psalms.

### Psalm 26

Judge me, O LORD; for I have walked in mine integrity: I have trusted also in the LORD; *therefore,* I shall not slide.

Examine me, O LORD, and prove me; try my reins and my heart.

For thy lovingkindness *is* before mine eyes: and I have walked in thy truth.

I have not sat with vain persons, neither will I go in with dissemblers.

I have hated the congregation of evil doers; and will not sit with the wicked.

I will wash mine hands in innocency: so, will I compass thine altar, O LORD:

That I may publish with the voice of thanksgiving, and tell of all thy wondrous works.

LORD, I have loved the habitation of thy house, and the place where thine honour dwelleth.

Gather not my soul with sinners, nor my life with bloody men:

In whose hands *is* mischief, and their right hand is full of bribes.

But as for me, I will walk in mine integrity: redeem me, and be merciful unto me.

My foot standeth in an even place: in the congregations will I bless the LORD.

### Psalm 8

O LORD our Lord, how excellent *is* thy name in all the earth! who hast set thy glory above the heavens.

Out of the mouth of babes and sucklings hast thou ordained strength because of thine enemies, that thou mightest still the enemy and the avenger.

When I consider thy heavens, the work of thy fingers, the moon and the stars, which thou hast ordained;

What is man, that thou art mindful of him? and the son of man, that thou visitest him?

For thou hast made him a little lower than the angels, and hast crowned him with glory and honour.

Thou madest him to have dominion over the works of thy hands; thou hast put all *things* under his feet:

All sheep and oxen, yea, and the beasts of the field;

The fowl of the air, and the fish of the sea, *and whatsoever* passeth through the paths of the seas.

O LORD our Lord, how excellent *is* thy name in all the earth!

## 256. Old Barnum's Tears Success Rite

As I have mentioned and you have hopefully learned from experience, olive oil is a holy and sacred oil. It will draw spirit, and with it luck will swing your way. This rite combines its metaphysical prowess with that of dragon's blood. Old Barnum's Tears is another name used by traditional Hoodoo practitioners[64] for dragon's blood, which is derived from a type of palm, a sacred tree in parts of Africa.

Gather these items:

- ¼ cup fresh olive oil (Make sure it's fresh. Olive oil gets rancid easily.)
- 3 small chunks of Old Barnum's tears

Is there a song that incorporates rain as a part of its motif that you like? How about a song that uses the word rain repeatedly in its lyrics? Find a song that uses rain in music and put your device well away from your shower but close enough and loud enough to hear.

Set up a little altar to burn your Old Barnum's tears. This will include a white silk or satin cloth and an incense censer. Light your charcoal. After it seems very hot, add the pulverized tears from a spoon and let burn as loose incense.

Take off your clothes, imaging you are shedding bad luck and the old you. Step into the shower and lather yourself up. Rinse with downward motions to further accentuate the fact that you are shedding. Repeat eight more times, for a total of nine.

Get out of the shower and apply the olive oil in dabs, from the crown of your head to your feet, moving downward constantly. Towel yourself dry.

Dress for your day, knowing you're going to be powerful, influential, and able to win people over all day with the help of your sacred substances.

---

64. Hyatt, *Hoodoo, Conjuration, Witchcraft, Rootwork*.

## 257. Lucky Dishrag Magick from Algiers, Louisiana

When the *Oprah Winfrey Show* was on, I remember having an aha moment over her aha moment about dishwashing. Historically, I've been notoriously hateful toward the activity. I have old plumbing, and yes, I still do the dishes by hand. Anyway, on her show, Oprah gave this beautiful account of how she cherished dishwashing. She felt that through it she remembered who had eaten with her, what they ate, and how they laughed and shared. She even lit a candle and had it nearby as she washed away. Okay, I know it's hard to picture anyone choosing to wash dishes by hand, let alone a celebrity, with the wide availability of dishwashing machines today, but still. Whatever the case, I like this rite she put into my mind.

Now I wash the dishes prayerfully at one of my witching hours—3:00 p.m. It is at that time that in the fall and winter, the sun is noticeably changing its position. The skies become mellower on most days at that time, and I love it. Plus, I have a gorgeous array of cacti in the window above the sink and squirrels outside keeping me company. I always try to do what she suggested: use dishwashing as a sacred time of remembrance and celebration.

We've done several dishwater rites so far this year. Today, there are a couple of Southern ones I want you to try. The first is from Algiers, Louisiana, and the second from Wilmington, North Carolina.[65]

1. To give someone good luck for a job interview, a new endeavor, or an undertaking, squeeze out the dishcloth that

---

65. Hyatt, *Hoodoo, Conjuration, Witchcraft, Rootwork*, 548.

is with your dishes and throw it after the person (not at them!).

2. If you want to keep your role at work, wash your face with a dishrag directly after washing the dishes with it.

## 258. Candlemancy and Success

You'll probably want to do this success candlemancy work on the weekend or during your time off, if you work regularly. Otherwise, do it when you are moved to work toward your success. It is designed to draw energy, specifically to draw customers.

You'll need the following items:

- A red, a white, and a blue candle (tapers or 4 x 6-inch columns)
- Silver or silver-colored candleholder(s)
- An earthenware plate
- Blue satin cloth
- Seashells
- River rocks
- Lighter/matches

We know good things come from the sea, and many enchanted beings reside there, filled with love and kindness. This altar and ritual is evocative of the sea and encapsulates the elements of earth, fire, air, and water.

Today you're going to create a little altar to bring success, and if you're in business, it will help you draw customers.

Put the three candles in the candleholder(s) on the plate, and the shiny blue cloth beneath it. Arrange seashells around the candles, and have the river rocks create a barrier around the shells.

1. Burn the white candle from 7:00 a.m. until 9:00 a.m.

2. Light the blue candle from 9:00 a.m. until 3:00 p.m.

3. Have your red candle lit from 3:00 p.m. until 9:00 p.m.

Pinch the wick with wet fingers to extinguish each of the candles. Do not blow it out. Stick to these times strictly or you might get sick.

### 259. Hoodoo Gardening: Parsley and Garlic

When you think of these two herbs, your mind might immediately wander into the kitchen. Culinary herbs, right? Yes, but they can be so much more. These two are so common and easy to grow that I want to discuss their uses and benefits more than their habit and propagation.

Garlic figures into the Hoodoo's repertoire in many different formulas. One popular way it is used is in four thieves vinegar. From its use in poultices to tisanes, parsley does so much more than simply accompany food on the plate.

Parsley is easy to grow in your garden, in pots, or even in a window, roof, or terrace garden. There's really no excuse not to have parsley in your life, and why would you want to when it's so useful.

We know from the folklore of various cultures that garlic keeps away evil people and supernatural spirits, like vampires. It has many health benefits and is hard to beat in many recipes.

Here are a couple ways to use the two in tandem for your career and job.

1. Slice a clove of garlic into nine thin pieces. Wear them in your shoe to work, with a piece of parsley in there as well. This is success foot track magick.

2. Sprinkle some steel dust in the soles of your shoes to take away work anxiety when you get home. Remove the garlic and parsley you wore to work and make a few little beads out of it. String it and wear it around your ankle, below your knee, or in your shoe. This is designed to help you leave work behind, enabling you to relax until the next day.

### 260. Eight Days Till Your Next Job

When you're unemployed, one week of waiting for a callback or email can melt into another and yet another—that is, if you aren't proactive. You can use your Hoodoo magick to take matters into your own hands.

Candlemancy figures prominently in success, career, and employment magick, and why not? One of the quickest ways to set up an impromptu altar is by using a candle. Further, lit candles bring the power of the element of fire into your space. Then, too, the light of the candle opens itself up easily to prayer and meditation. There is much promise in that small object—the humble candle.

This rite is simple and utilizes numerology. You will go through an entire week of having your white candle lit for an hour at sunrise and an hour as the sun sets. Be sure to burn it as you pray or meditate or, at the very least, set your most powerful intention for employment. Then, when the hour of reflection is over, snuff out the candle by pinching it out. Do not blow it out.

According to traditional NOLA Hoodoos, if it is meant to be, by the eighth day you'll get that job you've had your heart set on.

## 261. New Orleans Success Spiritual Floor Wash

In NOLA, Van Van oil reigns supreme. One of its most effective methods of dispersal is as a spiritual floor wash. If you want to usher in all the success you can handle, dissolve a blue anil ball in a bucket of spring water. To this, add Van Van oil (in an amount to lend the fragrance you desire).

- Van van is energizing. It opens magickal pathways we don't truly understand.
- Blue anil balls are lucky and cleansing and have a high spiritual vibration for lending peace to wherever their water is spread.

You can't go wrong with this wash. Use it alone or with the following lucky incense.

## 262. Business Luck Incense Work

Burning incense is a spiritually satisfying, healing activity when used in ceremonies, rites, or spells or on your altar. Quite naturally, incense has inherent power, as it brings together air, ether, fire, and earth elements into one evocative elixir. There's a type of incense I find very conducive to spiritual work. It is copal. Copal is a relative of frankincense and myrrh. When ground and lit, it emits profuse clouds of smoke. That smoke can take you for a ride up and into the ether. You will find yourself leaving the mundane earth rather easily with its assistance. This smoke is also meant to remind you of your higher power, enveloped in the smoke, rising into the heavens.

First, source an authentic source of copal. Grind up about two tablespoons of copal with a mortar and pestle. Set out a censer, a plate, and some petrified wood or a fossil, atop of which you will set a bamboo charcoal. When you see flicks of white, you know it is hot enough to ignite the copal.

As your copal incense burns, talk to it. Ask out loud for what you need to be successful and to have luck, adding longevity to your good fortune.

### Good Luck for Your Business

Use the same equipment, but only on Wednesday and Thursday. Let your copal smoke bathe the front steps of your business. Then wash them down with salt water. Carry out this ceremony at 5:00 a.m. and at noon. This will draw customers to your establishment.

## 263. Enemies Underfoot Spiritual Wash

There are several different reasons you might need to take a bath in this potent brew. Perhaps someone is sabotaging your attempts to get the job you love. Maybe you want to get an edge on your competition. Whatever the reason, there comes a time when you need to crush your enemies underfoot. According to Hoodoo lore, here's what to do if these scenarios sound like they apply to you.

Get five quarts of water (rainwater or spring water will do nicely)and add to a stock pot or cauldron. Put a nickel's worth of saltpeter and a tablespoon of table salt in the water. Stir with your best wooden spoon. Turn on the heat and cook until it is reduced by half. (Let it condense—this makes the ingredients even stronger than they were individually.) Let the mixture cool slightly, just cool enough that you can take a bath. Bring this to the tub. Plug up the tub and add the potion. Take off your clothing and lie down in the shallow bath soak. Concentrate on the victory you deserve over your enemies and competition. Save all the water in a bowl or bucket.

This spell should be done outdoors, preferably on your property. As you throw the water east in small increments, chant these words three times, with sincere intent:

*Evil, peel away from me.*
*May I be shrouded in goodness and light.*
*Blessed be!*

## 264. Louisiana Saint Work

We have mentioned St. Anthony at the crossroads. Fortunately, working with this saint is ongoing and multidimensional. Today, reflect on your employment. Are you doing what you desire? What do you need to be doing to be happy? Do you need a job or a job change? Well, St. Anthony is here to help.

This is the saint known to open the way, particularly in traditional Algiers-style Louisiana Hoodoo. St. Anthony helps bring clarity and action to follow up on your vision. To invoke this saint, burn a brown candle during your strongest witching hours only on Tuesday and Thursday.

Next comes St. Espidy work from NOLA. For travel and moving you'll want to employ a red taper candle. Create an altar using a small sword (a knife or scissors), plastic snakes or real snake skin, and a small statue of a horse. Rap on the candle three times to call it to attention. Burn your taper on the altar you created. Concentrate on your wishes and watch in the coming days for signs that they are about to come true.

## 265. North Carolina Tree Magick

Do you knock on wood, literally or figuratively, when you are thankful for your luck? Wood is an important and in some cases sacred aspect of our spiritual and metaphysical lives. This belief in the magickal powers of wood and trees is cross-cultural. It has been passed down over the centuries, from one culture to the next.

One of the most heralded and plentiful trees of the Southeast is the white oak. These are beautiful, strong trees that are useful in mundane life and spiritual practice. As you know by now, in Hoodoo we like to use directionality to power our magick. Here is one such luck amulet you can make:

1. From the north side of a white oak tree, take a small bit of the root. This must be taken from a part of the tree close to the trunk.

2. Wrap up the root in a piece of white satin cloth.

3. Tie with twine in the shape of a crossroads to fix firmly.

4. Hang with twine over the main door of your business.

This good luck charm works well from home, so it is good for telecommuters, the self-employed, entrepreneurs, and others selling anything at all from home.

## 266. Money Nation Sack

Eggs are marvelous, aren't they? They are a contradiction—extremely delicate and yet strong enough to support life. No wonder eggs are viewed with respect and wonder in Hoodoo. This nation sack is designed to yield abundance and prosperity. It is based on a women's mojo bag originally from the Memphis,

Tennessee, area. You will need to take several steps and wait a while before using. Why not start now, so that when you need it, it will be ready.

1. Get a white egg.
2. Poke a hole in the top of the egg.
3. Let the egg dry out completely.[66]
4. Once the egg is all the way dry, break it open carefully.
5. Put the dried yolk only inside a flannel you've sewn yourself using white thread.
6. Fix this to a string that is long enough to fit around your waist.
7. Wear the sack underneath your clothing, tied to your waist, to cultivate abundance in your life.

## 267. Crone's Dishwater Spell

A few days ago we really engaged in thinking about dishes and dishwater in a new light. Over the next four days, we continue that line of work with two different spells that incorporate the power of the Crone. These spells are derived from accounts by an informant to Harry Hyatt from Little Rock, Arkansas.[67]

Crones have a special kind of wisdom, thus they hold a place of honor on many pagan paths and in various types of folklore, such as Hoodoo. These wise women are a part of our holy tril-

---

66. This step will last however long it takes for your egg to become light and feel empty. This will depend on the type and size of the egg, the season, and the weather/temperature.

67. Hyatt, *Hoodoo, Conjuration, Witchcraft, Rootwork*, 383.

ogy. They have traversed the eras of Maiden and Mother and are now Crones. Their wisdom is notable, mystical, and powerful.

For this spell you'll need these items:

- Used dishwater (that you create through intention)
- A work clothes outfit
- A basin or cleared-out sink
- Scissors
- Shovel

Wash your work clothes outfit in used dishwater in a basin or sink. The used dishwater shouldn't be water from your dirtiest dishes. Simply create the used dishwater with intention by washing a few dishes or objects from your altar that are in need of refreshment.

With scissors, cut off a piece of the clothing from a discreet location and bury it. Hang the outfit up to dry on a clothing line, in a drying rack, or in the bathroom. This outfit will serve you well on special occasions when you need the insight and help of the dishwater and the crone. At those times, wear this outfit to summon the wisdom.

## 268.–270. Crone's Dishwater Three-Day Rite

For clarity and strength, wash your crown (the top of your head) with holy water. Soak your body in a shallow bath of used dishwater. Take three sips of the water. Repeat for a total of a three-day rite. Again, there is no need to use the dishwater from your Sunday night spaghetti dinner for this. Intentionally create your used dishwater. Also, you should be showered well prior to soaking in the dishwater. Taking three sips of the water will be more manageable if you have prepared with intention.

## 271. Go Get a Job: Foot Track Magick

No matter where you live, this rite will take you back to the South, to an earlier day and time, on the delicate wings of aroma. Here is a soothing, healing, calming, and deeply spiced concoction to make that you will combine with prayer and the anointing of the feet. This age-old practice reported in Hyatt's folklore collection[68] will give you the confidence you need to be influential over others and land the role of your dreams.

Gather these ingredients:

- High John the Conqueror root
- Honeysuckle (absolute or flower)
- Bottle of crab apple (Bach flower essence)
- 1 tablespoon honey
- 9 allspice berries
- 3 cloves
- 1 tablespoon good whiskey

Add the first four ingredients to a Mason jar. Grind the spices with a mortar and pestle until fine and add them as well. Stir. Add the whiskey. Stir again. Let the mixture steep for a week on your kitchen windowsill so it can soak up the light of the sun and moon. Swirl every day. Get into a peaceful and meditative state by praying to the Goddess, saying the Lord's Prayer, or just reflecting on the light of a white candle. Prayerfully anoint your

---

68. Hyatt, *Hoodoo, Conjuration, Witchcraft, Rootwork*, 4,298.

feet with this mixture at sunrise. Put your socks or hose on inside out. Wear them all day. Let the soul healing needed to repair illness or remove roadblocks aid your success.

## 272. New Orleans Floor Wash

This formula, updated from an original Hoodoo account,[69] is extra-strength. It is bound to bring success to your business. You know what else? It is a spiritual floor wash shared by an informant from NOLA that ensures prosperity and draws success. You can't go wrong with these ingredients, so noted for their ability to produce pleasant results.

Gather these materials:

• Red brick powder

• Queen Elizabeth root, pulverized

• Cinnamon essential oil

• Van Van oil

• 9 buckets of fresh running water (from a river or stream, not tap water)

This work needs to be done on your day off, when things are nice and quiet, so no one disturbs your work. Place the last four ingredients in a nonreactive bowl. Scent it to your taste. If you feel the need for a strong cleanse, you will need more drops of cinnamon. If you want people led to your space, amp up the Van Van oil. If you desire inner strength and protection, go a bit heavier on the red brick powder. Getting the hang of it? Then add drops from the bowl to the buckets of water and use to wash the floor.

---

69. Hyatt, *Hoodoo, Conjuration, Witchcraft, Rootwork*, 711.

This is a self-designed formula for your personal needs. One size doesn't always fit all—especially not in Hoodoo.

The other element of this work is secrecy. Don't tell anyone you're doing it. Just do it!

Wash your floors with this spiritual floor wash and be prepared for some very positive changes.

## 273. Memphis Success Perfume

Let's face it, High John the Conqueror root is the strongest and most highly sought-after curio for rootwork. Luckily there are varied ways of using this root that don't require the entire root to be used as a one-off, like in this perfume, for example.

When you're going to an interview for an important role that you really want to land, perfume will come in handy. You might like to start making this perfume today, because with jobs being so uncertain, you never know when you might be needing it.

1. Carefully select your High John the Conqueror root. Make sure it calls out to you as "the one" to become a part of your work.

2. Get a Mason jar or other sterilized wide-mouthed jar, and add a small bottle of Hoyt's Cologne. This is a high-vibrational, attractive scent that is beloved in Hoodoo.

3. Put the root in the jar. Keep it there for this month at least.

4. Swirl daily to release the energy of your High John into the cologne.

5. After this month has passed and you're ready to use your perfume, use only the liquid, which will be a combination of Hoyt's kissed by High John—a strong blend indeed.

## 274. Success Mojo

I've been interviewing lately after suddenly losing my day job. It is a daunting task, and at times it makes me very nervous. It is sort of like dating. You never know whether you'll hit it off with the other person. There are so many elements that come together, some under your control and some more of a spiritual nature.

Mojo bags are wonderful little helpful collections of power. Having one on your person in your pocket, bra, or bag or tied to your leg (underneath pants) lends so much hidden support. These bags build confidence, particularly those with herbal ingredients, curios, and bodily fluids combined.

This is one such mojo bag—here referred to as a flannel. You will need these ingredients:

• Cinnamon essential oil

• Your he and she (matching lodestone pair)

• Saliva

• Red flannel

Sprinkle nine drops of cinnamon essential oil atop your he and she and the same amount on the bottoms. Spit on your he and she and tuck them inside a red flannel. This is updated from a mojo bag shared by a Hyatt informant from Waycross, Georgia.[70]

## 275. Workin' It

A notable aspect of Hoodoo is that it requires your attention. You must roll up your sleeves and be prepared to work early in the morning until late at night, as the spell or rite requires. Here

---

70. Hyatt, *Hoodoo, Conjuration, Witchcraft, Rootwork*, 4,301.

is some candle work that is to be done Monday, Wednesday, and Friday.

To start, you need a Van Van formula you love and trust. I like mine to have a bit of pyrite in it and some sort of grass, either broom straw or lemongrass. Once you have your trusted source, pour some in a crystal glass bowl. Get a large green candle and light it. Hold the candle over the Van Van while you pray for success in every aspect of your life. Burn the candle at 6:00 a.m. on Monday—all the way down. Light a new one at 9:00 p.m. on Wednesday and let that burn as you pray with full intent. On Friday at midnight, burn yet another one.

Workin' your candle magick in this way will bring prosperity, luck, and overall success. This work is inspired by a Hyatt informant from Memphis, Tennessee.[71]

## 276. Memphis Abundance Magick

This is a beautifully simply ritual you should be sure to carry out for abundance and prosperity. It is designed for times that are truly lean, when you don't have enough food for your family to eat and ways of obtaining it are not apparent.

I have found engagement with brooms and broom straw to be especially effective for bringing success where I didn't think it was even possible. Broom is mysterious and is connected to the wildest of all forces of nature.

You will need these items:

- 9 broom straws from your personal magickal broom
- A thick green column candle

---

71. Hyatt, *Hoodoo, Conjuration, Witchcraft, Rootwork*, 836.

- A new needle
- Lighter

Take the nine broom straws and break each one into nine pieces. Lay these down on a plate in a spoke shape around the green candle. Carve the words "abundance" and "food" on the candle using a new needle. Light the green candle every morning for twenty to thirty minutes, for nine mornings in a row. Now you'll never go hungry. Your family will have food and abundance will flow.

## 277. Wishing Bottle

Remember when we discussed and made a jomo during the first month? If not, please review day 30. Today you're going to make a jomo for success in your career and at work. Make a jomo full of High John the Conqueror root, with three devil's shoestring roots tied up in it. Every morning, place your jomo in a bottle of whiskey and make your wish. Then, while holding the bottle overhead, repeat the wish thrice. Next, move the wishing bottle across your chest cross-like an additional three times. Finally, put the bottle behind your back and make the wish thrice.

Your jomo is stuffed full of powerful intent, with roots renowned for their strengthening potential and the sign of the crossroads. Whiskey keeps your jomo alive, and all the spirits drawn to it are left feeling good every day.

This work takes time. Wishes don't just fall out of the sky—if only! Repeat this rite every morning (as early as possible) until your wish comes true. Concentrate, be relaxed, and stay hyperfocused.

# SECTION III
## DISTURB ME KNOT:
## SHIELDING, NOTICING &
## UNDOING NEGATIVITY

Every component of Hoodoo in all three of the sections of this book is significant. I have, however, saved one of the most critical aspects of this work for this third section of the book, "Disturb Me Knot." In this section, issues that frequently bring people into the fold of Hoodoo are found, including protection magick, justice, hexes, and unhexing.

Our world has changed drastically since the early twentieth century, when much of Hoodoo was recorded. Still, there is the primal wish to stay safe and protected and be treated fairly. Sadly, as time goes on, many of us are treated increasingly unfairly, and that's where Hoodoo's strength is reaffirmed.

In this section you will do lengthy work that takes a week or longer to complete. This is due to the serious nature of the issues covered. There will also be your usual daily work. The overall goal of section 3 is to help you build confidence in yourself, your world, and your place within it. With that confidence you will have the strength to undo negativity placed in your path and in the paths of those you care for. We finish this book going through some negative and heady subject matter with the hope that in the end your light will shine even brighter than you could have imagined.

# CHAPTER 10
# PROTECTION MAGICK:
# DAYS 278-306

Since the beginning of time, people have been concerned with their own safety and the safety of their homes and families. We can see evidence of this in history books and in the beautiful and effective weaponry displayed in museums.

Worldwide spending on security technology is projected to reach $91 billion in 2018.[72] Security is a concern at the forefront of our minds, to say the least, and collectively we are willing to pay billions of dollars just for a sense of safety.

A hundred or so years ago, when much of Hoodoo lore was collected, there was still a desire for protection, with some spells, rites, and tricks even utilizing gunpowder and its components, such as saltpeter. The beautiful thing about Hoodoo, however, is within it we go beyond a reliance on conventional weaponry. In this section we'll delve deep into the psychic warfare against spiritual harm placed in foot tracks and the numerous ways those enveloped with evil create unnatural illness. We will not

---

72. International Data Corporation.

dwell in negativity or try to get into the mindset of those who seek to do harm.

Hoodoo presents a holistic approach to war. We are well aware that our enemies sometimes seek to attack our minds, bodies, and spirits using herbs, curios, incantations, and chants. These harmful inflictions will be addressed in the very last chapter, which focuses in on unhexing and banishing. This chapter provides you with ways to participate in the Hoodoo's holistic world of protection magick.

## 278. Devil at Your Feet

While I am not at all religious, I am deeply spiritual. Still, being that there is such a large volume of work in Christianity, I will consult it when need be. Psalms are especially helpful. I have also found out that angels, chiefly archangels, are nondenominational. They will come to those who speak directly to them. We begin this month's work with the archangel of protection—Michael. Michael is buff, tawny, and beautiful by most standards in painted and sculpted depictions. His brawny muscles are capable of shouldering any of your fears, for his existence centers around protection.

I have Doreen Virtue's deck of angel cards. I keep them close by. They are very helpful in my daily life. Just this morning I tried one of her Michael affirmations, and sure enough I felt his warmth at my back. The sensation was penetrating and soothing. You truly don't need any sort of special mode of communication when it comes to Michael—just an open, honest call to him will do nicely.

One of Michael's symbols is his powerful sword. This sword is used to slay your enemies and keep them, in the Hoodoo's way of phrasing, "underfoot." We love this imagery, and it ties into foot track magick.

Michael helps with protection of your job security. He helps support your stability and inner strength, possessions, vehicles, and so forth. If you call to him using the words that come to you from spirit, he will come. Warmth will be felt at your back, just as it was when I sat here and wrote these words. You'll know it's him because the type of heat felt will be enveloping, kind, and gentle.

Beyond the sword, Michael is seen with a bright purple light around him, and he is the bringer of the heat needed to make change in various situations.

Take a moment right now and call to Michael in the following way:

*Michael, I seek out your presence today.*
*I ask for your protection in every aspect of my daily life.*
*Come forward and let me bask in your soul-fortifying heat*
*and purple light.*

If you feel this heat anywhere on your body after calling out to Michael you'll know he is with you and you are henceforth protected. Another way to make contact is to randomly find a feather on your path, which may have fallen from his back. If people drop out of your life once he enters it, rest assured that he is clearing them and their negativity out of your way. You don't need those folks. Finally, going forward this month, listen for the name Michael being used (by a waiter, teacher, new colleague, relative, or whoever). When you hear that name or have people with it drop into your life, you'll know you are protected by the might and love of this special archangel.

## 279. Michael Altar Rite

Today, here is another way to engage and invite Michael into your life, building on the observations and affirmation from yesterday.

Purchase an image of Michael. This may be an image on a candle or a small statue.

Obtain a purple and a white candle. Put these tapers in silver candleholders on a silver or white plate.

Set out small crystal bowls of holy water in the four corners of your room.

Before 6:30 a.m., burn the candles while saying this:

*Michael, I call to you with genuine spirit and an open heart.*
*Guide me where I should go.*
*Keep me safe.*
*Shield me from all that is harmful.*

Wash your hands in the holy water and say the prayer again. Repeat once more so that you have done this ritual three times.

## 280. Child's Protection Charms

There is nothing more painful than when harm is brought to your child, or someone else's, for that matter. Innocents need to be protected until they can do so for themselves. Devil's shoestring is a rootworker's charm that is perfectly suited to keeping harm from coming to young ones.

1. It is thought that babies cry at times because they are frightened by negative-energy spirits.

2. To protect a baby or toddler from evil spirits, tie a piece of devil's shoestring around their neck—only while you have

your eyes on them the entire time. This will drive away evil.

3. When a child is teething, devil's shoestring is there to help as well. Sucking and chewing on the root is soothing.

## 281. Old Conjure Man's Curio Outfit

Old is hip, sage, and new again in the case of this outfit. Listen to the wisdom of the ages. There are oldies but goodies that we return to repeatedly as Hoodoos. This curio outfit, inspired by one in a King Novelty catalog, is no exception, for it brings together lodestones, horseshoe nails, and Hoyt's Cologne to deliver results.

Apart from the potency of the other ingredients used here, lodestones deserve your attention. They are emblems of security and talismans against evil that allow you to say goodbye to an enemy's tricks and be free from the influence of evil intent. Protected by this bag, you are assured to have vitality and good health.

Gather these items:

• 2 carefully selected lodestones (charged in salt)

• A red flannel

• 2 horseshoe nails to which you are drawn

• A thimbleful of Hoyt's Cologne

Charge your lodestones by burying them in a mound of salt. Leave them that way for three days, then remove them from the mound. Brush off the salt so hardly any is remaining. Put them in the red flannel, along with the horseshoe nails. Pour the

Hoyt's Cologne inside the flannel, as soul food to nurture the magickal potential held, bringing it to life

This collection of curios that are well known for their strength will bring protection to your life while warding off evil influences. It will also bring good luck to its respectful owner.

## 282. Drive Away Evil:
## Recitation with Incense Burning: Psalm 4 (Day1)

The unpredictable nature of evil makes it a great source of unhappiness and worry, which creates space for mistakes to take root. Making a simple altar on which you can burn sweet, uplifting incense, such as frankincense, brings about happiness and positivity. There are several psalms that Hoodoos utilize to drive away evil. Without evil influences you are largely safe from harm.

Over the next three days, say the following psalms with a clear heart and strong intention. Do not rush this. Say one psalm for each day while tending to your sacred altar.

Today, lay down a white cloth, set up your brass-colored censer, and light a few small charcoals inside it. Sprinkle some ground frankincense from a spoon onto the charcoal. Then recite Psalm 4:

### Psalm 4

Hear me when I call, O God of my righteousness: thou hast enlarged me when I was in distress; have mercy upon me, and hear my prayer.

O ye sons of men, how long will ye turn my glory into shame? How long will ye love vanity, and seek after leasing? Selah.

But know that the Lord hath set apart him that is godly for himself: the Lord will hear when I call unto him.

Stand in awe, and sin not: commune with your own heart upon your bed, and be still. Selah.

Offer the sacrifices of righteousness, and put your trust in the Lord.

There be many that say, Who will shew us any good? Lord, lift thou up the light of thy countenance upon us.

Thou hast put gladness in my heart, more than in the time that their corn and their wine increased.

I will both lay me down in peace, and sleep: for thou, Lord, only makest me dwell in safety.

### 283. Smiling Meditation: Psalm 8 (Day 2)

Today, light some fresh incense and meditate. Set out a handwritten version of Psalm 8 (see days 254–255).

Your incense should be airy and light. I suggest an uplifting Nag Champa stick or a 2:1 homemade ground version of frankincense and myrrh. You will want to use ⅔ frankincense because it is ethereal and connects us to the heavens, whereas myrrh is more grounding and connected to the earth.

This is a type of meditation that works well with the burning of your uplifting incense. It takes you into positive and strengthening territory, even if you are feeling down or weak. Sit in a comfortable place, preferably outside. Breathe slowly and rhythmically, 6–8 counts in and 6–8 counts to exhale. On the exhale, push away negative and bad vibes out from the soles of your feet and through your chest, throat, and mouth. Meanwhile, on the inhale, smile as you conjure a collection of pleasant memories with each breath.

Soon enough you will find yourself anticipating each inhalation, with its bolstering happiness, while appreciating the opportunity to cast off darkness through your exhalations.

Wiggle your toes and fingers to bring yourself back to the physical plane. Open your eyes slowly after about ten minutes. Take about five slow, deep cleansing breaths, focusing your eyes on Psalm 8 before you. Read this out loud three times, soaking in the significance and spiritual meaning of the words.

## 284. Continue Your Reflection and Prayer: Psalm 10 (Day 3)

Once again, light a beautifully fragrant incense. This will aid the high spiritual vibration of your work.

### Psalm 10

Why standest thou afar off, O Lord? Why hidest thou thyself in times of trouble?

The wicked in his pride doth persecute the poor: let them be taken in the devices that they have imagined.

For the wicked boasteth of his heart's desire, and blesseth the covetous, whom the Lord abhorreth.

The wicked, through the pride of his countenance, will not seek after God: God is not in all his thoughts.

His ways are always grievous; thy judgments are far above out of his sight: as for all his enemies, he puffeth at them.

He hath said in his heart, I shall not be moved: for I shall never be in adversity.

His mouth is full of cursing and deceit and fraud: under his tongue is mischief and vanity.

He sitteth in the lurking places of the villages: in the secret places doth he murder the innocent: his eyes are privily set against the poor.

He lieth in wait secretly as a lion in his den: he lieth in wait to catch the poor: he doth catch the poor, when he draweth him into his net.

He croucheth, and humbleth himself, that the poor may fall by his strong ones.

He hath said in his heart, God hath forgotten: he hideth his face; he will never see it.

Arise, O Lord; O God, lift up thine hand: forget not the humble.

Wherefore doth the wicked contemn God? He hath said in his heart, Thou wilt not require it.

Thou hast seen it; for thou beholdest mischief and spite, to requite it with thy hand: the poor committeth himself unto thee; thou art the helper of the fatherless.

Break thou the arm of the wicked and the evil man: seek out his wickedness till thou find none.

The Lord is King for ever and ever: the heathen are perished out of his land.

Lord, thou hast heard the desire of the humble: thou wilt prepare their heart, thou wilt cause thine ear to hear:

To judge the fatherless and the oppressed, that the man of the earth may no more oppress.

## 285. Mighty Hand

Mighty hand is a deceptively simple mojo, updated from one marketed years ago in a King Novelty catalog, that provides a wide variety of helpful fortification. It contains High John the

Conqueror root, which you know by now is one of the Hoodoo rootworker's strongest and most protective tools. It has the drawing power, in an assortment of areas, of the he and she's realm. To catch your luck and manipulate it, you'll notice that this hand contains salep root, also known as lucky hand root. To help you see the world more clearly, it contains Van Van oil. Finally, it has devil's shoestring to keep the devil at bay and trip him up.

To create a mighty hand, gather these items:

- High John the Conqueror root (male)
- A matching pair of lodestones (your he and she)
- An intact salep root, if possible (otherwise, do the best you can)
- 5 pieces devil's shoestring
- Red flannel
- Van Van oil

Add the first four curios and roots to your flannel, concentrating on the qualities of each. Sprinkle some Van Van oil onto the bag. Now you have a mighty hand to do your bidding.

### 286. Buckeye Health Plan

If you are craving health, prosperity, and safety, you'll need to add this bit of tree medicine to your repertoire. It is called a buckeye.

Since this month is devoted to protection, it's a good idea to deploy this nut as a guardian. Buckeye also aids in the following:

- Brings good luck
- Helps your money matters
- Brings luck in games of chance and gambling
- Wards off evil
- Restores health by bringing about healing

For these purposes, carry buckeye in a flannel or in your pocket as a magickal charm for protection of a variety of sorts. When you are in need of a luck boost or feel like ramping up your protection, simply put your fingers to the buckeye in your pocket and rub and twirl the smooth nut between your fingers.

## 287. Dragon's Blood Incense

Dragon's blood sounds mysterious and powerful, and it is. If only we could obtain the actual blood of a dragon! Who knows what mystery and power it would hold. Rather than being the blood of a dragon, this is a resin from a type of rattan palm tree originally from Southeast Asia.

Resin is the compressed, readily usable essence of a tree, capable of delivering valuable tree medicine. This substance should be used mindfully and with great respect for the trees from whence it comes. Resin (such as dragon's blood) literally protects the trees from which it is rendered, and helps them heal. This is one of the reasons it is such a respected substance in our magick.

Dragon's blood incense has many different uses in Hoodoo, one of which is protection. We also believe it can be used to bring peace and happiness to the home, body, mind, and spirit.[73] The scent is deeply earthy but with some musky patchouli-like notes.

Seek out some dragon's blood resin today. Add the smaller chunks to your censer, containing bamboo charcoal, or grind it first with a mortar and pestle for a powder that produces a smoother burning incense. To amp it up a bit, add floral notes by crumbling rose petals into powdered dragon's blood, and to lighten, burn it along with amber.

## 288. Protection from People

People are complex. They are capable of incredibly deep and abiding love as well as horrendous acts of violent destruction. You'll be comforted to know that in Hoodoo you can take matters of protection into your own hands. With a good rag and strong herbs, you can find shelter. We have many different types of mojo bags, for example, that enable you to proactively strengthen your being from harm.

This is a particularly strong-smelling and effective protection mojo.[74] Use it for especially dicey situations and when in the presence of people known to be very dark in their intentions.

Get three sticks of asafoetida and wrap them in a black cloth, called a black rag by early Hoodoo informants. This black rag will serve as your mojo, so make sure it is strong and serviceable. Increase this rag's efficacy even further by praying or saying an invocation, to invoke deity to come forward. Feed this protection mojo one week with chamber lye and the next week with whiskey. Feeding, of course, keeps the bag happy and reinforces its inherent powers.

---

73. *King Novelty Company Curio Catalog*, n.d.

74. Hyatt, *Hoodoo, Conjuration, Witchcraft, Rootwork*, 414.

## 289. A Week of Shielding (Day 1)

Physically, spiritually, and metaphysically, the world is a dangerous place. You can live joyfully and without fear, however, if you are properly prepared. To prepare for all forms of treachery that might arise, I suggest shielding yourself. Over the next week, we will explore various ways you can add Hoodoo shields to your everyday apparel—your personal protection.

- As you prepare yourself for any type of warfare, consider the numerous spiritual baths we've worked with. Many are protective.

- Certain colors are protective:

  Red is a power color beloved by Hoodoos, as evidenced by the pervasive use of the red flannel to create mojo bags.

  White is a color the ancestors and positive spirits find attractive.

  Black is a good color to make yourself invisible to harmful people.

  Brown aligns you with animal spirit energy.

- Mojo bags of the various types we will explore over the next few days are very important additions to your squad of protectors.

- Remember your foot track magick and how you learned to be observant of your daily path? This is a type of magick specific to Hoodoo that is extremely helpful to you if you suspect you are under attack, so utilize your knowledge!

## 290. Shielding (Day 2): No Harm Mojo Bag

There is no need to long for no harm to come to you. You can take matters into your own hands. This is a "no harm" mojo bag inspired by the account of a Hyatt informant from Charleston, South Carolina. It has been respectfully updated. Follow these steps exactly. Use the mojo for your personal protection.

Gather these items:

- 3 dimes
- Graveyard dust
- Elder bark, flowers, or root
- 3 matches
- 3 new pins
- River or rainwater
- Gunpowder
- Dark cloth

Take the dimes to your preferred cemetery. Pay the graveyard for your protection. (Leave dimes on the premises respectfully). Gather some graveyard dust and elder bark, flowers, or root. Once you return home, use three matches to light a fire either on your gas stove or outside in a barbeque pit with kindling and charcoal. If working outdoors, use a cauldron or a caste-iron Dutch oven. Boil the graveyard dirt and elder with a bit of river or rainwater. Mix this with gunpowder. Strain and sew the wet remnants into some dark cloth. Put this cloth in your mojo bag. Wear it either around your neck (tucked into your shirt/dress) or tied around your waist, underneath your clothing.

### 291. Shielding (Day 3): Magical Cloth Spell

Previously you engaged with coins and spent a week working pennies (beginning on day 245). Today we return to penny work. Did you ever imagine there were so many things to do with these seemingly useless coins? This is a magickal cloth spell inspired by the account of a Wyatt informant from Savannah, Georgia, and updated for contemporary practice.

Pennies capture the attention of the ancestors and spirits around you. It is a way of employing them to help you. So try this simple way to make a cloth imbued with their magick.

Get yourself a new piece of cloth. Soak it in a glass of lightning water for about an hour. While the cloth is soaking, return to your coin collection. Find a beautiful penny—perhaps an Indian Head, if you have one, or one with a date that is special. Squeeze out the cloth. Open it. Breathe your magickal intent and power into the cloth. Work on this for a least a half hour. Bring your cloth to life and implore it to do your biding. Next, put a penny in the middle of it. Using a brand-new needle and white thread, sew it up. Put this around your neck or waist. You will be protected from harm.

### 292. Shielding (Day 4): Coin and Foot Track Magick

Again, we are engaging your coin collection. Today, you are going to go to your jar of coins, mindfully. Sit with your coins for a while. Breathe intently into the collection. Take breaks. Remain relaxed. Talk with them about your concern for your safety or that of others.

Which shoes do you wear the most? Pull them out and bring them to the area in which you are working. You know by now that coin and foot track magick go hand in hand.

Your shoes are deeply imprinted with your power, will, intentions, and way of being in the world. You'll need some steel dust and High John the Conqueror root powder.

Sprinkle these two potent powders in the soles of your shoes, but only on the heel parts. Next, fish out two Mercury dimes, or take your time and find the oldest pair of dimes you can. Put the dimes under the soles of your shoes.

Another way to do this is to drill a hole into the dime and then string it. Tie this around your ankle and wear it as a protection anklet. However you do it, this is a well-respected way of harnessing foot track and coin magick for protection from ill-meaning people.

## 293. Shielding (Day 5): Protective Flannel

You're getting it by now—Hoodoo uses numerology, special days, special numbers, colors, directions, and curios to do the trick when it comes to protection. Here is a fairly easy-to-make flannel derived from traditional Hoodoo days, numbers, and curios. It is designed to keep you out of harm's way.

1. On the next Friday from today, get a new sewing needle.

2. Break it into three parts.

3. Sprinkle magnetic sand onto your lodestone pair (your he and she) that were previously fed whiskey and left to dry.

4. Attach each part of the needle to a lodestone, using the attachment quality of the magnetic sand.

5. Put this all in a red flannel.

Carry this with you however you can, such as in a bag or your pocket.

Now you're safe. No one can do you any harm with their Hoodoo or Voodoo.

## 294. Shielding (Day 6): High John Protection Mojo

However much you think you know about Hoodoo, make sure you don't forget about the plethora of curios at your disposal. There are plenty, but often we come back to the celebrated one: High John the Conqueror root. When you are in a precarious or dangerous situation, your well-fed High John can be invited to protect you.

This protection mojo is simple and very effective. High John is the preferred curio for rootwork involving the need for strength, courage, reinforcement, and protection. Charging it through feeding it Hoyt's Cologne ensures that your root will be enabled to do what is asked of it.

The only additional aspect you will notice about this hand is that it profits from the mystical power of a trinity, such as Maiden, Mother, and Crone or Father, Son, and Holy Ghost. You can insert the trinity with which you relate strongly as you create this protection mojo.

Take three pieces of High John the Conqueror root and soak them in Hoyt's Cologne in a glass bowl overnight, outdoors or on the windowsill. Lay them on a towel to dry slightly, then turn them over to blot dry the other side.

Add these to a red flannel, with reverence and respect for the herbs' potency.

Now you have a surefire way to keep yourself safe from harm.

### 295. Shielding (Day 7):Take an Inventory of Your Mojos

As you've seen, mojo bags, flannels, hands, tobies, jomos, nation sacks, etc., are wonderful shields in your daily life. It is important to keep your mojos undercover most of the time, as has been mentioned. Today is a day dedicated to taking an inventory of your mojos and how they work best for you.

Each type of work calls for you to wear or carry your bag in a certain place. Always stay mindful of those directions.

Here are some ways to have your mojo on your person:

- Hanging from your waist, beneath your clothes
- Hanging from your waist, outside your clothing
- Cross-body
- In your purse, backpack, or briefcase
- Tied around your knee area, preferably beneath your trousers
- Tucked in your pocket, over your heart
- Hanging from your neck above or below your heart
- Tucked in your bra (nation sack)
- Inside a chamois
- Hung from a nail (less commonly)

Think about the answers to these questions:

- So far, as you've traveled through the year, in which ways have you carried around your bag?
- What types of bags have you used in these various ways?
- Which type of bag is most effective for your work?
- What were/are the most memorable results yielded from your mojos?

## 296. Hoodoo Gardening: Blacksnake Plant

Blacksnake is commonly called black cohosh outside of Hoodoo circles, so you may have it in your garden already, and as an herbalist you might be familiar with it. Its botanical name is *Actaea racemosa.*

Blacksnake plants are native to the East Coast of the United States, all the way south to Georgia and west to Missouri and Arkansas. It grows well in zones 3–8, in a variety of woodland habits. It is also found in openings in the woods.

Blacksnake is a smooth herbaceous perennial plant that has compound leaves stemming from an underground rhizome and root. The leaves grow as large as three feet three inches. The flowers can grow up to eight feet tall and are lightly clustered, as well as being considered unpleasant in fragrance by many. The white flower spires are attractive, set against a dark background, which also sets off the fernlike, dark-green foliage. The height of the plant is 4–6 feet, and it needs to be planted 2–4 feet away from other plants or trees. It prefers acidic soil that is kept moist and fertile. The plant needs a medium amount of water. It is resistant to deer and rabbits. This herb is also noninvasive. It must have attention each week to ensure moist soil. If the soil dries out, the leaves might scorch and be unpleasant-looking.

Blacksnake grows slowly. It is also called bugbane because of its natural insect-repelling qualities.

## 297. Black Snakeroot Charm

People of various cultures have used blacksnake rhizome (which is referred to as a root) medicinally, including African Americans, Native Americans, and people with European heritage. It is used for female gynecological complaints, particularly during perimenopause and menopause. It has also shown promise in treating depression.

In Hoodoo, black snakeroot is well thought of for its protective abilities, among other magickal qualities, such as serving as a roadblock to prevent evil from entering your home. I suggest you add it to your Hoodoo garden for its showy quality and multiple magickal, visual/spiritual, and mundane uses.

If you buy a bare-root plant, be mindful about where you plant it. It would be nice to plant three plants, and the trio would make a wonderful show in your garden or wooded area. Once your blacksnake plants are well established, you can tap the rhizome occasionally to be used in your Hoodoo practice.

An easy-to-create charm would be carrying some black snakeroot in your pocket. You might also like to use the power of knots by tying six knots on a long, strong string from which your bit of blacksnake rhizome hangs. This charm can be used for the following purposes:

- To keep other people's ill will from bothering you
- To make it safer for you to venture into wild spaces and woods
- When you feel a need for protection

### 298. Cork Protection Amulet

Cork is at the heart of this protection amulet, and why not? There are numerous ways cork is able to protect itself. Let's first think about cork as a tree medicine. It is the outer bark of *Quercus suber*, meaning "cork oak." This tree grows predominantly in Southwestern Europe and Northwest Africa, specifically Portugal, Spain, France, Italy, Algeria, Morocco, and Tunisia. Portugal is where the tree flourishes, and the Portuguese are the leaders in its growth.

We are bringing cork into our discussion about protection magick because it is a protection master. It is one of the very last trees to ignite in massive forest fires. In its everyday existence, it is lashed by sandy and salty wind, but it lives on. It has very low conductivity to heat, sound, and vibration. The outer bark is used to make cork products every nine to ten years. The tree regenerates numerous times and lives to be about two hundred years old. Its qualities are lightness, immunity, shielding, stopping, buoyancy, resistance, and renewability. Think about these qualities and how cork helps all flora and fauna around it in nature as you make your protective amulet.

This amulet was shared by a Hyatt informant from Jacksonville, Florida.

You'll need these items:

- A new gold eye needle
- A bottle cork
- String

Push the needle through the cork. Put enough string through the cork so you can wear a low-hanging amulet necklace that hangs right below your heart. Thanks to the impervious nature of cork, you will be protected from the elements, and evil intentions as well.

## 299. Tree Magick (Hickory)

Trees are one of my favorite things. I like them and respect their ashe so much that I wrote an entire book dedicated to them called *A Healing Grove*. The wood of trees warm us; it can also be prepared in such a way in Hoodoo that it fortifies and heals. Tree bark, roots, berries, pods, leaves, and flowers all have unique possibilities. When it comes to Hoodoo medicine, healing, and magickal rites, as well as spells, it's hard to find a more diverse resource than the tree. Never mistake them for being ordinary. Also listen to their messages, observe them, and feed and preserve them in your neighborhood, land, or city.

Hickory trees grow in many different areas of the United States. They are a strong, hardy tree, with resins within the bark that lend a wonderful flavor to food. In the spring, the sapling can be used in your Hoodoo for protection.

Scan the tree visually and see which springy, young part of it calls out to you. Twist this limb, tying it around itself. On the bit that is a loose, use your knife to create a point. Stick the pointed end in the ground. Now you are protected and can consider yourself safe from meddling, interference, and harm.

## 300. Herbal Kingdom's Protection

Knowing more about plant-based medicine and lore will help you become more secure in the world. From the use of herbal remedies for common illnesses to the fortification you gain against spiritual illnesses resulting from your engagement in the plant world, you will find yourself growing sounder each day.

Our world is growing increasingly more artificial. This is noticeable in the places where we live and work, our modes of travel, the manipulation of the foods we eat before we even take them home, and even the substances we drink. This is not the Hoodoo's way, however.

Hoodoo asks you to return your attention to the simplicity of nature. Once you do so, you will notice that certain plants and animals make you feel fortified, peaceful, or strengthened as a warrior.

Here are three different methods to engage natural medicine in the Hoodoo way for your daily protection:

1. Drill a hole in a nutmeg. String it up and wear it around your neck. With the help of nutmeg, you will feel strong and it will be very difficult for others to harm you with bad juju.

2. Drill a hole through an acorn and string it on strong material. Acorns protect you from evil.

3. Burn red onion peels with a pinch of sulphur until nothing is left but ash. (Do this with the door closed.) If you wear this ash in your shoes for your foot track magick, no one can harm you with their Hoodoo.

## 301. Curio of Note: Gourds

Previously you learned about planting and growing gourds in the Hoodoo garden. I hope that felt good to your spirit and was helpful. Isn't it good to know that these gnarly and multifaceted vegetables have many more uses than simply being Halloween decorations?

Gourds are symbolic of our deep connection to the ancestors. They are very useful on altars, in soaps (luffa), and as kitchen utensils, to name just a few of their applications.

### Preparing Gourds for Ritual and Ceremony

Wash your gourd(s) in warm, soapy water to which 12–14 drops of tea tree oil have been added. Wash the gourds well with a sea sponge or clean rag. This will remove the types of soil-borne bacteria that cause the gourds to quickly decompose. Place them on old towels or newsprint (newspaper without the print) in a warm, dry place. Continue to turn daily and replace the towels or newsprint with dry material for a week. Turn the gourds regularly so they air out on all sides.

Now that your surface is dry, cut off the top of the gourd with a very sharp chef's knife or electric carving knife. Pull out any loose matter using a fork. Do this gently so as not to tear the outer surface. Be very meticulous.

The last stage of preparation includes preserving, disinfecting, and more drying. Wipe the gourd inside and out with pure tea tree oil applied to a soft rag. Put the gourds atop more newsprint or fresh towels in a clean, dry place for an additional month. Turn each one occasionally. Now the gourds are preserved, and you can wax them by melting beeswax pastilles in a double boiler or microwave until fluid or apply furniture wax. Brush the wax on the inside and outside of the gourd with a soft cloth and then polish it. This will help preserve it further. Do this last step every other month.

If you are feeling unhealthy in any sort of way, drink your various medicinal teas out of a hollowed-out gourd. Remember, gourds are protective of you, your home, and your possessions. Keep the connection between your ancestors and your practice alive through engagement with gourds.

## 302. Hoodoo Gardening: Rattlesnake Master

The next few days are dedicated to rattlesnake master. While there are several plants with "rattlesnake" in their name, *Liatris squarrosa* is the type I'm going to discuss here, as it is highlighted by a Hyatt informant from Brunswick, Georgia. *Squarrosa* is derived from the Latin *squarros*, meaning scaly or rough, and we can interpret that as snakelike for our purposes.

Rattlesnake master is native to the east coastal regions of the United States and grows abundantly in the coastal Piedmont states. This is a tough plant. I've grown it for years, and it returns despite our harsh Chicago winters. It grows from a half foot to 2 ½ feet tall and should be planted 6–18 inches away from other plants.

This wildflower delights in sunny spaces. The plant is attractive to bees and butterflies, adding to the overall effectiveness and beauty of your Hoodoo garden. It also attracts hummingbirds, with their many mystical qualities.

It is a fast grower and will grow well in a drier location than others of its species. The profuse though odd flowers bloom from July to September. Start this plant from bare root or seeds.

### 303. Rattlesnake Master Bottle

For protection, add some dried, cleaned-off rattlesnake master root to a bottle filled with Hoyt's Cologne. Cap it with the connected screw top or spring top. Put this on a shelf for a full cycle of the moon, checking on it occasionally. Swirl it to release the potent root into the cologne. Feed this potion from your bottle to your mojo bags, apply it to your clothing, or spray it lightly onto the body. With this potion from the rattlesnake master bottle on you, no one can harm you, according to a Hyatt informant from Brunswick, Georgia.[75]

---

75. Hyatt, *Hoodoo, Conjuration, Witchcraft, Rootwork*.

## 304. Rattlesnake Master Toby

One of the most helpful aspects of Hoodoo is that it addresses specific concerns as well as general ones. Within protection magick, for example, there is protection of property, children, possessions, employment, and relationships.

But Hoodoo doesn't stop there. We must go into wild spaces, brush, and bush, places others would dare not enter. You need inner courage for such movements, as well as a bit of help from the herbal kingdom.

Rattlesnake master can ward off snakes and other varmints in the woods. You need to go into the woods for reflection to connect with trees and to forage for your magickal herbs. Here is a toby to assist with your journey. [76]

### Toby Construction

- High John the Conqueror root
- Rattlesnake master (dried)
- Red flannel square or chamois cloth (small)
- A silver dime
- Lodestone(s)
- Thread and needle

Take a small piece of High John the Conqueror root and a pinch of dried rattlesnake master and place on a red flannel or a piece of chamois cloth. Add to this a dime and a lodestone (a single one or a he and she). Sew this up to form your toby.

---

76. Hyatt, *Hoodoo, Conjuration, Witchcraft, Rootwork.*

Don't let anyone touch this and it will protect you from snakes.

### 305. Curio of Note: Saltpeter

Comb through the annals of traditional Hoodoo and you are bound to come across the spiritual ingredient called saltpeter. It goes further back than Hoodoo, into the area of alchemy. Its first known use was during the fourteenth century BCE.

The name saltpeter sounds unusual, but it is another name for potassium nitrate. In some circles it is called Chinese salt, Chinese snow, nitrate of potash. It is a common compound with the chemical formula $KNO_3$.

Since you need saltpeter in your Hoodoo practice, it's good to know how it will look when it arrives. It should be a white powder or white crystalline solid. Keep in mind that magnesium nitrate and calcium nitrate are sometimes referred to as "saltpeter," although they do not have the same chemical composition as pure saltpeter, or potassium nitrate.

Saltpeter is the principle ingredient in gunpowder, which consists of saltpeter, charcoal, and sulphur. It is used as a food preservative and is an additive to fertilizer. It helps fireworks and rockets oxidize as well. Saltpeter is used in soaks and baths. It is appreciated for its protective qualities.

### 306. Perfumed Crystals

Salt is a substance we use daily to flavor and preserve food. It is also a wonderful ingredient in healing spiritual baths. In Hoodoo, salt has a holy connection to the divine. Here is a way to defeat evil spirits that may be lurking in your home by using salts.

Perfumed crystals are a type of salt sprinkled about the home. This blend of salt, herbs, and essential oils is designed to drive away evil spirits and bring luck, prosperity, abundance, and overall success.

To a glass bowl, add the following ingredients:

- 1 cup pink (Himalayan) salt crystals of a medium grind
- 1 cup medium grind sea salt
- ⅓ cup crumbled (dried) rose petals
- ¼ cup crumbled (dried) five-finger grass
- ¼ cup (pulverized dried) lemon verbena
- 9 drops rose oil (absolute is fine)
- 9 drops vetiver essential oil
- 9 drops cinnamon essential oil

Mix the ingredients well. Put in a sterilized wide-mouth jar with a spring top or screw top. (Make sure every surface is clean and completely dry.) Let steep for 4–6 weeks, shaking occasionally.

After the mixture has matured into a complexly scented sprinkling salt, disperse the crystals in the four corners of your rooms, hallways, and dresser drawers.

## Chapter 11

# JUSTICE JOBS: DAYS 307-335

When it comes to justice, injustice, and black folk (who were the primary informants and shapers of traditional Hoodoo), where do we begin and where must we stop? This is a very dense and loaded topic for our community. The need for justice and to be treated fairly weighs heavily upon us at the time of the writing of this book and seemingly forever.

The quest for justice was at first intimately tied to our desire to be freed from enslavement. We also wanted justice served for being enslaved in the first place. Through and since colonialism, we have turned to the arts, especially music. We've sung our Negro spirituals and gospel songs, and vented and celebrated through the blues, jazz, and R&B. Now, with hip hop, we trudge onward with our quest for justice for the brutality and unfairness perpetrated against us.

Incarceration is a separate though similar arm of justice. The statistics of how many black folk are on lockdown in the United States compared to our actual population is terribly skewed. Do we want justice when it comes to the law? And how!

The old folks who set the tone for Hoodoo wanted justice of every type, and they took matters into their own hands. Though the immediate circumstances may look different through the lens of time, the basic need and desire are the same. We have been oppressed and treated unfairly by the justice system, yet we persist in seeking our piece of the American dream.

During this eleventh month of work, we are going to explore justice rites, tricks, spells, jobs, and candlemancy inspired by traditional work and updated for today's concerns. To that end, we will engage in the art of making mojos, talismans, and amulets, plus invocations and prayers, mainly from the Psalms of David.

After reading this and working your way through the month, physically, mentally, and spiritually, you will gain knowledge of a wide array of methods for seeking justice and dealing with the justice system using Hoodoo magick and spells. With this information in your repertoire, you can help yourself and others, regardless of race or ethnicity.

## 307. Justice of the People: Noticing

During the development of traditional Hoodoo, black men, women, and children, for that matter, were treated unfairly by the legal system. Laws and even the Constitution of the United States denied basic rights and humanity to a large group of people. This was further aggravated by vigilantes like the Ku Klux Klan. Out of a spirit of self-determination, so present in Hoodoo, people sought justice and found ways of dealing with laws using their knowledge and beliefs in herbalism, animism, metallurgy, candlemancy, and the elements. Hoodoos were after their own type of justice, both unique and powerful.

As you move through this month's work, get your Hoodoo journal out, and notice the following:

- Reflect on how the past informs the present.
- Observe the persistent need for justice, from the past to the present.
- What do you see happening today that is bothering you about the legal system or in terms of justice?
- What would you like to change and in what way?
- Think about the positive forms of expression and movements (of the past and present) that work toward change.
- As a Hoodoo, how do you think you can use your presence and will to make this a better world?

## 308. Keep Police Away

Folklore and remedies abound for keeping the police away from homes and businesses. You'll notice that in this ritual, invocation is combined with metallurgy, coin magick, and numerology to keep the po po (police officers) at bay. Without being judgmental of the reasons someone might want their place of residence or shop clear of officers, I present this possibility, inspired by a Hyatt informant from Tampa, Florida.

### *Preparation*

1. Get a drill with a very small jewelry bit.
2. Gather four pennies of various ages, including an Indian Head penny. (Use a clamp to hold the pennies, if possible.)
3. Bring out a good-weight, small hammer and four nails.

Do you have the need to keep the law away from you while you work some things out? If so, focus on your intention to obtain this goal. Meditate for about ten minutes, working hard to clear all thoughts about the past or future from your head. Concentrate on being present. Once you have gathered the required materials, done your prep work, and meditated, you are ready to begin:

1. Place each penny in a clamp/vice.

2. Drill a hole in the center of each penny.

3. As you drill through the first penny, say this affirmation:

*This time is mine.*

Second penny:

*This space is mine.*

Third one:

*Officers of the law, see my goodness and light shine.*

Fourth penny:

*See not my wrongs, only my engagement with the divine.*

## 309. Law, Be on My Side Candle Spell

People make mistakes. If you feel you've made one and you need to catch a break, try this black candle spell.

Dress in all black, from top to bottom. Take a brisk walk, if you are able; otherwise, try meditation to clear your mind. During the walk, go as fast as you can. Work up your energy. See and feel yourself reversing the course of your actions. This will show itself through your perspiration. The distance doesn't matter. It's all about the effort.

Gather these materials:

• A clean white shirt

• A black candle with a fireproof burner

• Olive oil

• 6-inch square of brown paper

• Lighter or matches

1. Take off your shirt when you get home and put on a dry white one.

2. Get a black candle.

3. Anoint it with holy (olive) oil. Rub it from middle to the top and middle to the bottom. Put the candle in a fireproof burner.

4. On a clean sheet of brown paper, write "judge" and police officer's names using a #2 pencil.

5. Put this paper underneath the candle burner, facing upward.

6. Before the court case or trial, light the candle for thirty hours exactly.

This will encourage police to be on your side. The judge should dismiss the case.

### 310. Clear Me Mojo and Bottle (Day 1)

Hoodoo bottles can hold some mighty strong mojo. Think about it: In a bottle, you are allowing a special group of ingredients that have been prayed over and blessed to meld together. From the numerous individual parts comes a powerful new whole. Pairing this power object with another well-loved strong medicine, like the mojo bag, makes it all the stronger. This bottle/bag combo is even more effective because it contains your will, elements of the crossroads, steel, saltpeter, and the aspect of time, coupled with numerology.

When someone you care for is locked up in the penitentiary and you believe it is unjust, you'll need a heavy-duty mojo and bottle pair containing formidable enough juju to help the situation change. For them, you'll need the following components:

- Crossroads soil
- White cane sugar
- Steel dust
- Saltpeter
- A glass bottle with a well-fitting top
- A red flannel
- Parchment
- Pencil
- A St. Agnes candle or general good luck candle
- If the case is especially complex, clear two crystals by burying them in salt and setting them out under a full moon overnight.

### 311. Clear Me Mojo and Bottle (Day 2)

Nine days before the court case comes up, walk to your nearest crossroads with soil. Dig up some of the soil from each of the four corners of the crossroads, then take some from the center.

This way, you'll have quincunx power (strength from the five directions).

Bless your crossroads dirt, sugar, steel dust, and saltpeter in the name of your path's holy trinity.

Add these four ingredients to the bottle. Shake gently to mix.

Put the bottle in a red flannel.

Write the name of the person you're trying to help on the parchment.

Roll the paper toward you seven times, tightly. Keep it that way until the day the case comes up. The pair (bottle and paper) can be kept on your altar or placed somewhere safe in the house.

For a full discharge or pardon, pray over your bottle inside the mojo bag next to a St. Agnes candle or general good luck candle, which may be adorned with images of horseshoes, four-leaf clovers, and a rabbit's foot.

If the case still seems to not be progressing in the right direction, add the two charged-up crystals to the bottle and shake it again as you pray to your path's holy trinity (for example, in the name of the Father, Son, and Holy Ghost, if you are Christian).

## 312. Portal Charm (Day 1)

In Hoodoo, we love portals, as they are entryways into all sorts of spaces we need to traverse. Often this attention is paid to opening the way in a spiritual manner, with such mixtures as the famed Van Van oil. On this day, we will dwell on the actual portal home to your innermost sanctum and sacred space—your home.

You'll notice that throughout the year, we've dressed, spiritually cleansed, and done rites around the doorway. This time, let's once again address this sacred portal, but now with an eye toward justice.

When you wish to keep the law at bay or desire good judgments to be delivered, you need a dependable charm to enhance the efficacy of the wish. Charms sometimes are created from what others look upon as mundane objects. In this case, we turn to the humble yet well thought of bone—the wishbone. As the remains of an animal whose life has been sacrificed for your nourishment or spiritual work, the wishbone is an easy-to-obtain, accessible tool to reinforce justice magick.

## 313. Portal Charm (Day 2)

On day 210 you learned of the procedure for drying and charging your wishbone. Now that you are familiar with how to do that, repeat the steps given using a fresh bone, being sure to adhere to the lucky three days in the instructions.

Invocations give power to your intentions. You can use them to directly address your concerns and to pay homage to the life force within the helpers you employ. For your portal charm, once you've made your plea, use the invocation given here.

Once you have your bone ready to use, talk to it as though it is as alive as you. Tell it your legal problems and the type of person involved with the law or judgment you want to stay away from your door:

*This I ask with sincerity,*
*marked with my truth for making this request.*
*I ask you on all I hold dear and in threes,*
*keep my home clear of the law, three times three times three.*

With all the strength and belief you have mustered through the invocation, drive a nail into the upper part of your door. Hang the cured wishbone from your nail. It will help you stay on the right side of the law.

## 314.–315. Prayerful Walk (Days 1 and 2): Memorization Exercise

Memorization is an important tool for your subversive activities. After all, there are times when you don't want everyone to know what you're up to. When you have something to do with a court case, you'll benefit from having this psalm of David. Commit this to memory over the next two days. (It's okay to write it down, if need be.)

### Psalm 35

Plead my cause, O Lord, with them that strive with me: fight against them that fight against me.

Take hold of shield and buckler, and stand up for mine help.

Draw out also the spear, and stop the way against them that persecute me: say unto my soul, I am thy salvation.

Let them be confounded and put to shame that seek after my soul: let them be turned back and brought to confusion that devise my hurt.

Let them be as chaff before the wind: and let the angel of the Lord chase them.

Let their way be dark and slippery: and let the angel of the Lord persecute them.

For without cause have they hid for me their net in a pit, which without cause they have digged for my soul.

Let destruction come upon him at unawares; and let his net that he hath hid catch himself: into that very destruction let him fall.

And my soul shall be joyful in the Lord: it shall rejoice in his salvation.

All my bones shall say, Lord, who is like unto thee, which deliverest the poor from him that is too strong for him, yea, the poor and the needy from him that spoileth him?

False witnesses did rise up; they laid to my charge things that I knew not.

They rewarded me evil for good to the spoiling of my soul.

But as for me, when they were sick, my clothing was sackcloth: I humbled my soul with fasting; and my prayer returned into mine own bosom.

I behaved myself as though he had been my friend or brother: I bowed down heavily, as one that mourneth for his mother.

But in mine adversity, they rejoiced, and gathered themselves together: yea, the abjects gathered themselves together against me, and I knew it not; they did tear me, and ceased not:

With hypocritical mockers in feasts, they gnashed upon me with their teeth.

Lord, how long wilt thou look on? Rescue my soul from their destructions, my darling from the lions.

I will give thee thanks in the great congregation: I will praise thee among much people.

Let not them that are mine enemies wrongfully rejoice over me: neither let them wink with the eye that hate me without a cause.

For they speak not peace: but they devise deceitful matters against them that are quiet in the land.

Yea, they opened their mouth wide against me, and said, Aha, aha, our eye hath seen it.

This thou hast seen, O Lord: keep not silence: O Lord, be not far from me.

Stir up thyself, and awake to my judgment, even unto my cause, my God and my Lord.

Judge me, O Lord my God, according to thy righteousness; and let them not rejoice over me.

Let them not say in their hearts, Ah, so would we have it: let them not say, We have swallowed him up.

Let them be ashamed and brought to confusion together that rejoice at mine hurt: let them be clothed with shame and dishonor that magnify themselves against me.

Let them shout for joy, and be glad, that favour my righteous cause: yea, let them say continually, Let the Lord be magnified, which hath pleasure in the prosperity of his servant.

And my tongue shall speak of thy righteousness and of thy praise all the day long.

## 316. Prayerful Walk (Day 3)

Now that you have Psalm 35 under your belt, here's what to do with it.

Do you have a trial coming up or know someone with one whom you'd like to help? Well, today is the day you can practice your Hoodoo in such a way as to influence the court case. This is one of the awesome aspects of your practice. You don't just have to sit around and hope for the best. With practice and strong will, you can make things happen!

Make a wish on a dried wishbone. Put it in a cast-iron skillet or cauldron on a stove or live fire outdoors. Cook it on medium-high heat; burn it down until nothing is left but ash. Add a handful of dried rose petals and let them smolder and burn too.

With your intention concerning the court case close to your heart, walk nine steps backward, sprinkling the ash in the ninth footstep.

When you (or your friend, family member, or client) go before the judge, you (they) should recite Psalm 35 mentally at your altar the night before and in the courtroom the day of the trial.[77]

### 317. Trouble Journaling

Everyone has trouble occasionally. Being observant of yourself and those you care about the most can help keep this trouble from mushrooming until it is too hard to turn around. Today is the day to take a personal inventory and see who is in trouble in your life.

This trick uses something known as automatic drawing. A less intimidating name for this could be spiritual doodling. You don't need much to do this, apart from a very clear, well-rested mind and a piece or two of parchment paper and a pencil.

Pick a time today when you are relaxed yet receptive. Sit in a high-backed, hard chair at a table (kitchen or dining room). Put the paper on the table next to the sharpened pencil. Take your shoes off and get comfortable but stay very alert. (That's why you're in a rigid chair.) Close your eyes and take a few

---

77. Hyatt, *Hoodoo, Conjuration, Witchcraft, Rootwork*, 1,003.

cleansing breaths. Turn your eyes inward toward your third eye, our usual meditative inversion. Stay in this position, with your hands turned upward and open, resting on your thighs. Keep your mind as clear as possible. After about fifteen minutes, you can open your eyes gradually.

Take the pencil, and on the parchment draw freely, any way that is comfortable to you. After your drawing is completed, have a hot cup of your favorite tea with some relaxing honey to taste. Now do a reading on the drawing. Take stock. Who is it revealing to you, and how does the drawing guide you into helping them?

## 318. Healing Hand and Foot Magick

When someone you love is in trouble, the emotions can run from humbling to horrifying, especially if this trouble involves the law. It is fortunate that as Hoodoos, we have so many blessed tools to help in such matters. Working on behalf of friends and loved ones is a hallmark of this practice, and one we'll draw on today.

You should have a good stock of sage on hand by now, since it was shared on day 233 as part of your Hoodoo garden work. This herb is a beloved multipurpose healer. Spirits are moved by its drawing, clearing, and blessing prowess. You may also have a Bible on hand, as much of Hoodoo takes wisdom from the Psalms of David.

You will need sage, a Bible, holy oil, and a red flannel for this work to get your friend out of trouble.

Rip out Psalm 9 of the Bible and burn it to ash, along with nine sage leaves. Once they are ash, add a single drop of holy oil and rub into a paste form. Put this in a tiny red flannel. Have the person wear this in their sock.[78] They'll start moving away from the trouble they've been in and toward the light.

### 319. Murder Novena: A Week of Study and Practice (Day 1)

Having the life of a loved one snuffed out by brutality resulting in murder should be unheard of. Rather than being relegated to the dark ages, where such an act belongs, it is becoming increasingly prevalent in many areas.

As is the case with so many contemporary ills, traditional Hoodoo has a way of addressing the darkest parts of human nature and unspeakable acts such as murder. The noteworthy rite and ceremony that I want to share with you from an early Hoodoo informant, recorded by Harry Hyatt, warrants a week's worth of devotion and study.

This week we are going in depth into the terminology, practices, origins, and activities that come together for a meaningful and hopefully transformational rite to find more clues about a specific murder that has impacted your life or that of someone close to you.

Horrendous acts are shocking and can leave you feeling powerless and hopeless, but that is not the way of the Hoodoo. Instead, you are going to prepare for the worst. Knowing what is behind this ritual and ceremony and how to practice it offers a sense of empowerment. In a dark time, it provides a sense of hope and will hopefully lead toward resolution.

---

78. Hyatt, *Hoodoo, Conjuration, Witchcraft, Rootwork*, 1,009.

## 320. Novenas (Day 2)

The murder ritual and ceremony you will soon perform requires a novena, so it is good to have a proper fix on what it is, where it comes from, and why it might be useful. *Novena* is a word you've probably seen in your spiritual work. It is a type of Catholic ritual with ancient roots that is also relevant and used in Hoodoo. The noun *novena* is derived from the Latin *novem*, which means "nine." Novenas are used in Hoodoo and in the Roman Catholic Church in the form of worship containing nine successive days of special prayers, as a petition of some sort, and in thanksgiving (gratitude) prayers.

The nine days are in recognition of the number of days the Virgin Mary and the apostles spent praying between Ascension Thursday, when Christ ascended into heaven, and Pentecost Sunday. Pentecost Sunday is a very ancient feast of the church, celebrating the fiftieth day of Easter. The feast is one of solemnity.

This is the day when the apostles were granted the gift of the Holy Spirit. On this Sunday, the descent of the Holy Spirit occurs. *Novena* has come to stand for any series of prayers. The practice of nine days of prayer or other spiritual work has pagan origins and is utilized in many different ways in Hoodoo.

## 321. Petitioning (Day 3)

When the inconceivable occurs, you want the proper tools in place to set things right. This, after all, is the way to facilitate justice. Unique prayers come in handy. Today you will be given two psalms to memorize.

### Petitions

You can use petitions to speak frankly and earnestly to your higher power on behalf of others. It is a request for something wanted, frequently in the form of a simple, heartfelt request for courage or strength.

### Supplication

Another similar but separate form of prayer is supplication, where you are bearing your soul and self to deity. It is a practice of asking your higher power for something directly for your own needs rather than on behalf of others.

In Hoodoo, psalms are selected for these kinds of prayers. Some are aimed at courage, leadership, mercy, and so forth. Following are two such psalms.

This first one, Psalm 4:1, is for mercy, something desired by those seeking justice.

### Psalm 4.1

Answer me when I call, O God of my righteousness! You have given me relief when I was in distress. Be gracious to me and hear my prayer!

Psalm 5:8 is for seeking clarity and direction.

### Psalm 5:8

Lead me, O lord, in your righteousness because of my enemies; make your way straight before me.

## 322. Prayer and Ceremony of Thanksgiving (Day 4)

Some only consider Thanksgiving a holiday, but it is also a form of prayer. It is a way of showing gratitude and appreciation for what you've been given, not just your gifts. Prayers of Thanksgiving consider pain, struggles, and challenging issues such as what we are facing this week in the form of a murder.

You should always be appreciative of your ancestors, deities, higher power, nature, or however you see and experience spirit.

In the case of someone being taken from you, what sort of thanksgiving comes to mind? This will be deeply personal, depending on the case and on the reason for them being taken from you. Take some time today to write an appreciation prayer. Your prayer of thanksgiving can be as long and elaborate or as brief as you want it to be.

I generally start this sort of prayer with the words "I am grateful for...."

## Ceremony

This prayer lends itself readily to a family and friend ceremonial rite. Light a candle on behalf of the person who is the recipient of the prayer. Then say, "I am grateful that _____ was in my life because _____." Pass the candle to the next person in your circle, and they will repeat the prompt words, adding their personal statement and then passing along the candle.

## 323. Our Lady of Perpetual Help (Day 5)

The use of icons in spirituality and worship is not only Catholic but also has pagan origins. In paganism, we are especially fond of the divine feminine, goddesses, mothers of the earth, and certain plants and places.

The originators of Hoodoo took inspiration from the Catholic Church. We incorporate icon worship, and this relates back to many different ancient practices in West Africa and elsewhere, as was explored during your first month of this book.

Our Lady of Perpetual Help is a depiction of the Blessed Virgin Mary painted on a wooden panel. Its earliest appearance was thought to be during the Byzantine period of the thirteenth century CE, when it was called Our Lady of Perpetual Succour (the British spelling of *succor*, meaning assistance in the time of need).

The image is rich in iconography and symbolism. It depicts our Blessed Mother Mary holding baby Jesus. Archangel Michael (whom you've recently conjured) floats in the upper corner, to the left. He holds instruments of the Passion, including a sponge dipped in wine, the crown of thorns, and a spear.

Archangel Gabriel is to the upper right. He grips the nails and cross of the crucifixion. This image is believed to symbolize the way Christ defeated sin and even death. The baby Jesus is comforted by his Blessed Mother, as will we be when we turn to her in the face of murder and death.

### 324. Our Lady of Perpetual Help Prayer (Day 6)

You might find comfort in this traditional prayer to Our Lady of Perpetual Help. This is a modern English version by St. Alphonsus Liguori. [79]

Mother of Perpetual Help, behold at your feet a sinner who has recourse to you and has confidence in you.

Mother of mercy, have pity on me. I hear all calling you the refuge and hope of sinners. Be, then, my refuge and my hope. For the love of Jesus Christ, your Son, help me.

Give your hand to a poor sinner who commends himself to you and dedicates himself to your lasting service. I praise and

---

79. "Novena to Our Lady of Perpetual Help."

thank God who in His mercy has given to me this confidence in you, a sure pledge of my eternal salvation.

It is true that in the past, I, miserable and wretched, have fallen into sin because I did not have recourse to you. But I know that with your help I shall be able to overcome myself. I know, too, that you will help me, if I commend myself to you. But I fear that in the occasions of sin, I may neglect to call upon you and thus run the risk of being lost.

This grace, then, I seek of you; for this I implore you as much as I know and as much as I can: that in all the attacks of hell I may ever have recourse to you and say to you: "O Mary, help me. O Mother of Perpetual Help, do not let me lose my God."

(Three Hail Marys.)

Mother of Perpetual Help, aid me ever to call upon your powerful name, since your name is the help of the living and the salvation of the dying. Mary most pure, Mary most sweet, grant that your name from this day forth may be to me the very breath of life. Dear Lady, do not delay in coming to help me when I call upon you, for in all the temptations that trouble me, in all the needs of my life, I will ever call upon you, repeating: "Mary, Mary."

What comfort, what sweetness, what confidence, what consolation fills my soul at the sound of your name, at the very thought of you! I give thanks to the Lord, who for my sake has given you a name so sweet, so lovable and so mighty. But I am not content only to speak your name; I will call upon you because I love you. I want that love to remind me always to call you Mother of Perpetual Help.

(Three Hail Marys.)

Mother of Perpetual Help, you are the dispenser of every grace that God grants us in our misery. For this reason, he has made you so powerful, so rich, and so kind that you might help us in our needs. You are the advocate of the most wretched and abandoned sinners, if they but come to you. Come to my aid, for I commend myself to you.

In your hands, I place my eternal salvation; to you I entrust my soul. Count me among your most faithful servants. Take me under your protection; that is enough for me. If you protect me, I shall fear nothing. I shall not fear my sins, because you will obtain for me their pardon and remission. Neither shall I fear the evil spirits, because you are mightier than all the powers of hell.

I fear only that through my own negligence I may forget to recommend myself to you and so lose my soul. My dear Lady, obtain for me the forgiveness of my sins, love for Jesus, final perseverance, and the grace to have recourse to you, at all times, Mother of Perpetual Help.

(Three Hail Marys.)

## 325. Murder Novena (Day 7)

Today, your previous reflection, study, and practice come together in a murder novena for justice.[80]

Go to the cemetery where the murdered person is buried. Nine days in a row, pray close to the headstone, holding in your hands a picture of Our Mother of Perpetual Help and two eggs

---

80. Hyatt, *Hoodoo, Conjuration, Witchcraft, Rootwork*, 869.

(one in the left hand and the other in the right). On the ninth day, bury the eggs to the left and the right of the grave (where the hands would naturally fall). Put the Mother's icon on the headstone, and pray the Mother of Perpetual Help prayer you learned yesterday as many times as you need to for closure.

## 326. Curio of Note: Ice

I favor spells that capitalize on the elements—particularly water. In Hoodoo, we use magickal waters in our baths, teas, spiritual floor washes, and bottles of a variety of types, including war and peace.

Using water is an ancient pagan practice that is seen flowing through various African diasporic practices as well. Many different types of water are helpful, from rainwater to running water (rivers, brooks, falls), lightning water, urine, vinegar, and spring water.

Solidified water in the form of ice is utilized for various forms of Hoodoo magick, from love magick to justice magick, which is our focus today. Ice, being frozen, is used sympathetically to freeze acts, actions, judgments, relationships, and more. The water can of course be taken from a variety of sources. The source should match the purpose of the spell, trick, or job, or help facilitate it. Tap water is seldom, if ever, used.

Today we are going to prepare twenty-five to thirty pounds of ice for tomorrow's ritual. If you are using a standard ice maker, this means you will use a bit less than three gallons of water total. Otherwise, you will need your normal clean and dry ice cube trays. (Don't buy premade ice cubes.) You want to state your purpose over the water. Yes, its spirit can hear and understand you! You will keep filling, emptying, and refilling until you have about a basin's worth of ice. While the source of water is not specified for the upcoming work, I suggest using running water (from a natural body of flowing water, not from the tap).

## 327. Justice Trick from Algiers, Louisiana

Have you or someone you are working with been subpoenaed? Well, today you are going to freeze the action on the subpoena with an updated traditional spell from Algiers, Louisiana.[81] Put the twenty-five to thirty pounds of ice you prepared yesterday in the kitchen sink. Put the subpoena on the ice. Light a black candle and safely burn that atop the subpoena. Whatever ill action was set to be rendered against you will not happen, or whoever was set to testify against you will not do so.

## 328. Don't Mess with Me Bottle

Are you in trouble? Is someone you know having legal troubles? Well, today is the day you'll learn an additional method of helping yourself or others struggling with legal problems. This is a fragrant herbal bottle developed from one that was originally reported on from New Orleans. It's a "Don't mess with me" bottle.

Here's what you'll need:

- Cinnamon stick, powdered with a mortar and pestle
- A few sprigs of parsley
- A few lumps of white cane sugar
- Thimbleful of Jockey Club cologne
- 3 drops geranium essential oil
- 3 drops ylang-ylang essential oil

---

81. Hyatt, *Hoodoo, Conjuration, Witchcraft, Rootwork*, 842.

• 3 drops tangerine essential oil

• A small bottle with a cork top

Add your ingredients in the order given to a small bottle with a cork top. You can play around with the amounts of each, using however much you desire. Shake gently to mix. Place this outside on the east side of your home in the corner. The law ain't going to mess with you now.

### 329. Curio of Note: Saw Palmetto

Saw palmetto (*Serenoa repens, Serenoa serrulata, Sabal serrulata*) is a celebrated component in Native American medicine, especially that of the Seminole and Lumbee, as well as the African-American Gullah people. Naturally, with its habitat being in the Southeast coastal regions from South Carolina to Florida and in Southern California, it made its way into Hoodoo as well.

It is a fan palm, which is alternately termed a "tree" or "shrub." It has a slowly spreading, horizontal habit that extends up to ten feet, flourishing in zones 8–10, which are very warm. It contains verdant green, saw-toothed leaves, which extend from thorny stems. Its blooms are white flowers, which contain yellow berries that eventually turn coffee-brown when ripe. These berries are dried and used medicinally.

The reason saw palmetto is included in this discussion is because it is a systemic strengthener and tonic—perfect medicine for someone enduring a lengthy trial or the debilitating effects of injustice. It balances the metabolism, stimulates appetite, and returns sexual vigor as well.

## 330. NOLA Palmetto Hand

This is a fascinating and effective hand in accord with one reported years ago by a Hoodoo from New Orleans.[82] To start, you must obtain a "he" (spear-like/phallic-shaped) palmetto root. This should preferably come from the wild, personally foraged, if possible. It grows along the coast from South Carolina to Florida and in Southern California, so that's where you need to go to get it.

With a very sharp knife, cut three slits into the palmetto root, working from its bottom to the top (head). Write the names of the defense attorney and the prosecuting attorney backward nine times on paper. Put these cut-out pieces of paper into the three slits. Wrap the entire thing in a flannel. Wear this hand in the pocket on your dominant side.

Now the law will stay away from you or the person you're helping. This hand was designed for bootlegging, but use your imagination—it has many other applications.

## 331. Discharge Ritual

For some, a discharge would be a huge relief. It would be a reprieve from a huge burden. There are all different circumstances for receiving a discharge from a judge, but you can help influence it to be handed down.

Here is a ritual involving the novena rite of worship you worked with for a week a few days ago.

Gather the following items:

• 2 cigars (John Ruskins, if possible)

---

82. Hyatt, *Hoodoo, Conjuration, Witchcraft, Rootwork*, 607.

- 25 pounds of ice, made the way we discussed in the ice curio profile on day 326
- A glass lamp base (empty)
- 9 white votive candles
- 9 shot glasses (as holders)
- Matches

Put your two cigars in the glass lamp filled with the ice and then into a bathtub. Put your candles in little shot glasses as holders. Have a trusted friend or family member light the candles and say a prayer for you when you go to court. Make sure the two cigars are burning in the middle of this assemblage. At court, you will be discharged by the judge.

## 332. Curio of Note:
## Little John to Chew/Court Case Root

In Hoodoo, greater galangal (*Alpinia galanga*), an herb with some resemblance to ginger, is aptly called court case root or Little John to Chew. Native to Java, it has a very lengthy history, going back to at least 1000 CE in China. Called a root, as it is used like one in rootwork, it is a very wholesome rhizome. We carry it as a charm to guard the wearer. It is also chewed on, and the secretions from it are spit out, to do our bidding in court.

Medicinally and spiritually, it works as one. When setting out for court cases and trials, you will most likely experience nervousness, anxiety, and even an upset stomach. Take your court case root/Little John to Chew as a warm decoction before setting out, or slice it up thinly and chew it along the way. You can discreetly spit out a bit of its juice when you get to court and along your way.

This root is valued for its ability to treat stomach pain and digestive issues and its use as a stimulating tonic. You will find your courage and strength grow as your energy is revved up from this herb. Besides, it has been used in Western medicine since the Middle Ages in a variety of ways, including as a snuff.

This Hoodoo curative addresses a wide array of issues. It sharpens your thinking—a very good feature to have when in court. Little John to Chew will get rid of the foulness of impending doom. It naturally deodorizes the body and the mouth, specifically, after you chew or drink it. Your words will come across forcefully and effectively with Little John to Chew.

To use, make sure you are using Little John and not one of the other Hoodoo Johns. You can determine this by checking the botanical Latin name.

Use a sharp knife to splinter the root. Grind it in a spice grinder or dedicated coffee grinder or by hand, with your trusted mortar and pestle. The taste upon chewing or drinking it is earthy, citrusy, and heated but not overly spicy, for it lacks capsaicin.

### 333. Little John to Chew Job

As discussed and hopefully experienced earlier on in this work, bodily fluids have an important place in your Hoodoo practice. Saliva, for example, is used along with herbs to effect change by many different paths. Your spit can be combined with herbs, softening them and rendering their various parts useful medicinally, in healing work, for spells, rites, and remedies. One such preparation that can quickly be made from chewing an herb is an instant poultice. You can use spitting, particularly when paired with roots, to make things happen. One very effective way to use your rootworking herbs, saliva, and spitting in justice Hoodoo is to employ Little John.

You can chew Little John from your Hoodoo garden before a judgment, court case, or trial. Then spit it along the way as you approach the courthouse. Used the same way, it is also good for getting a job and for general luck magick.

## 334. Injustice Incense and Purification Ceremony

The noted historian and scholar Tim Samuelson of the Chicago Cultural Center loaned me a precious tome on incense. It is over a hundred years old! Within it I found some inspirational types and methods of using incense for divine worship, along with psalms for reflection and incantation, that are relevant to your justice work today.

After an injustice has been done, undoubtedly it will affect your home as much as it affects you. Injustice has a foul spiritual odor reminiscent of death, because in many ways it is killing off freedom. Today, take a journey back in time through this work inspired by age-old wisdom. Purify and protect your altar and home against this foul intrusion in the following way.

Purify your altar with holy water. Set out wine libations and then set out Hoyt's Cologne. Recite:

*Hoc incensum ad omnem putorem nocuum exstinguendum.*
*Dominus benedicat, et in odorem suavitatis suae accendat.*

Or in English:

*May the Lord [eclectic Pagans may insert the word "Goddess" instead] bless this incense for the removal of every harmful stench, and kindle it for the perfume of its sweetness.* [83]

Lay out a rich offering of homemade or various types of breads and high-quality beer and wine on your cleared altar.

Next, burn a thimbleful each of Queen Elizabeth powder, pulverized cedarwood, and storax.

Cleanse yourself by sprinkling yourself lightly with ashes from your blessing incense (just burned) and salt. Sip a bit of red wine.

Sprinkle a stick of dried hyssop (like a sage smudge stick) dipped in holy water over your body, then say this part of Psalm 51:

*Purge me with hyssop, and I shall be clean.*

Dry yourself with a freshly laundered towel.

Now you and your altar and home are cleansed and purified, and you are ready to move on in a clear light.

### 335. Justice Check-In

Everyone, at a certain time in their life, needs justice, or assistance with a trial or court case. This is part of the human condition and modern living. It is nothing new. Justice has been a longstanding issue in the community; therefore, there are long-standing, time-tested methods of influencing justice and legal outcomes devised by traditional Hoodoos.

Now, as the eleventh month of your work comes to an end, it is time to take stock of where you stand with the justice work in your life. Please take out your Hoodoo journal and revisit the in-

---

83. Atchley, *A History of the Use of Incense in Divine Worship*, 203.

ventory you made at the beginning of the month. Consider the following questions:

1. Where do you stand with your original problems and concerns?

2. Who have you helped?

3. How have you helped them?

4. What problems have you learned to deal with?

5. What herbs, rootwork, and curios did you enjoy employing the most?

6. How did you use these items that resonated with you?

7. What issues do you have remaining that still need to be resolved?

8. Devise a plan for how to meet your goals. Use bulletpoints, a numbered list, or full sentences.

9. Continue to work toward achieving justice and being brave in the face of court cases and legal judgments as you strengthen your Hoodoo through hands-on practice!

# CHAPTER 12

# CLARITY: UNHEXING & BANISHING WORK: DAYS 336-365

First, congratulations to you! You are a dedicated practitioner of Hoodoo, and as remarkable as it may have seemed in the beginning, you are now on day 336. I am certain that you have experienced a great deal of change and empowerment as you've studied and practiced Hoodoo.

Our work is not over, however. This is an incredibly important month for your work. If you thought you could start to coast, get that out of your head. Don't take your foot off the gas pedal yet. Our twelfth month focuses on clarity. Is there anything more beautiful, spiritually, than to have a clear mind and spirit? In the case of our work, the clarity we're going to work is going to be envisioned and conjured by understanding the power of unhexing and banishment.

A strong hex stands between you and your sanity. It can negatively impact your mind, which also leads to cluttered space and muddled efforts in your Hoodoo practice. Hexes are called many different things and appear in varied forms. When you are hexed, you know it. You might want to deny or question it, but in your gut you know the truth. Hexes, and their negative entourage of spiritual clutter, are unmistakable.

Rather than dwell in the negativity of the sources or types of hexes, we are going to trust your instincts, or the instincts of those you are working for, and work on busting their clutter. When you work through these spells, rites, affirmations, tricks, and ceremonies, you will be able to free your life of mental chaos. You'll have a fresh mind, and the stronghold of hexes will be broken.

Sometimes, however, things are just not as simple as we'd hope. The person or people spreading hexes will not go away. These pains in the you know where want to ruin your life, your efforts, your home, love life, career, and more. The same is true for negative spells aimed at you and people who won't take the hint and get out of your life. You have a variety of reasons to choose banishment, to be sure. This chapter, with its final section on the clearance of toxicity, will focus on the various modes of banishing.

### 336. Visioning Hexes

Hexes can be negative or positive, depending on how you look at them. Wait … did you have to go back and read that sentence again? Do you wonder if perhaps at the end of this year of study, I'm starting to lose my grip? Well, think again.

Hexes are overrated. They are distributed by a person consumed with darkness. How can they overcome your light? They can win only when you feed them with attention and fear.

You must be aware by now that my work faces the light. It embraces it and then reflects it back out into the universe. If you've made it through this book up to the twelfth month of the year, chances are you too are a lightworker.

### Vision Quest

Today, dip your gourd deep down into the endless well of light. Take this light in the form of healing well water and pour it over your head. Bathe in the light. Let all ills drain down from your crown, exiting at your feet. Be clean and go forward in the spirit of light.

Now go back to the month devoted to protection (chapter 10). Reread the section on shielding (beginning on day 289). Buff up your shields and choose the ones to utilize that are most suitable to the occasion, but keep your shields up and working.

## 337. Were You Hexed?

Have you experienced the ill effects of a hex? Let's explore the ramifications of hexes. Do you wonder how to know? Chances are, if you are seriously wondering if you've been hexed, you have been.

There are looming telltale signs of a hex:

• Lethargy

• Natural and unnatural illness that seems to spring up without cause

• Paranoia

• Fear

• General feeling of malaise

• Luck, love, prosperity, and abundance seem out of your reach.

Yes, these symptoms and effects of hexes are daunting, but you can win. You are dealing with someone with a weak mind, and I don't mean you—it's the one who laid the hex. Those who hex have issues. They decide to turn their negativity out and pour it into the world and your inner sanctum. People consumed with bad feelings toward people and the world are typically unbalanced and vengeful. They are ruled by their emotions.

But that's enough about those who hex. We are not going to spend time diagnosing people's issues or trying to figure out a twisted mind. This is personal space for your Hoodoo practice. Stay strong and grounded in these lessons and you can move about without fear.

## 338. Anti-Hex Work: A Week of Study (Day 1)

We will focus this part of the month of our study on considering the traditional methodology of unhexing using Hoodoo. Time will also be spent on recognizing hexes and unhexing when necessary.

One of the best ways to foil the evil intent held in hexes is to have inner strength and fortitude. The goal is to make yourself impervious to psychic attack. Unbalanced people will most likely throw their negativity your way. This can be done by simply saying certain words to you or looking at you with an evil eye. Hexes can also be more elaborate and measured, depending on the perpetrator. If you are sealed off from negativity, you will be able to help not only yourself but also others in your life.

Building up your inner spiritual energy, training it like a muscle, enables you to walk over evil. Obviously, this takes a long time and great dedication to accomplish, longer than a week. We will, however, dedicate this amount of time for guided study and practice to help you along the way.

### 339. Understanding Your Core (Day 2)

One of the ways you can get a strong sense of the Hoodoo's knowledge and interest in Eastern medicine and spirituality, primarily that of India, is through the attention to the navel shared by yogis and Hoodoos. Today we are going to explore this shared interest in the navel area. This is philosophical grounding before moving on to a traditional Hoodoo rite involving this important area of the body.

Let's begin with the chakras. Chakras are central areas of spiritual energy we all have in our bodies. The navel area is of one of the seven chakras and is called the manipura, *mani* meaning "gem" and *pura* interpreted as "city." This area is very important because it correlates with the ego. As a power center, it controls the following:

- Empowerment

- Energy

- Willpower

- Personal identity

- Metabolism

- Self-worth

- Self-esteem

- Relationships

- Digestion

- Liver
- Colon

If you want to engage your navel energy (your manipura, or third chakra), say an affirmation as you lightly touch it with your dominant hand:

*I feel the entry and exit of my spiritual power.*

Stop now and see how that makes you feel. Repeat this affirmation twice more. You will need to be in touch with this area and keep it clear, acknowledged, and happy to stay free of hexes.

People with out-of-whack energy in this area are dominating and controlling, have low energy, feel weak, become manipulated, and are generally unpleasant because their energy source is blocked.

## 340. Strengthening Your Manipura (Day 3)

Hexes leave you feeling powerless and uncomfortable with yourself and others. A hex is a relationship-wrecking and all-consuming malaise that good energy and luck cannot flow through. With a negative stage set and no access to good vibes, you begin to gravitate toward things that make you suffer more, such as bad relationships, overspending, substance abuse, and more. This can all be avoided if you have a strong manipura.

### Strengthening Rite

The purpose of this rite is twofold. You want to relax enough to let in good energy, recognize your positive qualities, and identify your goals. You'd be surprised at how simple this recognition and relaxation process can be when herbs are involved.

Gather the following:

- 1 teaspoon each rosemary and chamomile
- 8 ounces spring water

Rosemary is an herb celebrated for its ability to help us remember. It is the herb of memory. This herb is included in this tea to help you recall your self-worth, goals, and days before the hex, when you were more energetic.

Chamomile is known for its relaxing qualities. Bring the water to a boil. Turn the heat down to medium. Crumble the two herbs, working vigorously with your hands. Keep your inner power at the fore and your intentions in mind.

Sip the tea. Take out your Hoodoo journal. Write down today's date and describe how you are feeling.

## 341. Anti-hex Incense (Day 4)

Certain herbs are respected for their ability to help align and strengthen a weakened third chakra. You are going to be getting in touch with those specific herbs now. Today you will create an invigorating, spiritually charged incense using resins, wood, and herbs.

Gather these ingredients:

- ¼ cup frankincense beads
- 2-inch chunk of myrrh
- 2 tablespoons finely cut sandalwood
- 2 tablespoons cut and sifted (dried) rosemary
- ¼ teaspoon rose absolute
- ½ teaspoon rosewood essential oil
- ½ teaspoon frankincense essential oil
- ½ teaspoon sandalwood essential oil

- ¼ teaspoon myrrh essential oil
- 1 teaspoon Queen Elizabeth powder

Before you begin this work, clear your mind of worries. I know this is hard to do because you may well be dealing with the negative impact of ill will. Work on increasing your lucidity by taking a brisk walk, run, or hot shower, or do meditation, as you have done throughout your work—perhaps you need to try more than one of these.

Once you are feeling lucid and ready to work, thoughtfully but assertively grind the frankincense, myrrh, sandalwood, and rosemary with your mortar and pestle until you have a fine powder. Impregnate the herbs with your wish to remove any hexes upon you by breathing steadily into the mortar as you work the pestle. Move this powder to a glass dish or stainless steel bowl. Sprinkle on the absolute and essential oils from a stainless steel spoon. Mix well. Sprinkle on the Queen Elizabeth root powder as a scent preservative and spiritual strengthener. Store the incense for tomorrow.

## 342. Manipura Altar (Day 5)

This might just be the single most important altar you can build when it comes to rectifying a downward spiral in your life. It encompasses elements important and well respected in Hoodoo that are recommended in both Hindi and Western practice. The manipura altar uses individual pieces that come together to feed, restore, and fortify the navel area. This area is the central focus this week because it is the part of your body that is sensitive and susceptible to ego injury. These types of injuries have a wide-ranging variety of sources. Overall, they leave you open and available to hexing; therefore, this area needs ample attention and care.

1. Clear off a table near where you sleep.

2. Lay down a bright yellow or orange silky cloth on the table.

3. Put fresh red roses inside a crystal (or glass) vase with clean water.

4. Set out a censer with charcoal and matches.

5. Place charcoals inside the censer and light them.

6. Sprinkle the charcoals with your incense from yesterday.

Practice going to your manipura altar, repeating these steps, and contemplating the peaceful, invigorating, and strength-building quality of the altar. Go to this altar to find peace of mind and healing whenever needed.

## 343. Unhex Spiritual Wash (Day 6)

There are different types of washes in Hoodoo, such as spiritual floor washes, spiritual baths, and hand and foot washes. This unhex wash is exceptional in that it deals solely with the hands, feet, and navel.

**Hands:** Hands need to be cleansed because they are sensors and doers. We make and feel things through our hands. Having them spiritually cleansed can lead to clarity, vigor where once you felt weak, and the power required to unhex.

**Feet:** You've worked through an entire month of foot track magick, so you're familiar with ashe. Not only are the feet practical in terms of carrying you through your life journey, but they can also connect you with nefarious items left on the ground to foil your direction and cause chaos. The items are there specifically to hex you.

**Navel:** Your navel area (solar plexus), as you've learned, is a power center. This is the space in the body that is controlling your outlook and way of functioning in many regards. If you are seeking empowerment, this is the place to keep stoked.

### Unhex Spiritual Wash

You will need these tools:

- Basin or plugged sink
- Hot water
- 1 tablespoon saltpeter
- A white washcloth

Fill the basin or sink with water as hot as you can stand and add the saltpeter. Wash your hands in the saltpeter water.

Recite the first affirmation:

*I feel my vigor returning.*

Using the washcloth, wash your navel with the spiritual wash.

Say the second affirmation:

*I recognize the return of my power.*

Wash your feet mindfully as you say the third affirmation:

*I move forward in life with mindfulness, purpose, and strength.*

Reminder: Set your alarm for a half hour before sunrise tonight when you go to bed, to be up and ready for day 7 of this anti-hex work.

### 344. Unhex Ritual and Ceremony (Day 7)

Today is the day to bring together in a ritual and ceremony the six elements of unhexing through the third chakra. It's best to do this early in the morning just before the sun rises since it is a magickal time for Hoodoos. With your foresight and preparation last night, you should be up at the right hour.

Move your altar to the bathroom carefully and respectfully, piece by piece.

1. Light your unhexing incense.

2. Take another saltpeter sitz bath.

3. Practice deep belly breathing: Push your belly out and suck in, breathing slowly and rhythmically through your nose for about five minutes. Lightly trace around your navel area in a circular pattern. When you are done, extinguish the incense.

4. Anoint yourself in holy oil (olive oil) while still wet. Dry off and put on a red robe (or dress or shirt). Go outside barefoot (weather permitting).

5. Perform this ceremony:

    Say: "I am whole."

    Rub your hands together.

    Say: "I am sound."

Caress your navel area with your hands.

Say: "I hold my ground."

Stomp your feet.

Say: "I walk only in the light."

Hold both arms to the sky.

Now repeat and do all these actions twice more.

Say: "Blessed be!"

6. Go inside. Anoint yourself with a few dabs of rosemary essential oil to your temple area. Put your daily mojo on.

7. Change into blue clothing. Wear blue all day. This color will shroud you in peaceful healing energy. This is a way to celebrate your ceremony and seal off your sense of peace.

## 345. Hex Reversal Work (Day 1)

Hoodoo harnesses the power of movement. We examine and utilize different types of movements, for their promise for our work. This is how it is now and how it has been from the beginning.

You are familiar with foot track magick now after spending a month working on it. By now you realize there is potency in the footstep. Your feet hold the ability to make things happen just by the mere fact of how, where, with what, and why you walk. You are now stepping into a contemporary riff on a traditional spell from Brunswick, Georgia.[84]

For this work you will need these items:

• A live crab

• A cauldron and a stock pot with a cover

---

84. Hyatt, *Hoodoo, Conjuration, Witchcraft, Rootwork*, 395.

- A heat source (stove or outdoor fire)

- Sugar

- Cayenne powder

- Salt

- Hot water

### Prayer of Thanksgiving

With your live crab contained in a covered basket or pot, say a prayer of thanksgiving:

*There is beauty and majesty in all of Mother Nature's gifts.*
*Crab, coming from water, with your unique ability*
*to creep in all directions,*
*I thank you*
*for sharing your life force with my work.*
*Highest praises to you.*
*Thank you for all that you have done and will do.*
*Blessed be!*

### Directions and Rite

Quickly blanch the crab in some spring water in your covered stock pot. Move it to the cauldron (or similar sturdy pot). Put in the oven. Cook it all the way down until you are left with just ash. (A low temperature and slow approach works best.)

Add the sugar, cayenne powder, salt, and a bit of hot water (enough to make a good paste).

Take your crab ash paste outside, barefoot. Hold it to the sky and say: "Thank you!"

Rub this paste on your temples. Take nine steps backward. Recite: "No harm."

Rub the paste on the palms of your hands. Recite: "No harm." Take nine steps forward.

Rub the paste on the soles of your feet. Recite: "No harm."

Walk backward, back inside your house. Rub some of the paste on your navel area. Recite: "No harm."

## 346. Hex Reversal Work (Day 2)

If you've been Hoodooed, here's a surefire way of reversing the negative energy you feel, ridding yourself of the hex once and for all.

Go outside a bit before sunrise (skyclad, if you'd like).

Take nine steps backward and chant the following a total of nine times:

*Unhex, unhex, unhex, unhex, unhex,*
*unhex, unhex, unhex, unhex.*

Do this nine mornings in a row to cleanse yourself of the hex.

## 347. Hoodoo Gardening: Asafoetida

Though asafoetida (plants from the genus Ferula, including *Ferula asafoetida, Ferula narthex,* and *Ferula scorodosma*) is sometimes called giant fennel, it is not the culinary herb. Sometimes referred to as devil's dung because of its unpleasant odor, this herb has an important place in magick. It is one of the nine plants traced back to the tenth century and invoked in the Pagan Anglo-Saxon "Nine Herbs Charm." Enslaved Africans in America recorded many uses for asafoetida, some of which filtered into Hoodoo.

In *Slave Narratives: A Folk History of Slavery in the United States from Interviews with Former Slaves,* compiled by the Federal Writers' Project of the Works Progress Administration from 1936 to 1938,[85] formerly enslaved people refer to numerous folk remedies involving asafoetida and the magickal ways asafoetida was used. The asphidity bag, for example, was filled with asafoetida and other herbs to ward off various illnesses. This Hoodoo herb is cross-cultural. In Appalachia, giant fennel has been used in much the same way, pinned to the underwear, for example. It is also used in the East Indies and has early recorded culinary uses in Persia.

With giant fennel or other Ferula, it is the sap released from the stem that is of interest. It is put in mojo bags, with its fetid, potent, and persistent odor used as a preventative against illness. Sometimes it is combined with oil of turpentine in a special formula with sugar lumps as a cure-all in African-American culture, taken internally. Worn around the neck or ankle as a mojo, it is sometimes combined with garlic, another cure-all against various illnesses. Historically, it was especially useful in helping heal childhood illnesses. Asafoetida is noted for warding off spiritual illness.

### 348. Asafoetida: Power Walk

Hexes make you feel weak and take away your energy. Here is a way to regain your strength and spark.

*Mojo*

Put some asafoetida into a red flannel. Invigorate it by feeding it with a bit of gunpowder. Sprinkle this over it, into the bag. Then

---

85. Federal Writers' Project of the Works Progress Administration.

tie your mojo off on a piece of string and wear it near your heart under your clothing.[86]

### Foot Powder

Take this one more step and you'll surely be protected. You can walk over an enemy's evil intent by sprinkling asafoetida and gunpowder into your shoes.

With your mojo bag and foot track magick, your enemies don't stand a chance. You are dressed and well equipped for any type of psychic warfare. If you've been hexed, chances are you're lying low, spending a lot of time in the house. Break that cycle. It is debilitating. Today, with your full-body protection, go outside and take a power walk. This activity, done every day, will rebuild your energy, self-esteem, and sense of well-being.

## 349. Asafoetida: Heart Mojo

The heart is the center of our emotions, vigor, health, feelings, openness, and strength. We worked the navel area—the third chakra, also called the manipura—a few days ago. Now let's turn our attention to the heart center.

When you are hexed, you begin to shut down. Nowhere is this closing-off more present within the body than in the heart area. It is an all-inclusive location that nourishes different bodily systems. The heart is a critical spiritual area of our being.

I love the forms of yoga that focus on the heart center, as feeding, opening, and nurturing this place is vital to good health. Hoodoos are well aware of the healing and strengthening nature of the heart. We seek to feed it and keep it protected. One such way is with a good mojo that sits near the heart center.

---

86. Hyatt, *Hoodoo, Conjuration, Witchcraft, Rootwork*, 414.

*Anjali Mudra*

A good time to be attentive to this important zone in the body is before you put your clothing on for the day, directly after your shower. You can put your hands in a prayer posture, also called a mudra—to be specific, the very well-known *anjali* mudra. This looks like prayer hands, and this gesture is typically accompanied by saying "Namaste" (which translates roughly to "I see and honor the light in you"). Once your hands are put together in this posture, touch your thumbs to your sternum, with fingers facing upward. This way, you are doing so much in a single gesture. You are uniting the left and right, yin and yang, male and female. You are offering yourself up to the divine. With all the unhexing work you've done, it's time for your compassion and love to once again be released.

To further open up your heart while doing this posture, put your hands behind your back and press them together, toward the center of your back. Breathing in a rhythmic manner, you should feel relaxed, empowered, and connected to the divine. Your heart is now very open.

For one last step, add this "keep enemies away" heart mojo. Simply put a piece of asafoetida in a red flannel. Wear it hanging from the neck so it grazes your heart during the day or in your left pocket. This is a protective heart mojo developed by traditional Hoodoos.

## 350. Walk Over Your Enemies Rite

Today, let's continue this anti-hex work by creating a charm. This charm combines familiar ingredients, such as the silver dime (with its numerous metaphysical properties), with oil of turpentine, plus the spiritual nature of the number nine. Oil of turpentine is an important curative in African-American medicine and is worth a closer look.

Turpentine and kerosene-like petroleum products have been used medicinally for a very long time. They are recorded as having been used in ancient Babylon as a stomach treatment, for example. The oil's distillation process is described in literature from the ninth century in Persia as well. Today, a majority of Nigerians use some sort of petroleum product medicinally. Oil of turpentine is drawn on to treat many ills that are the hallmark of hexes, including parasitic growths.

Enslaved Africans in America used a teaspoon of turpentine poured over several lumps of sugar and chewed this as a medicine, washed down with plenty of water for yeast infections (candida). Turpentine comes from pine resin, and when you use it, be sure it's pure and organic and contains no other ingredients. Diamond G Forest Products brand is a good type.

Pines are well-respected trees in our medicine. They seem ever-lasting and protect themselves, with their resin, from fungi and parasites. One of the biochemicals they contain is similar in action to that found in neem, tea tree, pau d'arco, and eucalyptus. Thought of as a cure-all, it has been used to treat fungal infections, arthritis, gout, the sinuses, pathogens, stomach pains, and even cancer.

We are employing oil of turpentine today to curtail harm aimed at your well-being and so you can walk over enemies.

Gather the following items:

- A silver dime with a hole drilled in the middle
- 1 quart spring water or rainwater
- Cord string

- Oil of turpentine
- A glass bowl
- A cotton ball

Boil your dime, uncovered, in a quart of spring water or rainwater. Reduce the water (through boiling) until there is only a cupful left. Set aside. As it cools, tie nine knots in a strong string. Hemp string works well. Soak the string in a small bowl of high-quality oil of turpentine. Lay it on a paper towel to soak up the extra liquid. Dab the soles of your feet with a cotton ball dipped in the cooled dime water. Tie off the string firmly and wear it, confident that you can walk over enemies.[87]

## 351. Hoodoo Gardening: Slippery Elm

Slippery elm *(Ulmus rubra, Ulmus fulva)* is a tree that grows well in many areas of North America. It can grow sixty feet high and has a deep-red heartwood that has led to it also being called red elm. The inner bark is used medicinally. The bark is harvested during the spring, taken from the trunk and branches. The stringy bark is pliable though strong and smells like fenugreek. Just moisten it and it will swell, becoming mucilaginous. It is dried and used in a variety of preparations, from teas and poultices to suppositories.

This is one of the first herbs I learned to use. I continue to use it because of its numerous healing qualities. It is an official drug of the United States Pharmacopeia. Highly thought of, slippery elm is an expectorant, demulcent, diuretic, and nutritive. It is included in this conversation because it is soothing and healing and revives just about anyone, even those who have been hexed.

---

87. Hyatt, *Hoodoo, Conjuration, Witchcraft, Rootwork*, 484.

A gruel can be created from a paste from this herb and then thinned with boiling water. The taste of this oatmeal-like substance benefits from the addition of cinnamon, lemon, honey, and cayenne pepper.

Slippery elm helps those who have been destabilized to get centered. It is known as a communication herb. It is used in Hoodoo for its effects on the throat and as a systemic tonic. Burned as incense in our usual way on a charcoal, it stymies gossip from anyone meaning you ill. Taken orally, it drives away bad juju. It protects against the evil eye and is a superior guardian.

## 352. Slippery Elm Tea

Let's fully engage slippery elm by making a "run away bad juju" tea. You can either purchase powdered bark or pulverize it yourself using a mortar and pestle. Bring a cup of water to a boil, then turn off the heat. Add a tablespoon of the powder, then cover and let steep for twenty-five minutes. Take this twice a day.

This slippery elm tea is considered a remedial. It relaxes and helps you sleep. Slippery elm draws out impurities and irritants placed by others.

## 353. Curio of Note: Mistletoe

The fact that mistletoe (*Viscum album,* family Loranthaceae) is known as a love charm used at Christmastime to attract kissing attests to its magickal qualities. It does more than draw people together intimately; it is both a magickal and a medicinal herb used in Hoodoo.

Mistletoe grows very well in Japan, Northwest Africa, and Europe, where many of its uses have been recorded. There are thirty species besides *Viscum album*. The American type *Phora-dendron leucarpum* is seldom used medicinally.

The physical complaints treated by mistletoe include those felt by people who have been hexed. It eases anxiety, treats headaches and dizziness, and lowers blood pressure. Mistletoe, in minute doses—administered only by a professional, as it is poisonous—is used as an antispasmodic, tonic, and nervine. It helps with delirium, hysteria, debility, and giddiness. The German Commission E (a scientific advisory board) approved it for help with degenerative and inflamed joints, as well as malignant tumors. It has been called a cure-all or all-heal by the Celts and Gauls since earlier times. It plays a prominent role in Druid practices because it is a parasite that feeds off the celebrated oak tree, among others.

## 354. Keep Away Evil Mojo

To continue your immersion in thoughts about mistletoe, today you're going to make a mojo bag containing it, developed from that of a Hyatt informant.[88] It is easy this time of the year to get mistletoe (if you're in December) because this is when it is used in kissing rites for the holiday season. You can obtain your mistletoe from a nursery or florist (fresh).

Dry the mistletoe by hanging it from a nail. Drying prevents mold from getting in your flannel. Once dry, spritz it with Hoyt's Cologne and put in your flannel bag. Now you have a mojo that keeps away evil, such as hexes.

## 355. Purging Hand Wash

Soap is intimate and can be luxurious, especially when you make it yourself. This sturdy soap incorporates the lovely scent of

---

88. Hyatt, *Hoodoo, Conjuration, Witchcraft, Rootwork*, 460.

ocean pine, complete with all the power of pines discussed. The soap also includes relaxing lavender and highly spirited rose oil. Its base is the holy olive oil. This soap is easy to make, effective for purging, and enjoyable.

- 1 pound melt-and-pour olive oil–based soap
- A microwave-safe (Pyrex type) glass bowl or a double boiler
- 2 teaspoons ocean pine essential oil
- 1 teaspoon French lavender oil
- ½ teaspoon pure rose oil
- Soap molds or muffin tins

Slowly melt your soap base in a microwave-safe (Pyrex type) glass bowl or a double boiler. Do this patiently, making sure the soap doesn't overflow. Remove from the microwave or heat source when melted. Mix in the essential oils; stirring with a stainless steel spoon is preferable. Pour this soap into rectangular or hexagonal soap molds. Hexagonal soap, with its five sides, is considered especially effective and lucky. If you don't have molds, you can use large muffin tins.

Carve the name(s) of the person or people who have hexed you into the soap. Wash your hands with the soap multiple times. Keep washing each day. Just as the name(s) fade, eventually you'll feel that you've washed away the ill will and trouble they've sent your way. You can save some of the soap for another time, when needed, because you'll have quite a few to work with.

### 356. Breaking Ill Intent

Is one thing after another going wrong in your life? This is probably not a coincidence. It's time to take action and do a fast change on your luck. A good old-fashioned mojo bag can do wonders when it comes to removing bad luck, especially with the ingredients used in this one:

- Lodestone
- Red flannel
- Saltpeter
- Sea salt
- Hoyt's Cologne
- Hemp string

Put the lodestone in the red flannel. Sprinkle it and the area around it with saltpeter and sea salt. Spray the flannel with Hoyt's Cologne. Make a knot around it, creating a bag. Tie this mojo to your waist. Wear it for nine days. This is a traditional flannel that promises to break ill intentions, like hexes.

## 357. Bring Good Vibes Back Flannel

Today, let's continue to delve into our exploration of removing funky thoughts and evil deeds from your world. One of the things that happens with hexes generally is that they permeate the home. Suddenly your home seems dark and dank in spirit. The vibes are bad. No one wants to be there.

If this sounds like your situation or that of someone you know, try this sharp luck flannel[89] to bring back good vibes. You will need nine horseshoe nails and a red flannel bag.

Notice that you will be employing the power of the number nine. You will also put the nails in alternately, using the power of opposites. Bringing together opposing forces with our heart

---

89. Hyatt, *Hoodoo, Conjuration, Witchcraft, Rootwork*, 4,294.

work creates a dynamic space from which balanced power can emanate.

Place your horseshoe nails in the flannel in opposite directions: place one head up and the next down. Tie firmly in the flannel so they stay in this position. This will bring about a sharp change in luck and vibrations in your home.

### 358. When Is It Time for Banishment?

Much of our work in this chapter up to this point has been about mitigation. You've learned how to ease the disruption caused by hexes. Modifying your home to improve the vibrations has been another strategy. You've worked to alleviate the chaos that ill will brings and sought to bring relief to your situation.

As we finish up this last month of work, we are going to investigate something more drastic. There are times when only bold moves yield the desired results. What I'm speaking of is banishment. That's right—removing someone or something from your life entirely. This relegates the troublemaker to another space. At your point of exasperation, do you really care where they go? Banishment keeps these perpetrators of malaise out of your life for good.

Banishment of someone meaning you ill—a toxic person or hant, for example—fits perfectly in certain situations. You need to be a good judge of this; after all, you are the gatekeeper of your life. You'll banish if you cannot otherwise rid yourself of the discontent and malady aimed at you, your space, and those you love.

Hexes are like cancers: little by little they spread and eat away at your sense of wellness. Banishment is a way of surgically removing your cancerous ill-wisher and sealing yourself off from their toxicity so they cannot return.

## 359. Sweep Away Spell

One of the stronger weapons in your Hoodoo arsenal is your magickal broom. Think of the symbolism: brooms sweep away physical trash and debris. They can go further than that. In Hoodoo, there have been many ways, recorded and still in development, wherein brooms and sweeping are deployed for serious work like banishment. People can be hit with brooms, and you can throw the broom out after them or sweep salt after them so they won't return. Brooms clear vibes, raise spirits, and keep away those who are no longer wanted.

This is a banishment spell inspired by an informant to Harry Hyatt.[90] It works on someone who has been in your home, frequently bothering you.

You will need your magickal broom and nine straws taken from your broom. Lay out the nine straws over your threshold.

Recite this three times directly over the broom straws:

> *You will come here*
> *no more!*
> *You will spread harm*
> *no more!*
> *I banish you from my home and hearth.*
> *You are banished*
> *forevermore!*

Remove any large articles from your floor. Set them aside, off the floor. Sweep each room of your home. Gather this together

---

90. Hyatt, *Hoodoo, Conjuration, Witchcraft, Rootwork*, 420.

at the back door. Take the rubbish to the crossroads and bury it there.

## 360. Drive Away Evil Rite

Great, you know the one who has laid hexes, so you can banish them. But what if you don't know? If this is the case for you at any time, today you'll learn a general banishment rite to drive away evil. This should work as a preventative, keeping you and your environment free of hexes.

Carefully select a High John the Conqueror root. You've come to know and love this root by now, and hopefully you have a great source for obtaining strong ones. Select one that calls out to you and that looks very powerful. This root is designed to bring unyielding strength. High John also advocates for freedom.

Charge and release the might of High John the Conqueror root into some holy oil. Get a sterilized jar with a spring top and fill it ⅓ full of fresh olive oil (holy oil) over the root. Close the top. Say the Lord's Prayer over it. Let steep. The magick of the root will seep out and into the oil for the full cycle of the moon. Shake and swirl gently from time to time to accelerate the seepage.

Once the root is fully dressed, take a bit of the oil with your dominant hand and, starting from the right, draw a line across your chest from right to left. Now starting in the center, make another line with the oil from center to top and from center to bottom. This is your shield.

Repeat the Lord's Prayer. Ask for the evildoer to be released permanently from your life. Now you've driven away the source of evil.

## 361. Banishment Egg: Get the Bleep Out of Here!

Today we return to one of my favorite features of Hoodoo—egg magick. We have worked with this throughout the twelve months. This rite is reworked from one described by an old-school Hyatt informant from the Memphis, Tennessee, area.[91] It employs running water, which, as you'll remember, is water from a natural source, such as a river, waterfall, stream, or brook.

These are the components you will need:

• An egg

• A waterproof marker (Sharpie)

• Knowledge of your hexing party

Just a final word: Make sure you really want this person banished. Combining egg magick with strong words and water magick ensures this person will surely be on their way. Most likely they will leave town.

On an egg, write the name of the person you want to banish nine times. Write all around the egg with the marker, being careful not to crack it. Toss this egg as far as you can into the moving water (a river will work nicely). As you send off your egg, make your wishes known with the strongest of words. Use your imagination, but remember the spirits respond to swearing. They hear your stress, strife, and strong intention.

For example, you could say this:

>  _____, *get the hell out of my life!*
> *I banish you from now until eternity.*
> *Take your dark practices and piece-of-shit hexes*

---

91. Hyatt, *Hoodoo, Conjuration, Witchcraft, Rootwork.*

> *and be gone. You are banished.*
> *Be gone forever from my life.*

It shouldn't be long before this person becomes a distant memory in your life, like the egg.

## 362. No Trespassers Allowed

Everyone wants to keep people who hex them away from their property. At this point in your Hoodoo practice, I hope you have built up knowledge and power as well as strong internal energy. Remember how each of your spells and rites calls for components? Well, the most important ones are your knowledge, power, and energy. You must have strongly focused intent for your Hoodoo to stick.

This unyielding intent means that items taken from you, such as those needed in this rite, are airtight. There are no holes in your body, mind, or spirit through which evildoers can penetrate. To see where you are with this, take stock through the following four questions:

1. Do you feel your power?

2. How has your power manifested and made itself known in your life?

3. Do you notice your magickal intent sticking now more than it did during the first month of this work?

4. What helps you get centered the best? Is it prayer, meditation, walking, writing in your journal, or some other activity?

Good. I'm glad you took the time to answer these questions and get in touch with your development. Now let's focus for two more days on dispelling.

### 363. Dispel a Hant

Hants are nebulous spirits. They are often troubled mischief makers that we're better off without. Here is a foot track magick rite for you to use to deal with them, drawing on the lessons from yesterday about being deep in touch with your inner being. This is a traditional way of dispelling hants.

From your person, cut a bit of your hair and a piece of your underwear. Then gather the following items:

- A shoebox
- 9 nails
- Dirt

Put the bit of hair and piece of underwear in the shoebox. Now push the nails through the box, one head up and the next head down, alternating until all nine are added. Bury the box under the front door: under the front stoop, under the steps (if the home is elevated), or near the door/front stoop. Use your left foot to drag some of the dirt over the box. This rite utilizes upward/downward magick, the power of opposites, and foot track magick to keep unwanted spirits permanently out of your life.

### 364. Dispel Hants at Bedtime

One of the reasons we wear black to funerals is to show respect for the dead. Another reason, on the spiritual side, is so spirits don't get confused and follow us home. This is a funerary rite designed to keep any hants or other spirits with evil intentions away from you after a funeral.

- Gourds are known to be protective, as you've seen through your work. I'm hoping you have grown some in your Hoodoo garden and have taken them in for the season.
- Horseshoe nails are strengthening and good protectors.
- Horseshoes bring good fortune to the home and property.

### Rite
After a funeral, go find a horseshoe nail and bring it home.

**Day 1:** Nail the horseshoe nail into your bedroom door, just like it would be going into a horse's foot.

**Day 2:** Hollow out a green gourd, being careful not to break it. Remove the top and bottom of the gourd.

**Day 3:** Hang the gourd up by your bed.

Now you have a luck and good fortune trifecta that will keep wandering spirits away.

## 365. Foot Track Brambleberry Spell
Another touching hallmark of Hoodoo is the way it uses various items around us, joined with alchemical and symbolic substances, to help us. This spell centers on brambleberries, which are berries that grow on canes with thorns or on trailing vines. You may very well already have some of these types of berries in your garden. They include raspberries and blackberries.

This foot track magick will enable you to show evil spirits that they are better off elsewhere. It is a way for you to show contempt for evil. With this spell, developed from a traditional

Hoodoo practitioner from yesteryear,[92] you are saying, "I am above and beyond your petty acts. Move on. Get out of my life and stay there! You have no effect on me."

Gather these items:

- The sole of a shoe burned up entirely so nothing is left of it, apart from its ash.
- Handful of brambleberries (any kind)
- 1 tablespoon each bluestone and alum
- Spring water
- A cup

After you have burned the shoe sole and have its ash to work with, set it aside. Boil the brambleberries, bluestone, and alum for a few minutes in the spring water. Pour into a cup. Stir in the shoe ash. Sip and spit out small amounts of your potion, outdoors, three times a day. This shows you are fed up with the evil spirit haunting you and sends them away.

---

92. Hyatt, *Hoodoo, Conjuration, Witchcraft, Rootwork.*

# Closing Reflections

Now it is time to take stock. This is a mental space where you can consider how you started this Hoodoo work and compare that to where you are with it today. To that end, let's do a reflection exercise.

You will need these materials:

- Your Hoodoo journal
- A couple of lined pages provided to review Hoodoo work
- Ink pen

Return to the exercise at the beginning of chapter 8 in your Hoodoo journal. Reread your assessment of the way you wanted your home and your living situation to be. Reflect on what you have accomplished so far and what has changed. Take note of what has not worked and has not changed. Use this to plan what you will focus on as you begin a new year of Hoodoo work.

Turn your attention to your Hoodoo journey that began 365 days ago:

- What did you hope to accomplish?
- What did you accomplish?
- What did you hope to learn?

- What did you learn?
- Where will your practice go from here?

Remember, your Hoodoo practice has a solid foundation after the last 365 days of work, reflection, and study. There are several things to do now. You can go back through the book and bookmark your favorite and most problematic days. See if you have written any notes about the circumstance of those days. Then revisit the work of that day and try it again, thereby deepening your engagement.

Next, it is your turn to shape and mold your Hoodoo practice. To do this, expand your repertoire of herbs and curios, your understanding of the elements, and the types of practices you explore. Seek diverse applications for your work. Share Hoodoo with others (friends, family, and clients) if that is appealing. Understand that Hoodoo is a continuously growing and expanding group of folkloric practices. Respect and learn from the past while also looking at the present day as well as the future. Hopefully your knowledge and appreciation of these practices will continue to grow and expand.

Ashe from the crossroads! May the wind be at your back during your continued journey.

# BIBLIOGRAPHY

Anderson, Martha G., and Christine Mullen Kreamer. *Wild Spirits, Strong Medicine: African Art and the Wilderness.* New York: Center for African Art, 1989.

Anglican Church in Aotearoa, New Zealand and Polynesia. *A New Zealand Prayer Book = He Karakia Mihinare o Aotearoa.* Revised edition. San Francisco, CA: HarperSan Francisco, 1997.

Atchley, E. G. Cuthbert F. (Edward Godfrey Cuthbert Frederic Atchley). *A History of the Use of Incense in Divine Worship.* London: Longmans, Green and Co., 1909.

Courlander, Harold. *A Treasury of Afro-American Folklore.* New York: Marlowe & Co., 2002.

Federal Writers' Project of the Works Progress Administration, 1936–1938. *Slave Narratives: A Folk History of Slavery in the United States from Interviews with Former Slaves.* Washington, 1941.

Furlow, F. Bryant. "The Smell of Love." *Psychology Today.* March 1, 1996. Accessed August 2, 2018. https://www.psychologytoday.com/us/articles/199603/the-smell-love.

Hearn, Lafcadio. "New Orleans Superstitions." From *An American Miscellany*, vol. II (1924). Accessed August 2, 2018. http://www.sacred-texts.com/afr/hearn/nos.htm.

Hyatt, Harry Middleton. *Hoodoo, Conjuration, Witchcraft, Rootwork.* Hannibal, MO: Western Pub., 1970.

International Data Corporation. "Worldwide Spending on Security Solutions Forecast to Reach $91 Billion in 2018, According to a New IDC Spending Guide." March 27, 2018. https://www.idc.com/getdoc.jsp?containerId=prUS43691018.

Illes, Judika. *Encyclopedia of Spirits.* New York: HarperOne, 2009.

"Novena to Our Lady of Perpetual Help." Modern English version by St. Alphonsus Liguori. Our Lady of Perpetual Help Roman Catholic Parish. Accessed August 2, 2018. https://www.olphaz.org/parish/pray/novena-prayer.

Puckett, Newbell Niles. *Folk Beliefs of the Southern Negro.* Chapel Hill, NC: University of North Carolina Press, 1926.

Samuelson, Tim, curator. *Love for Sale: The Graphic Art of Valmor Products.* 2015 exhibition at the Chicago Cultural Center in Chicago, Illinois.

Thompson, Robert Farris. *Flash of the Spirit.* New York: Random House, 1983.

"Tulsi and Rudraksha." *Hinduism Today.* March 1997. Accessed August 2, 2018. https://www.scribd.com/doc/25116340/Hinduism-Today-Mar-1997.

# INDEX

## To Write to the Author

If you wish to contact the author or would like more information about this book, please write to the author in care of Llewellyn Worldwide Ltd. and we will forward your request. Both the author and the publisher appreciate hearing from you and learning of your enjoyment of this book and how it has helped you. Llewellyn Worldwide Ltd. cannot guarantee that every letter written to the author can be answered, but all will be forwarded. Please write to:

Stephanie Rose Bird
℅ Llewellyn Worldwide
2143 Wooddale Drive
Woodbury, MN 55125-2989

Please enclose a self-addressed stamped envelope for reply,
or $1.00 to cover costs. If outside the U.S.A., enclose
an international postal reply coupon.

Many of Llewellyn's authors have websites with additional information and resources. For more information, please visit our website at http://www.llewellyn.com.

# GET MORE AT LLEWELLYN.COM

Visit us online to browse hundreds of our books and decks, plus sign up to receive our e-newsletters and exclusive online offers.

- **Free tarot readings • Spell-a-Day • Moon phases**
- **Recipes, spells, and tips • Blogs • Encyclopedia**
- **Author interviews, articles, and upcoming events**

# GET SOCIAL WITH LLEWELLYN

Find us on   @LlewellynBooks

www.Facebook.com/LlewellynBooks

# GET BOOKS AT LLEWELLYN

## LLEWELLYN ORDERING INFORMATION

 **Order online:** Visit our website at www.llewellyn.com to select your books and place an order on our secure server.

 **Order by phone:**
- Call toll free within the US at 1-877-NEW-WRLD (1-877-639-9753)
- We accept VISA, MasterCard, American Express, and Discover.

 **Order by mail**:
Send the full price of your order (MN residents add 6.875% sales tax) in US funds plus postage and handling to: Llewellyn Worldwide, 2143 Wooddale Drive, Woodbury, MN 55125-2989

**POSTAGE AND HANDLING**

STANDARD (US):(Please allow 12 business days)
$30.00 and under, add $6.00.
$30.01 and over, FREE SHIPPING.

CANADA:
We cannot ship to Canada. Please shop your local bookstore or Amazon Canada.

INTERNATIONAL:
Customers pay the actual shipping cost to the final destination, which includes tracking information.

Visit us online for more shipping options. Prices subject to change.